GAMES AND THE FIGHT

AN UNTOLD STORY

GAMES

AND THE FIGHT

AN UNTOLD STORY

BENNY SINCLAIR

First published in 2022
Copyright © Benjamin Sinclair 2022

Benjamin Sinclair
Melbourne, Australia
Email: bennysinclair@hotmail.com
Website: www.bennysinclair.com
Instagram: @bennysinclair
Agency: Dime and Ruff

Cover and text design – Luke Harris
Printed by IngramSpark
Lyrics throughout written by Benny Sinclair.
Cover photograph by Marty Camilleri

ISBN: 9781922607980 (pbk)
ISBN: 9781922607997 (ebk)

NATIONAL
LIBRARY
OF AUSTRALIA

A catalogue record for this
work is available from the
National Library of Australia

This book is dedicated to all those who *believed* in themselves and the few who *believed* in me. It's a story about my life and a piece of social history. Some names have been changed to protect the privacy of the people I've come across. The late Chopper famously said, "Never let the truth get in the way of a good yarn." I've taken that onboard.

Photograph by Lucius Yin

ABOUT THE AUTHOR

Benny Sinclair is an author from a diverse background. A troubled youth: to a state champion boxer, chef, bouncer and trainer. He became a father: business owner, signed rapper, model and actor. Writing a memoir was a natural transition into the creative writing field for this determined Australian. His story delivers a bold message galvanising his audience towards a constructive focus: what one's heart is set on; to find contentment, spiritual elation and your own success. Benny captures past and emerging modern culture imbued with a theorist's perspective on the evolution of technology that subliminally changed the human perspective. He challenges society's narrative by raising questions of discernment and values that discriminate against the vulnerable or averse. His candid style prevails as a diversion through entertainment with insightful afterthoughts; proclaimed with language that sets a tone of authenticity and verity. From the playground to the boxing ring: quintessentially the title says it all. As a man of mixed heritage Benny is a passionate humanitarian. In 2012 he co-founded Team Africa to empower young African Australians through sport. Benny has been a mentor to many over the journey, his memoir is no exception; a highly reputable page turner by all accounts. This book is a must read for social and cultural historians.

BAD

MADE

BEAUTIFUL

CONTENTS

PROLOGUE

I t had been building for a while, the trouble in my life, and when it peaked it hit me bad. I'd come a long way from my juvenile days, so had most of my mates, we'd all moved on to bigger and better things. I was hustling flat out when it happened, flying most of the time, just tryna get that paper coz of the plan I had. I was gonna be more than I started out as. Life growing up hadn't been all that easy. There were things about me right from the start that made me different, and I never felt like I really fitted in. I made the most of what I had though, and made the system work for me as best as I could.

But just when I was finally growing into my own skin, ready to fight the world, and ready to make my music speak for me, things got hectic; all the heat I was trying to avoid hit me with a vengeance. I'm a fighter. I fight. I believe in what I do, and my story is one of redemption. What I'm about to tell you is my life story so far, well let's just say as close to the story as I can. From the dark side to the light side, I have lived through some interesting things. If you're getting nervous reading this don't stress, I'm not a dog, in fact my totem's a mandrill ... But I'm sure you know who you are; picture me pointing at you without judgement, don't take it personal!

COZ YOU WERE BORN A FIGHTER,
YOU GOTTA BELIEVE IT, YOU GOTTA EARN YOUR RIDE
UP

Nothing Comes Easy, *Assumptions* (2019)

The Auslanders

Mum was born in Nuremberg, Germany. She migrated to Australia when she was six years old with my grandparents and her siblings. She met Dad in Melbourne and married after falling pregnant with me. Dad found work in Shepparton as a teacher just before I was born in 1979. I was a blonde kid that grew darker, which makes it interesting now that I know about my heritage. Mum told me the nurses said "I had the loudest set of lungs in the hospital," referring to my vocals, even though I had severe asthma and I nearly passed away as a young baby, I fought on through. My mum missed the family support, so my parents moved back to Melbourne soon after my birth.

When back in the suburbs of Melbourne, my parents' relationship fell apart and they divorced before I was two years old. I don't have any memories of living with my dad, and I don't have any full blooded brothers or sisters. Since both my parents remarried, I have two half siblings from my mum and four half siblings from my dad.

My mum and I moved around a lot. I briefly remember having some stability living with my oma and opa who lived in housing commission flats in an inner Melbourne suburb called Prahran. My grandparents would look after me while Mum was working. They had some nasty arguments and fights with a drunk neighbour who used to beat up his wife. We had to leave the commission flats after my oma threw a brick through his window. She had a temper when it came to that sort of thing. Plus, the fucker had it coming!

We ended up finding a much nicer flat in a better street in Prahran and continued living together. They would speak German at home, and I was intrigued. I asked them heaps of questions about Germany and I learned how to speak the language.

I loved that neighbourhood. There was an enchanted tree to climb in the driveway, always kids in the street to play with, and a milk bar down the road, an awesome bakery, and the market wasn't too far away.

My grandparents would buy me all sorts of treats like chocolate eclairs, and ice cream from the Mr. Whippy van, that'd roll down the street playing loud carnie music. Our soft drink was Loy's. It was delivered once a week in crates straight off the truck; all the flavours you could think of. It was the best in summer. I used to love climbing people's brick fences on our walks, and we'd sing, "I'm the King of the castle and you're a dirty rascal."

Unfortunately living in that beautiful neighbourhood didn't last too long and for financial reasons, mum and me moved out to the suburb of Springvale with my aunty, uncle and three cousins, and my grandparents moved to Noble Park. My cousins and me were all similar ages, so we had fun times together. It was good to be around family. It made me feel safe and secure.

In 1984 I did my first year of school in Springvale, and I was enrolled under the name Benjamin Kaul; which is my mother's maiden name. It originates from northern India & parts of the Middle East, where our ancestors must have come from. I like to think I was enrolled under Kaul coz at that point of my life I grew up with the German side of my family. But the truth is, Mum was tryna move on from the past and in her mind it made sense. My aunty once wrote on my paper lunch bag over school holidays my name – Benjamin Sinclair. I said, "Aunty you got my name wrong, it's Benjamin Kaul." She said, "No it's Benjamin Sinclair. That's your name." I got upset. I wanted my last name to be Kaul like my grandparents.

I loved my grandparents and felt better about my life when I lived with them, or when they stayed with us. I have very fond memories of them and their own unique ways. They were ethnically different and had quite different personalities to many other people I knew at the time.

My oma was from East Germany, her birthplace was Breslau which is now called Wroclaw, in Poland and when I was young she worked in a chocolate factory in Prahran. My opa was born in Munich and later lived in rural Bavaria, he worked as a brick layer and gardener and had a great sense of humour. When he was younger he could walk on his hands. He loved soccer and tennis, especially when German teams or players were on TV. He could play the harmonica, most memorably on Christmas Eve; always enhancing our traditional celebrations. They also had an interesting record collection made up of artists like Boney M and Engelbert Humperdinck.

My Opa's father and family never accepted Oma when

they were in Germany as someone that he should marry coz she'd been working on his family's farm in Bergham near Bad Endorf in rural Bavaria, as a refugee during the war: her hometown Breslau had been invaded by the Russian's and she was separated from her family at the age of 15. Opa's family thought she looked like a Gypsy coz of her curly black hair. Defiant of his father, Opa married Oma and moved to Nuremberg where she was reunited with her parents and siblings. She then had four children, including my mother.

When Opa's father passed away, he left him no inheritance, Opa was heart broken. He contested the will but wasn't very successful. He got a small payout and with the money he decided to move Oma, my mum and the other kids to Australia to make a fresh start. They arrived by boat after a three-month voyage at sea, ironically on Australia Day; January 26, 1960.

It was a tuff time for the family after they arrived. They worked hard but my opa wasn't good at saving money and was bitter over the loss of his inheritance. He would give things away and work for cheap rates. They wouldn't live in the same home for too long, constantly moving around, never giving themselves a chance to get settled. He told me that when he was about 10 years old, he was in the Hitler Youth, a Nazi training camp for young soldiers. An older regiment of boys had bullied his group, a younger regiment. Opa's regiment, or maybe himself directly, stood up for themselves and reported the older regiment to their superiors. Adolf Hitler, who was visiting the camp at the time, heard about this and wanted to congratulate each boy individually for displaying the German *spirit*. He shook my opa's hand and congratulated him. My opa said to me, "If I could turn back the clock, I would spit in this bastard's face."

Opa became a lieutenant during the war. He spoke about serving in Greece, Bulgaria and Russia. However, he waxed lyrically about his beloved donkey and Greek girlfriends a lot! In Russia he surrendered during battle and was captured and sent to a Prisoner of War camp with the men he was in charge of. This was against orders, and his second in command threatened to tell the authorities when they arrived back in Germany. The penalty for disobeying a command was death by firing squad. He later escaped the camp, abandoned the army and marched back to his home in Bavaria, via Hungary and Austria, hiding from the authorities along the way. He wore a steel Edelweiss on a piece of leather as a good luck charm after he'd snapped it off his helmet, before burning his uniform.

I asked my opa if he shot anyone during the war and he said, "I just shot at the trees." His brother, who he was close with, went missing in Russia and never returned home. His sister suffered from depression. She was taken from her family and the family was told she was placed in a hospital. She was then given a lethal injection and murdered, due to the Nazi policy on mental illness. My oma had an equally hard time. Her father was sent to a compulsory labour camp, due to having ashkenazi heritage. He told Oma he survived by sucking on pebbles when he wasn't given food or water. And once separated from her family, my oma fled to West Germany, along the journey through the east she was almost killed during the bombing of Dresden. An air raid shelter that denied her entry was blown up only moments after she left to find another shelter with more room.

During my first year of school, a boy who was a grade older than me hustled me for a dollar at the school canteen. He told me I was too short, and the canteen lady wouldn't be able to see me. He then bought dim sims for himself and his friends, and I saw him walk by with the bag and steam coming out. He was laughing. Oma had given me the dollar and I told her what had happened. At the time I remember not really understanding what the boy had done, it was the first time I'd ever been hustled. I just thought he was strange. Oma came to the school the next day at pick-up time and questioned me on each kid that passed us to see if he was the kid that nabbed the cash. He eventually passed us, and Oma shook the six-year-old boy by the arm violently until he promised to bring my dollar back the next day. He did as he said. It was a good life lesson in not taking shit from bullies. But it was also a lesson in hustling.

My mother eventually bought a house of her own in the Melbourne suburb of Ashwood, and I moved schools again and put on a lot of weight. When I stayed with Oma and Opa during weekends and holidays while my mum was working, I was fed a lot of heavy German food and sweets. They believed the extra weight I gained would strengthen my immune system and therefore fight my asthma. It was an old school Euro trick, but it worked like a charm. I became a big strong kid!

Back in the day, Mum seemed happy in Ashwood. I remember she had a good record collection of Whitney Houston, Prince, Michael Jackson and some Aussie artists too.

She'd sing a lot and we both enjoyed watching music videos on TV. During this time she bought me heaps of toys and figurines to play with, like He-man, Star Wars, Voltron, Ghostbusters, toy soldiers and Matchbox cars. I'd set them up in a room and the toys would go to war and fight with each other. I felt loved and pretty spoiled in those days.

From the age of seven, I walked home from Ashwood Primary, which was a couple kilometres away from where we lived. I had a routine when I got home after school; I'd get my key out, let myself in, make a snack watch TV and wait until mum got home from work.

After a newspaper article appeared in a local paper about our large exotic goldfish getting pinched from our pond by some young vandals, which they tried to cover up by pouring petrol over the pond, my mum attracted a stalker. He called the house one afternoon when I was home alone. I still get goosebumps thinking about it. The eeriest thing about the call was that I initially thought it was one of my uncles or my dad, but the voice on the phone just kept saying "Guess, guess, guess." He knew my name too, coz of the newspaper article. I told Mum the moment she got home from work and for the next few weeks, she finished work early or picked me up from school. He never called again but the damage was done, and I started to understand how vulnerable my mother was as a single parent.

Once I learnt to throw and catch, I discovered I was pretty good at ball sports. I enjoyed cricket and was once asked to play with other school friends on a TV show called *The Early Bird Show* hosted by an Aussie rock star and his sidekick,

Marty Monster. I was also asked to join the state boys choir by some talent scouts who came out to the school and picked me out after an audition. I went there once but got a strange vibe about the place, some stupid kids behind me giggling and poking me and Catholic priests roaming the school yard in big white robes gave me the creeps. I just stood with my back against a pole during recess and told mum I didn't want to go back.

Briefly on weekends I competed in little athletics and for a big chubby kid with asthma, I did okay. I went to cub scouts too, but I only went to one camp and got sent home with bad asthma. I got a creepy vibe about that place too and didn't stick with it much longer after that. We had to do community jobs such as wash cars for the people in your street. I just preferred to wash their cars for two dollars of my own pocket money. Yes, the hustling instinct was strong in me.

I used to walk home from school with some friends. My best mate at the time was a small Aussie kid, I'd go to his place and play war games and stuff like that. One day we were walking home from school together, he was about 15 metres in front of me, and I'd found a large stick in my path. I picked up the stick and threw it as hard as I could, like a spear at his head. I think it was the inner warrior in me coming out. I just expected him to have superior skills like me and duck for cover, but he didn't, and it hit him straight in the forehead, knocked him off his feet and split his head open. I felt terrible. So, I helped him to his feet, walked him home and rang him up on his home phone flat out over the next few days to make sure he was okay.

Blackbird

wouldn't say I was bullied in school, but I can remember kids laughing at me behind my back every now and then coz of my weight. This hurt my feelings. So, I used to stand up for myself if people said things to my face that I didn't like, not necessarily physically fighting, but verbally stand up for myself.

At the age of eight, I was invited to a kid from school's birthday party. His parents were from Ireland. The theme of the birthday party was The Olympic Games, and all the kids at the party competed in races and other events. I lost in every event. Then the birthday boy said, "Now it's time for boxing." I put on the boxing gloves and beat the kids I fought by knocking them down. I then fought the birthday boy and gave him a blood nose, so I was awarded the gold medal. This was a sport that I knew I was good at, and I loved it. Plus, I loved watching boxing and wrestling, particularly Mike Tyson or the Australian boxer Jeff Fenech or wrestlers like Junk Yard Dog and Hulk Hogan.

In 1988, my mother fell pregnant to her boyfriend. He was Aussie with Scottish heritage. She'd been seeing him since I was about three years old. He was an ex-champion body builder and gym owner, who'd changed his occupation to a furniture salesman. He had aspirations. We'd go for drives on weekends, look at big houses and mansions in posh neighbourhoods and go to open for inspections. Mum's boyfriend wanted us to live that way. So, he convinced mum to sell her house and buy a rundown weatherboard house in Malvern, which is a wealthy inner south-eastern suburb of Melbourne. When we moved into the house there was no heating and rats that shitted everywhere. There were holes in the walls and plaster falling down from the ceiling, missing floorboards, scattered old newspapers which had been used as insulation and an outdoor toilet. It smelled old, damp and like piss. However, my mum's boyfriend convinced Mum we were better off now.

I needed to find a new school. I finished off the last few months of grade 4 in Ashwood, then said goodbye to my old friends and started grade 5 in 1989 at a new school in Malvern, under the name Benjamin Douglas, not Kaul, or Sinclair. The reason my last name was changed again was simply coz I was asked by Mum and her boyfriend to take on his last name. I was nine years old at the time, my first baby brother had just been born and they told me they didn't want people in the new wealthy neighbourhood thinking they weren't married. I was convinced the name Douglas was the coolest name going around. There was a Black Douglas Scotch Whisky add on TV at the time and it featured a battle scene with knights dressed in armour, and the narrator told the story of the great *Black Douglas*, who was killed while carrying the Heart of the Bruce. To me this seemed like a good enough reason to change my name. I'd always loved watching movies or cartoons about ancient warriors and historical battles.

In the early days I had a reasonable bond with Mum's boyfriend. He had weights, dumbbells and a bench press around the house, and photos of his bodybuilding days. He also had trophies of his championship wins, which I was really proud of. We'd wrestle, play fight, kick the footy and watch sports on TV. As their relationship progressed, Mum and her boyfriend would fight and argue a lot and I didn't like it, it felt uncomfortable. It was sometimes physical, with lots of swearing, pushing, and shoving. Mum would say he was a tight-ass with his money, and it was true coz he wouldn't want to pay or give her money for many things at all.

My dad was in and out of my life after my parents split up. I can't ever remember living with him and very rarely stayed the night at his place. It was more day visits on Saturdays or Sundays every now and then. I can remember day trips from the age of five where we would make comedy skits on his video camera. I was amazed. Dad was an aspiring actor and I can remember seeing him on a TV ad selling a highlight video for the 1984 Olympic Games. Oma and Opa told me to watch the TV coz my dad was on it. He also played small cameo type roles on popular Australian 80s soapies like *Prisoner* and *A Country Practice*. I thought that was pretty cool and was always happy to re-unite with Dad.

In 1985 he organised an audition for me in a Band-Aid commercial. The lady wanted me to cry at the audition, but I couldn't stop laughing. I didn't get the part, but I knew I wanted to do something like that with my life. In the early years of my schooling there was some consistency with seeing Dad and I'd see him almost every second weekend for a while. During the footy season we'd attend games and support our team, the North Melbourne Kangaroos. It was good bonding time. He bought me some cassettes and song books. I'd read the lyrics and practice singing the songs.

I wrote my first rap for Dad to perform on his answering machine during that time. Dad rapped it out and recorded it on his telephone answering machine and I can still remember most of the lyrics. Sometimes during school holidays Dad and I would visit my nana, Mary, and family in Corowa, a country town which borders Victoria and New South Wales. It was on these four-hour drives from Melbourne that me and Dad would have long talks. When visiting Corowa, I remember being shown an old family photo by my relatives who lived there. The photo was of Nana's mother, father and grandmother, Mary Anne Washington. It was an old black and white photo, but you could tell her grandmother was black and her father was mixed race. Unfortunately it was difficult to distinguish what their ancestry might have been and exactly how this heritage of ours originated, nobody knew the answer.

Family members have told me that Nana Mary was beaten by her father, particularly when she asked those kinds of questions about our heritage. From all accounts, he was ashamed of it and became violent. My nana's favourite saying was, "I was in the blues when I had no shoes, then one day on the street, I met a man with no feet."

My father has always felt the need to assure me he never cheated on my mother, but he's pretty sure my mother cheated on him. My mother says the opposite. I think their marriage was doomed from the onset; unfortunately there was a culture clash, and that made them question their values, the fear of non-acceptance a reality, so they pretended to make it work for my sake, until the pressure got too much, and they split!

On a long drive with Dad one day, he told me that when I

was younger, he'd wanted to again pursue a relationship with my mum and that Mum's boyfriend found out. Apparently he phoned Dad and said if he went near Mum, he'd "cut his throat." Dad said he was too scared to go near my mum after that. Mum's boyfriend was "on the juice" like a lot of bodybuilders, and no doubt was going through 'roid rage' at the time.

Years later Dad remarried — one of his ex-students more than 20 years his junior. His wife is Italian, she had a lot of control over Dad and I saw my father less as their relationship developed and they had children.

Dad regards himself as an atheist. To be honest, I don't really care; that's his business. Sometimes his advice has missed the mark, but often things he's said to me have had great value, after all he is my father and he's tried to be there at times when I've needed him, which I appreciate. Things are what they are!

FRESH KICKS

In January 1989 I was nine years old and just about to start the school year in Malvern. The place itself was in an older looking double story building, established in 1875. The playground looked old too, with gravel instead of a grass oval and a big basketball court. In the classrooms, I could see the old flip top desks, which I'd seen in the movies. There was also a big park with a duck pond and lots of trees to climb or play sport in. There was a junior campus of the school on the other side of the park whose back oval fence ran on to the south end of my street, not far from our creepy rundown weatherboard house, which before we moved in was known to have a beat-up version of an A-Team kinda looking black van, parked out the front.

On the first day of school, my mum styled my hair. She used to blow dry it and apply hair gel or styling mousse. I had thick dark hair, with a mullet and kinda spiky up on top. My hair is thick, it usually just stays up without blow drying, if I don't let it grow too long. This hairstyle was pretty cool in Ashwood. I wore a grey short sleeved school shirt and grey school shorts. I had shiny black school shoes that mums boyfriend Wayno polished for me. I thought, Dammnn this guy is really trying hard to impress these Malvernites, and he even bought me nerdy navy-blue socks. Still, I thought I looked sharp! I'd never worn a proper school uniform before. I arrived at school and met my teacher Miss Putana, who was blonde and come to think about it was probably a bit of a cougar, well maybe not quite, but anyway she was always nice to me. I was happy that my classroom was upstairs coz my last school only had one floor; this was something different for me.

Some kids in my class came up and spoke to me; they looked Aussie and I noticed some of them were Greek; and a couple were Chinese. I felt like each time I changed schools there were similar playground hierarchies. The popular kids were, most of the time, good at sport and dressed the best. And with the girls, the prettiest girl was usually the most popular.

I noticed only about half of the kids were wearing school uniforms, the rest of the kids were dressed casually. The school uniform sweater was a nice-looking navy and gold rugby jumper, and navy blue track suit pants. The sneakers they wore were mostly Nike, Reebok, Adidas, Converse or Puma, or skate shoes like Vision Street Wear. The kids that didn't wear the school uniform wore clothing such as Mambo or Quicksilver. Some of the Greek kids had mullet hairstyles like mine. The popular Aussie kids had under-cut hairstyles with longer fringes or bowl style cuts. Hardly anyone was wearing black shiny school shoes or grey school shirts and shorts, that Mum and Wayno told me I was supposed to wear, so I felt like a bit of a geek.

I made some friends that day that I'm still friends with today, one of them is Memo, a Greek kid that lived two streets away from my house. I also met some Aussie kids including Bronzer, Jackson, Daf, and Spinach who became an actor, starring in the Melbourne soapie *Neighbours* and later on gave Hollywood a crack.

On that first day, as the kids huddled around me during recess, I asked a few questions. Firstly, I asked, "Who's the fastest runner?" It turned out the fastest runners at Ashwood were the most popular kids in my year level. Someone said Spinach. That's great, I thought coz I'd just been assigned to my yearly desk seat position and I was sitting next to Spinach. However, I soon found out who the alpha males of the group were, and Spinach wasn't one of them. There were some deeply entrenched social politics at my new school. It seemed it was a battle between Jackson and Bronzer. And pretty soon, I'd be in the middle of it all.

"Who's that?" I asked, pointing to the prettiest girl I could see in our class. She wasn't the most popular coz she was quiet and shy. I never really spoke with her much coz of her shyness.

"What football team do you support?" I asked. Everyone at my last school went for the Essendon Bombers, but at this school they liked different teams. I told them I supported North Melbourne, one kid in the group yelled out, "Yeah," it was Daf, he was also a North Melbourne fan, so we became instant friends. "What music do you guys like?" I asked. I heard them say bands like INXS, Guns and Roses, and Run DMC. When they asked me, I said, "Bon Jovi." They all laughed! I didn't actually like Bon Jovi that much but that's what all the cool kids at Ashwood liked, so I thought it would be tuff to say that.

They asked me if I skated. I said "You mean roller skates? Yeh, I have a couple times on school holidays with my cousins and stuff." They said, "No Skateboard." so I said "Oh yeh I got a skateboard for Christmas." They said, "What kinda deck ya got?" I said, "Huh? Ya mean what kinda skateboard?" I figured these guys must be professional skateboarders with designer skateboards or something. "I got a Twister," I said. My skateboard was most likely something my mum found in the discount bin for a cheap price at Big W. It had the word Twister written on it. There must have been a designer brand like Santa Cruz Twister, coz they all said, "Wow cool," or they just had no idea themselves.

They asked if I had a girlfriend? I said "Nah." Jackson and Bronzer said they both had girlfriends. None of my friends in Ashwood had girlfriends or even spoke about girls. I'd be way too embarrassed to tell anyone if I had a girlfriend. They asked where I lived, I said, "My house is just down that way, it's the house on the bend." They said, "Ahh cool! The house that used to have the A-Team truck out the front?" At that point, I really wished the squatters who lived in the house before us didn't

20

own the truck and it belonged to us, coz everyone looked impressed by it. Disappointingly I said, "No, that belonged to the people who lived there before us." No one seemed to care though, maybe it creeped them out more than impressed them, I wondered to myself on a second guess, as there was no way it was as cool as the real A-Team truck. I used to have a model toy version and Mr. T figurines; I would know.

Jackson said, "I live near you, let's walk home together." I was stoked that I'd made friends so quickly, and I had a new friend who lived close by. I couldn't wait to get home and tell mum, about my first day at the new school.

I instantly felt confident at the new school, coz the neighbourhood wasn't as ruff as what I was used too. I didn't feel like I was getting picked on for my weight, but I was still self-conscious. I knew I didn't want to be chubby anymore. I'd seen some recent photos of myself at family functions and I felt embarrassed coz I could see fat rolls around my stomach through my t-shirt.

I decided to wear my runners to school the next day and asked Mum if she could buy me a school rugby jumper when she could afford one. I thought my Aerosport sneakers would cut it at the new school coz in Ashwood, most kids had them, and we all thought they were ace. Our mums would have bought them from Target or Kmart. I remember hearing a few smart-ass remarks in the classroom about Aerosport sneakers. I asked my mum if she could buy me some Nike's or Reebok's. She said they were very expensive and couldn't afford them, but If I was a good boy, she might be able to save up some money for some Reebok's for my birthday in April.

Every kid I met in Malvern swore like a fucken wharfie. I prefer to say 'wharfie' over 'trooper' coz wharfie's have always had a bad ass gangster reputation here in Melbourne due to the notoriety of the Painters and Dockers Union. The Malvern kids were often smart-asses to each other, so I didn't take the Aerosport sneaker comments too seriously. I just wanted fresh kicks.

One day Mum came home from shopping very excited. "Look Benji," she said. My mum, Oma and Opa always called me Benji coz they liked the movies about the golden mixed breed dog! "I bought you some brand-new sneakers like all the other kids have at your school and they were only $5." The shoes pretty much looked like Chuck Taylor's, except the print on the shoe was a black and white newspaper screen print, and the tag on the shoe was the red *Coca-Cola* logo. They were Coca fucken Cola shoes! I liked them and couldn't wait to wear them to my new school.

Almost as soon as I got to the front gate all the kids were waiting for me. "Nice new shoes," they said. Then someone said they looked like Vision Street Wear kicks or Chuck Taylor's. I said, "Thanks they're Coca Cola and my mum only paid $5 for them." They all started laughing, like a pack of hyenas. "Haha, Coca Cola shoes! Let me drink your shoes haha, only $5, haha." I was shocked. The way I was raised, was if you found something good for a bargain price, it was like you'd won the lottery. To the Malvern kids, it meant they must be trash or something a homeless person would wear. In reality, they were as good a quality as Chuck Taylor's, just the wrong brand, the cheap version. I kinda kept very low key at recess that day, and even quickly ran home by myself without my new friends, so they

22

wouldn't laugh at my shoes again. I took them off straight away and told mum what happened. We were both sad about it.

STAND WITH ME

On one of my first days when I was walking home from school with Jackson there were three older kids from grade 6 ahead of us, and Jackson said, "Stay away from those kids and watch out for them, they're bullies." I said, "What? Those kids over there, they don't look tuff?" And they didn't. One was shorter than me, one had red hair and was taller and dressed cool like a skater, and then there was the average built guy. It was strange that Jackson seemed scared, and I wasn't scared of them at all. I liked that feeling and thought Jackson was a bit of a pussy.

A few weeks later the shorter, so-called bully and his friends were standing in the middle of the school staircase stepping on all the grade 5 kids' shoes as they walked past. I thought, I guess Jackson was right, coz he was acting like a bully, and everyone was too scared to say anything. Then he went to step on my shoes. I stopped him and put my hand on his chest looked him straight in the eye and said, "Nobody steps on my fucken shoes." He looked scared of me and stopped what he was doing. After that no one in grade 5 had problems with the grade 6 bullies.

I became friends with some grade 6 kids and some younger grade 4 kids. There were a lot of Greek kids in the area and Greek school classes on Saturdays. Later in the year we were heading to an inter-school sports cricket match and one of the bullies had sworn or said something smart-ass to the sports teacher in charge. The teacher grabbed him by the arm and shook him violently for about 30 seconds, in front of both the grade 5 and 6 cricket players. He went red in the face and burst into tears. He was completely humiliated. I thought the teacher did the wrong thing but part of me thought he had it coming. This was maybe my first introduction to karma in action!

The walk home from school was a time for comradeship with my mates, telling jokes and clowning around. After awhile I called us 'The Walking Club'. Sometimes kids would bring bikes but just ride slowly, so we could hang out. My house was always the first stop. I started to feel like I'd formed a small posse.

I wanted to change my image, so I started growing my hair out on top a little bit and grew a longer fringe. This look suited me coz I have a natural cows-lick in the middle of my hairline, so the hair parted easily. I trimmed the mighty mullet at the back as well. I also decided it was now time to lose some weight. It was time to stop eating anything sweet or fried and eat less in general. I started jogging at the park near my school, doing sit-ups every day, push-ups and light weights. My mum and Wayno, who were also into fitness and used to run a lot, gave me some good tips. I didn't play football for my local club in 1989 but kept myself busy training every day. I improved in all sports too. Later I went on to play for a couple local footy clubs on weekends during the season and captain the school team.

We were a competitive bunch of kids at that school, music and sport were huge. I played everything, football, cricket, softball, soccer, netball, volleyball, four square and tennis. A game called long base was my favourite game at school. It's like rounders with a baseball bat and tennis ball, and each base was on the corners of the netball court. You would score a home run if you hit the ball over the fence. I scored many, and reigned supreme. Lunch times we played brandy, British bulldogs, basketball, and no-rules rugby. I couldn't get enough of those games.

The first time anyone ever complemented me on my weight loss was at school swimming sports at the Harold Holt Swimming Pools in October of 1989. The pools were named after a prime minister who had drowned in 1967, his body was never recovered. It took about eight months to get down to an average weight for my age. It was the illustrious Miss Putana who was the first to notice. She was pretty much the first person I met at the school, so she'd seen me at my chubbiest. She said, "Geez Ben, you've lost so much weight! Well done!" I was just in my swimming shorts at the time, so she really noticed the difference. It was a nice compliment, made me feel good and she could see my confidence grow.

I started to become a little naughtier with the influence of all my new mates. I now used to swear as much as they did. We were a pretty naughty class in general, so many big personalities that clashed with each other all the time. Although Miss Putana was rather nice to me, I thought she did some strange things. The issues first started for her when she decided to discipline Spinach by tying him to his desk with string. I think she was trying to be funny and cool, which is something sad adults do around kids. She used to tell us off for talking to each other too much and she'd get agitated when Spinach couldn't sit still, hence the string. I was a bit the same but not as obvious as Spinach. She also put masking tape over Memo's mouth one time. This display of twisted humour caused the class to retaliate against her daily, even the female students, who probably told their parents and thought she was being unethical.

One day, Miss Putana had to teach us about the health effects of alcohol abuse and using nicotine. But the lesson was railroaded when her cigarettes fell out of her handbag and the whole class erupted in laughter. "Hey! Miss Putana, why ya smoking?" "Hey! Miss Putana, you'll get lung cancer!" Some kids made fun of her and some kids were just mad coz she looked like a hypocrite for telling us not to smoke when she had cigarettes in her bag. Absolutely no one took her seriously after that, not even the quiet, nerdy kids. She used to burst out of the classroom in tears at least once a week.

It all came to a head, when she took off for a really long time one day. Before she ran off, she said, "Do whatever you like." Most of us took off to the playground, but Action Jackson decided to take it to the next level, stay in the classroom and eat his lunch sitting on the ledge of the window of the second storey classroom. Someone must have walked by the school, seen a kid hanging out the window eating his lunch and called the office. The School Principal, Mr Capable, rushed to the classroom, grabbed him off the ledge and dragged him down to the office. He was in big trouble. Later that day I asked Jackson why he did that, he said, "She told us to do what we like." We all ended up having to go to the office and speak about our behaviour with Mr. Capable, but I think Miss Putana was in more trouble for abandoning the class than we were. You can only hope she never took up a traffic controller's position on a busy freeway, after her teaching gig fell through.

The school was very proud of their music classes and teachers. One lady was a short Hungarian. She used to conduct the school choir and always used to sing the word, "Ready," in her thick accent before we started singing. My mates would mimic her. The other teacher was South African, and she played keyboard. The Hungarian teacher taught us how to play nursery rhymes like *Hot Cross Buns* and *Three Blind Mice* and maybe some Christmas carols on the recorder. I saw a meme not long ago with a picture of a recorder saying: *WTF did this do for my education, lol.*

Both the teachers would run the choir, and pretty much everyone in our class, minus some kids that had to go to Special Ed or stuff like that participated. I enjoyed it, not necessarily the song choices but the singing and performing. I think the South African teacher had an influence on the songs most of the time coz she was playing the piano or keyboard on songs like *The Banana Boat* song and *Cotton Fields*. I didn't mind too much. I often got solo parts, along with some of the girls and my mates who showed an interest.

We'd perform throughout the year, at different events the teachers organised. The annual school performance for parents and families involved dancing too, and the teachers went to a lot of trouble organising our costumes. The last performance of the year was in December, at the local shopping centre, where we'd be performing Christmas Carols. It was a very hot and humid day in Melbourne, and the teachers made us all wear our school uniforms, including the school rugby sweater.

The performance started well, but about 20 minutes in I could see the sweat dripping from the face of our conductor, aka the short Hungarian lady. Suddenly I felt a gush of wind behind me. A Greek kid with a bowl cut, fainted on the podium and face planted straight into the tiles of the shopping centre floor. He landed nose first and there was blood everywhere. The Hungarian lady rolled up her sleeves and tried to help him up. She had blood all over her white shirt and forearms, she looked at me for help. Some people were still singing, so we told them to stop and tried to help the teacher. I began to feel dizzy and so did about four other kids, we needed to sit down and drink water.

The shopping centre cleaners cleaned up the mess and we all got sent back to school. I got sent home from school early. I remember Mum had given me money for a lunch order that day. We didn't have a canteen, so your parents would put money in an envelope, and you could pre-order your lunch. I'd ordered a hamburger, which was the best thing on the school menu. I remember thinking, bonus, I get to go home early from school, and I can take this hamburger with me too.

WiLD STYLEZ

I used to enjoy art class and loved watching cartoons. During 1989, The Ninja Turtles were the biggest thing on TV. Batman had also made a revival with a new movie, along with lots of new merchandise, clothing, and toys which my grandparents had bought me. From a young age I loved drawing cartoon characters of my own or trying to draw the characters I'd seen on TV. I wanted them to look perfect; my family always said I was very good at it and I should be a cartoonist when I was older. I was given books to help me practice. As much as I enjoyed it, I think I lacked the patience or attention span for the finer details, and I was unable to perfect things the way I wanted to. I liked being a little more extraverted. I preferred the idea of being a performer of some kind. I liked singing just a little more than acting, coz singing always made me feel good and happy. It was therapeutic.

Bronzer invited me to his birthday party in August of that year and on the train ride to the movie theatre in the city, he pointed out some graffiti along the train line. I can remember the burner that stood out to me. It said *Hugh Dunit* and it had a picture of Pinocchio above it. He took a photo, and he took photos of more graffiti and of all us kids at his birthday party. He later showed me a scrap book he had with photos of all the graffiti pieces around Melbourne, he had taken. He also had some *Hype Magazines*, that he'd bring them to school sometimes. I started to appreciate graffiti as not being just random scribble or senseless vandalism. It wasn't long before I could identify different graffiti crews and tags.

During the first term of Grade 6 in 1990, after I'd turned 11, I'd made a new friend called Ike whose parents were Armenian. He had a crazy full colour range Posca collection; with all the different felt tip sizes. I got my hands on a couple through Jackson who had swiped some from the art room. They were the most expensive markers at the time and they were great for tagging, but worked best on smooth surfaces. The tips were measured in millimetres, and you could decide on round or flat tip. One Saturday afternoon, we decided to head to a playground near where some of our mates lived and go on a tagging spree on the equipment. My first tag was YOSP and I think Ike just wrote his name or an abbreviation. We were proud of our achievements and sat back and admired our tags at the playground for quite some time before we went home. Some of our mates brought up how their local playground had been 'bombed' over the weekend and at school on Monday morning it was the talk of the school yard, particularly with Bronzer, who I guess saw himself as the 'King of Graffiti' of the school. I braggingly told Bronzer that it was us that had tagged the play equipment, he looked shocked, and I guess jealous or something, coz he gave me a sour look, and didn't speak to me for the rest of the day.

The next day Bronzer rocked up to the school and said, "Mate you're in big trouble. A big-time writer my brother knows from the graff crew KSA (Kick Some Ass) writes YASP and he wants to come down to the school and beat you up coz you copied his tag." I went pale in the face and asked, "How old is he?" Bronzer said, "He's 16." I had only just turned 11 and looked like a little kid. I was stressing. I was expecting the guy to come down to the school that day, so I kept a low profile and spoke with Ike about what we should do. Should I go over the tags with something else, or should I fight the guy? He was scared too, but all the blame was on me coz my tag was YOSP, not his. I asked Bronzer, "Is he still coming to the school yard? Coz YOSP is different to YASP." He said, "Yep, he said that you're a biter and he's really pissed off." I said, "What does he look like?" He said, "He's a big black guy." He made me feel like I'd done the wrong thing in the graffiti world. I was scared, so after school, me and Ike went back to the play equipment with our markers. We went over our tags with different colours and made them look wack.

The next day I told Bronzer we'd gone over the tags with different tags. He cracked up laughing and said, "Haha, sucker you were shittin' yourself. I made it up, the guy writes YASP but doesn't wanna bash ya but maybe just change your tag just in case." Bronzer was a smart-ass, I felt like knocking him out, but was embarrassed coz I'd been scared and stressing so much. I just tried to laugh it off. If he didn't continually pull stunts like this, I think Bronzer and me would have been much better mates. After that, I started to think all the Anglo kids were lying smart-asses. But my mum always used to say there is good and bad in every race and I never forgot her words!

MARIO BROTHERHOOD

ronzer saw himself as the leader of the Grade 6 boys and during his reign, he certainly ruffled some feathers, especially Jacksons. They were tall kids for their age, but Bronzer was older than most of us. When I arrived in Grade 5 in 1989 everyone was a skater, and if you dressed like a skater and couldn't skate, the biggest insult you could be called was a fake skater but now we were tagging the biggest insult was to be called TOY or a biter. I remember a wild rich kid just ran up to another rich kid yelling, "Fuck you, ya fake skater!" and for no other reason just punched him straight in the nose. The kids nose opened up instantly and he started crying, his basketball that he'd been dribbling at the time just kept bouncing all the way down to the back of the basketball court. It was bad for the kid but for some reason I just couldn't stop laughing, thinking about how fucked up these crazy rich kids really were.

It didn't seem like we were in Malvern all that long before mum fell pregnant again & my second baby brother was born. I played an active role in raising my brothers over their early childhood. I started minding them regularly when my mum wanted a break and Wayno wasn't home. It was hard; my brothers would cry a lot when they were babies, and I would have to figure out how to keep them calm. There were no mobile phones back then and my mum didn't have a car. Sometimes she'd be gone for hours.

I felt like Jackson looked up to me, had my back most of the time and respected me. I was one month older than him, and we stayed friends. He was the first kid I ever saw shoplift anything. We were at the local milk bar after school one day, and I could see this look in his eye. The milk bar was owned by a Greek family, and my mum would talk with them, so I considered them our friends. One of the other kids that was with us ordered mixed lollies, it was between 1-5 cents per lolly and the server would individually place each lolly in a white paper bag, including spearmint leaves, raspberries, snakes and chicos. This distracted the milk bar owner while Jackson filled his pockets with Snickers and Mars Bars. I didn't even see him do it, I would have said something if I did. He offered me a Snickers and I said, "Nah man, that's wrong. They're family friends those people." The other kids grabbed some of the chocolate bars from Jackson's pockets and said, "Give me some, you tight ass." No one cared, I thought about it a little more as we walked past Jackson's house, en route to our houses. I asked him to break off some of the Snickers he was eating. I felt like I wanted to taste what stolen goods tasted like. To me it tasted cheap, like it didn't have value, but I ate it. I was surprised these rich kids in Malvern were stealing, coz why would they need to?

Throughout our first few years in Malvern, I did what I could to help Wayno renovate our house to a liveable state. We now had carpet and a heater in the lounge room, and some plumbers had moved our toilet indoors into the newly renovated bathroom. The inside of the house had been painted, most of the holes in the walls and roof repaired. We also started demolishing the front fence and replaced it with a white picket fence. Then we started painting the brown wooden weatherboards white. The house looked a lot better. It reminded me of something from the American movies based in the South, like *The Colour Purple* or something like that. I helped with most of the renovations. I also used to help out with the gardening. There was still a lot of work to go into the house, but it got worse before it got better.

One day I was sitting in the front seat of Wayno's car. We were on our way home from the fish and chip shop with dinner, when I heard the dopest track I'd ever heard on radio. It was *Wild Thing* by Tone Loc. I instantly told him to turn it up, and he was feeling it too. We just sat in the driveway with his stereo pumping, waiting for the song to finish and find out what it was called. I ran inside and told Mum, I'd just heard the wickedest song ever, and I said, "Could you buy me the tape?" We didn't get the chance to hear real rap very often on Melbourne radio, it was mostly Oz rock or pop music. Maybe a little bit of Run DMC or Beastie Boys from time to time and artists like Bobby Brown were starting to get some airplay. Also New Kids on the Block, but they didn't sound like real rappers. There were some comedians trying to rap, they were too gimmicky for me. Some MC Hammer songs were released, followed by Young MC with his big hit *Busta Move* and they were getting lots of airplay too. Salt n' Peppa were also breaking through. Then out of nowhere came Vanilla Ice's hit, *Ice Ice Baby*. Everyone in our school loved that track and Jackson was the first to buy the cassette single and get lines drawn in his hair. Memo got the lines in his hair too, coz he and Jackson became besties for a while, wearing their MC Hammer happy pants!

I gotta say I held off on that trend coz I preferred other rappers and a slicker look. I'd grown my hair longer and was starting to have a shaved undercut look and each time I'd ask the hairdresser to go higher and higher and cut less of my fringe. Bronzer and Ike started wearing Raiders and New York Yankees, hats and t-shirts and Mum bought me an LA Dodgers hat and some t-shirts when she could afford too. I started to listen to Ice-T and we all loved watching the gang movie *Colors*. Jackson also had the 2 Live Crew record, and we used to laugh at all the dirty tracks.

One day I rocked up to school and all of my mates were talking about a new gangster rap crew in the schoolyard and they were all laughing their heads off, repeating some of the lyrics on Daf's Walkman. "What are they called?" I asked. "N.W.A.," they said. I couldn't wait to hear it, so we headed to Ike's house on the weekend; his parents were divorced, so his mum was very lenient. She'd bought him *Straight Outta Compton* (1988), and he had a big ghetto blaster style Pioneer radio double cassette player. I couldn't stop listening to it. It had taken a long time to arrive in Australia, probably coz of all the explicit content. I can remember thinking Bronzer was kinda a hypocrite, coz just a few months before he was complaining about Tone Loc saying 'motherfucker' a coupla times on his LP. Now he was listening and laughing along to N.W.A with us; there must have been more to it all. This music was next level. The beats were dope and I felt like I was getting an education on how to become a man, a player, and a hustler. At the time it seemed like the best way to live. Who was going to tell me different? I wanted that lifestyle and I wanted it fast. I felt that kinda life was better than how I was living at the time. Plus, most rappers were of African descent, and coz I'm part Black, it was a sign that I could live that way too.

I guess my new life as a hustler had to start somewhere, and Ike's mum had a massive basket full of fresh eggs in their kitchen. We'd grab the eggs and while jumping on his trampoline in his front yard, then take pot shots at passing trams and cars. Sometimes we'd throw water bombs instead. I've always had a wickedly accurate throwing arm and would quite often nail the target I was aiming at. Surprisingly, the cops were never called. People probably couldn't work out where the projectiles were coming from. So, I guess we were free to scramble those eggs, without the bacon!

Another favourite weekend hobby was picking up the telephone book and prank calling random numbers like Bart Simpson did to Moe's tavern, but we started doing it just before The Simpson's came out on Australian TV. We'd say things like, "Excuse me Mr (whatever the surname in the phone book was), is your fridge running?" He'd say "Yes," or "Let me go check," and come back and say, "Yes, it is," and we'd say, "Well you better go n' catch it." Nick knocking was also a thing. Nothing could beat the thrill of getting chased by an angry baby boomer dressed in his wife's pink dressing gown at 7am on a Sunday morning. The early morning ghostly wake-up call was surprisingly never appreciated!

As I got a bit older, watching porn movies during school holidays became a tradition. My mate Devious was Greek Macedonian, and to the delight of my mates in our neighbourhood he would bring over his dad's Greek porn videos. Sometimes other friends would invite us over to do the same thing at their homes, when their parents weren't home. We upset one of the girls in my street once when we invited ourselves over to her house to watch a comedy movie like *Uncle Buck* or something and we played a Greek porn video instead. She never spoke to me again. It was a shame coz she was a nice girl and she had some cute friends.

It was a challenging game to steal porn magazines like *Penthouse* or *Playboy* from the local news agencies! Sometimes we'd get our hands-on the XXX rated ones and it would end up like that scene in *2001: A Space Odyssey*, when the Monolith appears, as all us little hood rats crowded around while someone flashed through the pages to the centrefold. We had our techniques too. We'd slide a magazine inside a newspaper and just pay for the newspaper or get someone to buy a Tatts Lotto ticket to distract the person at the counter. This would also become our technique when we were racking markers to write our tags on walls and trains and stuff, or spray cans from hardware stores for larger works of art!

STREET FIGHTER

Video games were a big part of growing up in the 80s and 90s. My first memories of playing any kind of videos games was in 1983. Someone had given me a Space Invaders-type game for Christmas. I could sit it in my lap and play. I used to love it. Not long after that I can remember visiting a place called the Fun Factory, which use to be, just off Chapel Street in South Yarra, which has always been a wealthy area in Melbourne. The Fun Factory did not reflect this. It was ruff outside and inside but had a big video arcade and pinball machines. There were video games like Pac-Man and Donkey Kong, which were huge during this time. Then the big games companies made the gaming machines smaller and kids would bring small games consoles to school and play at recess. Someone had lent me an old dusty games console in about 1986. It must have been from the '70s coz it had games on it like Pong and Galaxy Game.

I heard some kids talking about Atari in the schoolyard

and I'd played it a couple times at friends' houses. My best mate at Ashwood Primary had a Commodore 64 and I'd play with him and his brother when I'd visit. The games had the best graphics I'd ever seen. We used to play games like *Double Dragon* and *The Last Ninja*. Just before we officially moved into the Malvern house, we needed to get the squatters kicked out, which was a bit of a process. So, during that time, we briefly lived in a flat my mum rented not too far from the house. The block of flats was next to a small pinnie parlour (video games arcade), later to become, John's Pinnies. It was a small shop filled with a pinball machine, pool table, several arcade games and car games with steering wheels. There was a back room with a locked door and a thick sliding, glass reflective window. When you went up to the window to change your notes or coins an older Greek man who was maybe around 50 years old would greet you. He didn't speak English very well, and behind him, you could see an old card table in the back office where he'd sit. There were a few places like this around the neighbourhood, and they were all run by old Greek men. When I was older, I realised that the pinball and video games were just a front. These businesses were in fact gambling dens. Later down the track, when the casino opened in Melbourne, all the pinnie parlours went bust.

One day randomly outta nowhere my asthma flared up and I was sent back to hospital. I kinda got freaked out in the kids playroom area when a Middle Eastern girl, possibly from Iraq and maybe a little older than me, decided she was gonna get butt naked. This was the first time in my life I'd seen a naked girl my age. I guess I'll never forget it. I think she had some kinda condition, the nurses came running in and comforted, dressed and treated her, whilst I looked down at the ground embarrassed, and then rushed back to my room. Later that afternoon, one of the nurses checked in my room to see if I was okay and asked if I'd like to play Nintendo. I'd actually never heard of it, but I said, "Yes please." I played Mario Brothers and Duck Hunt all week, until I was well enough to go home.

I remember telling me friends at school about Nintendo, like I'd just had some kind of religious experience and Daf said, "We've had a console for ages! And we have Famicom, Sega and PC Engine." I didn't really understand what he meant at the time but thought he must be one of those super rich kids and he dressed okay too. He was a bit of a joker and used to make me laugh. We also supported the same footy team, so we were already mates. He lived right across the street from Bronzer but with zero aspirations to lead the juvenile rat pack of Malvernites.

Back in the day, Daf's house was a local hang out for kids of all ages in our neighbourhood coz of all the video games he owned. He also had an older brother who was pretty quiet, but he must have been smart coz he went to a school called Melbourne High, where you needed to sit an entrance exam and finish in the top 10% of the state to be allowed in. Most of his mates were of Asian descent and I was usually told that their parents were doctors or lawyers or something like that. When I first visited their house, it wasn't the wealthy Malvern house I was expecting. Instead, it was in about the same condition as my place, except there were cats and clutter everywhere. It didn't smell good either. I think Daf's mum may have been a hoarder. Daf and his brother were too coz they had so many video games, and toys like Transformers, WWF wrestling figures, and heaps of quirky stuff. The dude copped a lot of shit from kids at school, coz he was sensitive about his nerdy love of collecting things. It was common knowledge that a kid in the year below us in school had broken into Daf's house on more than one occasion and swiped his games and consoles, but no one could prove it. I think his mum must have had insurance and replaced everything.

Daf's mum looked very old. She was white and grey haired and shopped at the op shop, so never had any new clothes. Daf's dad left them when they were young and he told me he was rich and had run away with a younger woman. All the toys and games were a combination of his father feeling guilty and spoiling the boys or the mum spoiling them coz she was lonely. She must have been depressed. Daf would speak badly of his dad and also his mum. We would be sitting in his lounge watching WWF wresting or one of his favourite films like *The Adventures of Ford Fairlane*, and he would scream at the top of his voice, "Mum, where's the fucken Barbecue Shapes?" Or "Mum, bring me the fucken Barbecue Shapes! Now, you old Bag!" And stuff like that. It was crazy. Years later I watched *Wedding Crashers* and thought that Daf was just like the character Will Farrell played, screaming at his mum, "Hey Ma! The meatloaf. We want it now!" I sometimes wonder if Daf gate crashes funerals now, trying to pick up grieving widows, while his poor mum cooks him meatloaf and puts up with his shit.

PART BLACK MEN CAN JUMP

here was a epic graffiti crew called 3174 (Noble Park's post code), who were from Noble Park, the suburb Oma and Opa lived in, so I'd noticed their 3174 tag spray painted around from time to time. The notoriety of 3174 was big enough that my whole family knew of them. The story was that the gang of 100 teenagers had turned on the cops when they attempted to break up a party and flipped a police car with two cops inside. I was told by my aunty this had made the local newspaper. I did remember seeing similar scenes in the movie *Colors*, so I'm not sure if they copied what they'd seen in the movie, or if the movie sparked the rumour.

During the school holidays or weekends I'd sometimes catch the train from Malvern to my cousins' place in Springvale. We used to play in the street a lot and my eldest cousin had developed a crush on an older kid, who was around 16. My cousin was about 13. The older kid was an okay dude and always chill with me. I think he had a crush on my cousin too, but nothing happened between them coz he was respectful. I noticed he wore Raiders jackets and hats and my cousin told me he'd joined the 3174 crew. He also used to hang out with his own cousin and there were a few other friends that used to hang with them. They were of mostly Aussie and Latino descent.

There were some other kids in that neighbourhood we'd hang out with and go to their houses from time to time. I remember there were two sisters, our age, whose names I can't remember, who lived with their single mum, who spent most of her time out drinking. Their house was across the road from milk bar and fish and chip shop, where everyone used to hang out. Rumour was the cousin of our mate in 3174 had broken into their house one night and raped the youngest sister. The rumour got back to my uncle and aunty and they decided they were going to move out of the neighbourhood. So, they bought a block of land in an outer seaside suburb called Mount Eliza and built a brand-new house. But they were still in the neighbourhood a little while longer while waiting for the house to be built. They must have finally got out at the right time, coz a few months after they moved out, someone was murdered inside a local phone booth. We used the phone booth all the time, especially to call our families overseas. The rumour was that the Vietnamese gang, Springy Nips, were responsible for that crime, but I'm not sure if anyone was ever charged with the murder. This was my introduction to gang-related crime and violence in Melbourne and the toll it took on local communities. But back in my neighbourhood I had my own problems to deal with.

During this time Bronzer, who was bigger than me would go out of his way to find out when I was coming over to Daf's house. He was really starting to piss everyone off in the neighbourhood and was constantly picking on Daf, telling him his house smelled like cat piss and mothballs, so Daf didn't like him much. For whatever reason, Bronzer attempted to jump me several times in Daf's front yard. When I'd arrive, he'd be pushing and swinging punches in my direction, which I'd always dodge. I don't think he ever landed a punch. But I sure landed them on him, putting him on his ass almost every time he tried to pull this stunt. He'd kinda try and make out it was just sparring each time by saying, "Okay, okay round one. I'll get you next time in round two." But he didn't have the hand speed or intent when he was throwing his punches. My punches were faster, harder and more accurate than all my friends. I was never scared to throw them if I had to, apart from a couple isolated incidents that will always bother me.

NBA and even the Australian NBL became big in Melbourne in the early '90s, so we'd sometimes go to local games. I supported the North Melbourne Giants and other mates supported the Melbourne Tigers. It seemed a lot more entertaining than the footy coz they had music, cheerleaders, hotdogs and it was indoors. We'd play basketball almost every day after school, and some of the richer kids got Nike Air Jordans or Reebok Pumps coz they could, but it didn't make them better players. I was still getting around in my standard plain Reeboks, but to my surprise Bronzer gave me an old pair of his Nike Air TWs, which were too big for me. It was one of his acts of actual friendship, which at the time made me think wow, what a great mate he was after all! I embraced his gift and wore them until they almost completely fell apart.

Daf and me started collecting NBA basketball cards. We'd snatch rare cards from one card shop and sell them on to another card shop in another neighbourhood to make some pocket money. It was a big thing at one point. We also kept cards to trade with other kids. Jackson stole more than all of us and he'd end up giving me a lot of things he'd ripped off coz I guess he didn't value the stuff or really even want it most of the time. We watched NBA whenever we could, and Bronzer had some dope documentaries on video of Michael Jordan that we'd watch. He also introduced us to a porn movie called *Rolex Girls* which we'd watch at his place on school holidays. It was a neighbourhood classic.

After much anticipation, Daf convinced his mum to buy him an adjustable basketball ring and put it in his backyard. He made the ring only about seven or eight feet tall, so it was pretty easy to dunk, except he didn't have a paved yard, so we had to play on grass, which made it difficult to bounce the ball. Daf decided he was going to be different to most people, who usually liked Bulls, Lakers or Celtics. Instead, he supported the Phoenix Suns, coz he liked the player Charles Barkly and had a purple Phoenix Suns singlet he'd wear all the time.

The basketball games were like rugby matches. I guess we figured if you're running and not bouncing the ball, we had the right to tackle you. There would often be small scraps and arguments. The basketball matches at Daf's eventually got banned, when a neighbourhood kid who looked about 30 at age 13, named Bazza, lost his cool after Daf dunked on him and said, "In your face Bazza!" Bazza got pissed off and attacked Daf, who managed to avoid getting hit, ran off and locked himself inside his house. Bazza attempted to kick the door down and when he couldn't, out of frustration, punched through a glass window instead, severing the arteries in his arm. The blood spurted out everywhere like a fountain in a mall and Bazza screamed his ass off. Daf's mum called an ambulance, and Bazza was taken off to hospital.

Bazza was a crazy kid. Rumours were, he'd been shaving

since the age of 10 and he jokingly told everyone he'd been given rock cakes at birth by his mum. I think Bronzer told him to say this. Bazza spoke with a deep slurred voice and would get very excited if he saw you in the street and would scream his ass off. He was also extremely easy to influence and would do almost anything, particularly bad shit. He went to a local public high school called John Gardiner. He collected shopping trolleys for the local supermarkets and made good money. He was always talking about local gang fights between graffiti crews and other gangs, or about the mysterious man in the black hat. We used to crack up laughing hearing his crazy stories.

One day we were playing basketball near the Tooronga train station with Bronzer and a kid we called Grimace coz he looked like the McDonald's character of the same name. Suddenly, Bazza ran up all excited screaming, "He knows! He knows! He knows!" Bronzer thought he'd exploit Bazza's excitement and said, "Bazza, smash ya head on the basketball pole, real hard!" So, Bazza ran up to the pole, grabbed it with both hands and began to bang his forehead into the pole as hard and as fast as he could, until he split his head open, and blood came gushing out everywhere. Then he just stopped, put his hand on his head and ran off home. I couldn't believe it. Bazza came back to the same basketball court about a month later whilst we were playing 'three-on-three' with some other kids. Bazza again ran over to us screaming his ass off, but this time Bronzer said, "Hey Bazza see that 30 year old lookin' bloke over there riding his bike, go run over smash him in the head as hard as you can, and steal his fucken bike!" And just like that Bazza ran over, punched the man straight in the jaw, knocked him off his bike, jumped on it and rode off. We had to pretend we didn't know him and then we ran off pretty quick. Bronzer or his older brother probably ended up with the bike.

Down by the Tooronga basketball court, we could see the trains riding past and we could often see graffiti on the panels, or even inside the train. By this stage we were tagging a lot, mostly with markers and sometimes spray paint. We tagged a lot of laneways. I became Druid after the character in the Asterix books, and our crew was FTM which stood for Fuck The Met, as in the Metropolitan Transport Service. To live up to our name we'd sneak up onto the train tracks, fill our pockets with rocks and when the trains rode past, we'd throw rocks at them trying to smash the windows. The train tracks were up on a hill, so there were plenty of places to hide behind trees, or in the long grass. There was also a water drainage tunnel there that could take you through to the other side of the tracks, an easy escape route if we ever got chased.

THE GAME YOU PLAY AND MOST GET BURNT, MONEY FELT MY PAIN THEN SPENT UP ALL IT'S WORTH

Money, Don't Take It Personal (2018)

Bugzie Sinclair

With all the weight loss I was starting to notice girls a lot more and felt like some of the girls might have their eye on me. I went for my first double date towards the end of Grade 6. Jackson had a couple of different girlfriends since I'd met him and his new girlfriend was a friendly red-haired girl, and her best friend was a pretty blonde. My date was from a privileged background, and I felt a little too ruff around the edges for her. Most of the girls around Malvern made me feel that way, kinda like they were always judging me as a troublemaker, or perhaps a little underlining discrimination for my German and black heritage, but who knows. We watched the movie *Cry Baby*, starring Jonny Depp. Man was it awkward when they started talking about French kissing, I didn't even know what that was or if I should kiss my date. Before that I'd always thought a kiss just meant on the lips, I didn't get the whole tongue thing, but it did make me curious. Jonny Depp was on the verge of becoming a superstar back then, and 21 Jump Street was a great show we'd watch on slumber parties and at our friends' houses. River Phoenix was also a favourite amongst the school yard banter, until he tragically died outside Depp's club, The Viper Room. Everyone loved the movie Stand by Me coz it spoke on our level.

My first date had given me confidence, I'd broken the ice and could say I'd officially been on a date with a girl, and not feel embarrassed. I even told my mum about her and called my date a few times, on the old landline but had to speak to her mum or dad, "Hi can I please speak to…" in my unbroken little kid voice. Damn it's so embarrassing thinking about that. The invention of mobile phones has made life so much easier. There were definitely girls that weren't so shy, usually the girls who were one or two years older than us, and I quickly learnt you had to pick the right ones. Jackson was a month younger than me but caught on faster, probably coz he had older siblings, and I guess we didn't call him Action Jackson for nothing!

Leading up to Christmas time, I guess I was feeling pretty good about myself. I had many new friends, I'd lost weight, had an under-cut hair style, Reebok kicks, cool clothes, and it was summer in Melbourne and I had a tan. I've always loved the hot weather; I feel like I can breathe better when it's warm coz it keeps the asthma at bay. There was a school Christmas Carol function on at the park and two girls my age had caught my eye coz I caught them smiling at me under a swinging branch tree in the local Malvern park. A blonde and a brunette. They went to a very expensive private girls' school. I exchanged numbers with both of them, and all my mates got very jealous.

I did the whole call up on the landline thing and spoke with both their parents, but this time both the girls were interested in meeting up. I didn't know who to choose, so I arranged to meet up with both of them. It was already Christmas holidays by this stage, so I think it must have been a weekday in December. I tried to look my best and bathed myself in Wayno's cheap aftershave and for some strange reason we decided we would meet at the closest cemetery in East St. Kilda, I probably wanted them to think I was fearless.

It ended up being a great idea coz I had both girls on either side of me grabbing my arm and holding onto me coz they were scared. After walking around for an hour, we jumped back on a tram and headed back to the park and said our goodbyes. A couple of days later, my mum brought in some mail and said this is for you. It was two separate love letters from the girls, asking me to be their boyfriend. I chose to call up the brunette on the landline again and it all backfired. It was the blonde who had really wanted to be my girl. This was my first lesson in the complications of dating. I didn't learn anything at the time though. In fact, I'm still learning to this day!

My favourite movie back then was *Scarface* with Al Pacino. When we were living in Ashwood, Wayno brought it to our place to watch with mum one Friday night. I waited until everyone was out the next day and chucked it in the VCR. I was in awe. The chain saw scene where Al Pacino said, "Why don't you try sticking your fucken head up your ass and see if it fits," always stuck in my mind. The movies *Goodfellas* and *Mobsters* came out a couple years later and Wayno mentioned that Costas Mandylor, one of the lead actors in Mobsters, had been a member of the body building gym he owned when he was younger.

Every time there was a fancy-dress party on, or at Halloween trick or treating with my Malvern friends, I'd dress up as a gangster. Al Capone, the original Scarface to be specific, with a black shirt, white tie, and a black gangster style hat with a white ribbon around the brim.

I'd watch any gangster movie I could get my hands on. I also read a book based on Myer Lansky's life when I was about 13. It was Wayno's book and I'd seen it lying around the house. I learnt all about gangsters from the early days in New York, particularly Lansky's close associates, Lucky Luciano, and Bugsy Siegel. I could relate to the gangsters mentioned in the book due to their ancestry and the fact that they, or their parents, migrated to America from Europe. The book had a huge influence on me.

As did all the gangster movies from that era. Later in life, I bought the Godfather box set from a junkie who was desperate for cheese. There were some dope Chicano gangster movies too, like Blood in Blood Out. But one of the most memorable movies that I ever watched was Boyz n the Hood. This movie was the bomb and we would watch it ritually at Memo's place on Saturday morning's followed by New Jack City and Menace II Society.

During those times I'd figured out that we didn't need to pay to visit the cinemas anymore. Wayno had taken on a part time job as an usher at the cinema's in Southland. His business wasn't going too well coz Australia was going through a recession. He was also the supervisor of the video games area, which was dope coz he had the keys to the games and gave us free credits. I took my mates along with me a coupla times. Unfortunately, for me and the crew, Wayno didn't work there for long. I think he felt embarrassed doing a job like that. I thought he should just stick with it, coz at least there was some coin rolling in for a little while. We were still very poor for people living in Malvern and Mum, and my grandparents weren't too happy about what he'd put us through with all the renovations. So, we had to devise new ways of seeing movies for free.

We worked out that if you went to the movies with a group of three or more, and two people bought tickets, then entered the cinema and got the end of their tickets torn by the usher to signify they'd paid for entry – meant that others just needed to wait in the toilets until someone met you in there and passed you one of the tickets the usher had torn. You'd then walk towards the cinema with the ripped ticket and trick the usher into thinking you'd already been in the cinema, so they'd let you in. The other person that was still in the cinema would repeat the process to get the other person in and so on. The other thing we'd do was look for faulty exit doors in the back alley behind the cinemas and pry them open with our pocketknives. That way no one needed to buy a ticket, and we'd sneak in large groups of 10 or more. The best thing in life are free, BBD tell 'em' bout free.

Family Untied

One of the biggest events of the early '90s was that Mum and Wayno finally tied the knot and I was his best man. This meant he went from being my mum's boyfriend to being my Stepdad! At the time I didn't realise the wedding would change our family dynamic and I wondered if my stepdad saw me as a mate rather than his son. He wasn't a social person and didn't have many friends. I guess I was just filling the role of best man at the ceremony. As the years went on and the pressures mounted due to the responsibilities of minding my brothers, feeling like I didn't belong, the domestic arguments, the renovations and living without so much – feelings that lived deep down in me for a long time – I started to resent my life in Malvern and question who I really was.

The wedding was a humble Catholic ceremony in Malvern. Mum had been baptised Catholic in Germany and Wayno, his mum and sister were also Catholic. The reception was in a nice restaurant near the Royal Botanic Gardens in South Yarra. I can remember having a great time with my cousins throwing corks from the champagne bottles at each other and I was dressed in a shirt and tie. Mum let me have a small glass of champagne and I snuck in a few more in with my eldest cousin! All our immediate family was there, and it was a pretty good day. And that's all I've got to say about the matter.

I'd not been baptised at this point, coz it didn't really seem like a priority with mum but that all changed not long after the wedding and I got baptised at the same time as my younger brothers. Prior to the baptism, I had to visit the priest and get lessons to become a Catholic, at St. Joseph's Church in Malvern. Somehow I passed the lessons and the baptism ceremony took place at the same church. At the time I was just pumped that I got a gold chain with a gold cross just like my Greek mates. In reality it was a formal recognition of spirituality, which helped me decipher things I'd always felt through out my childhood and had naturally influenced so much of my life.

Drinking a little bit of beer, wine or sometimes spirits around my family, seemed acceptable from a young age. I can remember Opa giving me the froth from his beer glass to drink from when I was a little kid living in the flat in Prahran. He was working as a brick layer and on hot days he'd get home from work and crack open a coupla 'longnecks'. If it wasn't the froth, he'd give me a sip from his glass of the cold beer straight, but just one or two and I didn't ask for more. You couldn't get German beer in Melbourne back then, so it was usually VB or Fosters. Oma and Opa also used to smoke like chimneys, with big heavy-duty ashtrays around the house. They used to smoke Benson and Hedges. I can remember finding the cupboards full of cartons and opening the packets and playing with the cigarettes. The gold packets got my attention. Every adult I knew smoked, it was like drinking coffee or tea, but more frequently. No wonder my asthma got so bad. I think Mum drank and smoked for most of her pregnancy with me, until someone told her not to.

My dad's side of the family drank more than Mum's side did. Dad's brothers could rarely be seen without a drink in their hand. Nana Mary could drink glasses of beer straight from the jug, one after the other without flinching. She had a reputation of being able to out drink anyone in the family and would never look drunk. Dad used to say it was her Islander genes, coz islanders have a reputation for being able to drink a lot. So, it stuck and I assumed that was the answer to my black heritage questions. Both my dad and Wayno gave me beer, but mostly light beer from the age of ten, usually on a hot summer's night.

When my friends from Malvern started introducing alcohol to parties in Year 7, I was never one to say no. I felt like my family wouldn't have minded, and they didn't really. I felt like it's almost what they expected that that's what we'd be doing. I didn't have a helluva lot of discipline from anyone in my family, although I did tread lightly with what I told them coz I didn't want to upset them. Wayno would tell a lot of stories about fights and various things he got up to as a kid, so did my uncles, and I felt like I wanted to live up to and experience all the fun they'd experienced when they were young.

My opa gave me a Swiss Army knife for my 11th birthday. He said, "Here you go, if someone attacks you, just stab them like this," and he demonstrated how to stab someone with his own knife pinpointing the middle of the stomach as the best place of contact. He had many different types of knives and tools, and I was always fascinated with them. He would peel golden delicious apples with a pocketknife like a snakeskin and for a joke put it on my head and stuff like that. He had false teeth, which he'd remove to pick out the food with the knife then screw up his face like the old man did in the old cowboy movie we use to watch. Yep, for an old Bavarian veteran, he really knew how to make us laugh, but as they say "don't bring up the war", opa hated that shit.

He also used to use the pocketknife to clean up branches that could be used as walking sticks, swords, and weapons of any kind. He made me an awesome bow and arrow once that would have caused serious damage if he'd sharpened the arrows, but they were blunt, so I couldn't hurt myself or anyone else. He made a range of weapons for himself too. He hammered long rusty nails into the bottom of his walking stick and then concealed the nails by placing masking tape over the top. He demonstrated how he would crack the stick over someone's head and cut them open with the nails if they tried to rob him. He also liked carrying a medium sized bag along with him wherever he'd go. The bag contained several weapons. Some of the weapons were a small iron crowbar, a box cutter, and a pepper gun. The pepper gun was a piece of PVC pipe, with masking tape on either end, and inside the pipe were crushed peppercorns. Opa's theory was, like capsicum spray, if someone attacked you, just rip off the tape and throw it in their eyes and blind the attacker. Lastly, he made little booby traps around the house to take out any would be burglars, lucky for the burglars they never messed with my grandparents.

THE RAIDERS

In 1991 I was in Year 7, there were some exciting, yet turbulent years ahead. Upon reflection, life had been ruff at times but it was all still pretty innocent, and nothing stressed me out that much. At the end of the day, I was a happy kid.

A lot of my friends left the School after Grade 6 to attend expensive private schools that their parents could afford. A whole bunch of new kids started at our school that year as it also taught the first 2 years of High School. Being one of the only public schools in the area the population was generally made up of students whose parents couldn't afford to send them to private schools or kids whose parents were hoping that their marks would be good enough to get into the elite 10% that would be accepted into Melbourne or MacRobertson High, via a Grade 8 entrance exam we all had to sit. Ahh, and this is when an Aussie kid, Medium entered my life, kicking off a legendary feud.

Even though Bronzer ended up going to a private school in Caulfield, he stayed in contact and used to call me up regularly for long chats about sports and girls mostly, and we'd also catch up in the neighbourhood. He invited me to his school fete at the start of the year and I couldn't believe how amazing the facilities were. I knew there was absolutely no way my mum could afford to send me to this school. I thought to myself, If I ever have kids and could afford it, I'd send them there.

I met a few of Bronzer's friends from school and they seemed like good kids. Most of them were Jewish. I didn't know about my Ashkenazi Jewish heritage at this point coz my oma just identified as being German. She didn't tell us until she was an old lady, when I guess she felt it was safe. It was a sensitive topic, and it was simply just too dangerous to speak about it when she was young. Discussing it clearly brought back trauma. Her Jewish grandfather was wealthy and owned a factory in Breslau and her grandmother worked for him as a maid and became more or less a concubine. She fell pregnant and gave birth to Oma's father who was baptised a Lutheran. Oma was also baptised Lutheran but needed to convert to

Catholicism before she married Opa. She said she was treated poorly, so she avoided the Roman Catholic community and for that reason both my grandparents preferred not to attend church unless they really needed too. The practice of religion can often be more cultural than spiritual. But I believe they were both close to God in their own way.

There weren't many girls in our year level, it was like we were at an all-boys school in most of our classes. There were plenty of girls in Year 8 and the year below us, but they looked like little kids now I was in high school. The Year 8 girls were all over us younger guys and I wasn't really expecting it, coz they were a lot more physically developed and most of them taller than me. It came as no surprise that Action Jackson was in on it and was happily cradle snatched by some lovely lady and pretty soon after that I fell into my own cradle trap when her bestie asked me to be her boyfriend. She'd caught me by surprise, so I just said, "Ahh, yeh sweet" but I wasn't interested in being someone's boyfriend. However, I had worked out what the other guys were doing to take it to the next level. It was to go out with an older chick coz they put out, and when I say, 'put out' I'm talking about being in Year 7 here, so that meant 'getting on'. Getting on was the term we used to describe making out. After school that day my new girlfriend's friend, came up to me and said, "Would ya like to get on with ya girlfriend in the park dunnies." I remember thinking her friend was hot, but so damn clinical. I said "cool" and that was that.

It was like a big public event as my Year 7 mates and most of the Year 8 girls all walked with us to the park. Jackson and me were holding our girlfriends hand's, followed by the group like we were in some kinda village ceremony. I felt like a baby in the arms of a woman. Sex hadn't even entered my mind. Anyway, we all lined up against the wall of the female toilet block, as the crowd started taunted us shouting, "Go, Go, Go... Hurry Up... Come On!" Then suddenly, Jackson locked jaws with his girl, then my girl side glanced at me and like a giant python, opened her mouth and moved in for the kill. I was in shock; I didn't know what to do. I just kept twirling my tongue around in her mouth, eyes wide open, looking at Jackson who was more experienced. The show went on, and I guess I've always been competitive and never liked losing, so I made sure I was the last to finish 'getting on' with my girl. After what seemed like a lifetime, I reckon it couldn't have been no longer than 30 seconds, I was done and my 'getting on' virginity was lost forever. We then exchanged numbers and I walked home with what was left of The Walking Club. Let the games begin!

From that day on, I was a kid on a mission and over the next few years I was intent on getting as many girls' phone numbers as I possibly could. It was the thrill of the chase, and there were so many pretty ones out there, so it's fair to say, I went all out. Our crew would always be venturing out into different neighbourhoods getting up to mischief or just kicking back at parks, basketball courts, train stations, parties or underage clubs. It felt like I was on a Viking ship conquering the new world and I was leading the raid!

Every weekend my black book would be filled with new numbers. Most of the time I'd never see the girls again. I was getting too many to call them all, so I started putting an asterisk next to the ones I really liked to try to remind myself.

I was very attached to my black book. I remember hearing the term on an old 'Australian comedy sitcom called *Acropolis Now*. One of the main characters, Jim, had a black book and he'd write different girls' phone numbers in it.

I loved the show *Acropolis Now*. Although my mum's side of family was German, not Greek, there were a lot of similarities with the experiences of all non-English speaking Europeans who migrated to Australia. In the show, the Greek characters called Aussie people 'skips' or 'Skippy the bush-kangaroos', like the old TV program about the mystery-solving kangaroo. The southern europeans called themselves Wogs and there's no real explanation for that name, but I've definitely heard a few people try to make it up. Anyway my point is, it was the first time I'd heard those names used on TV, and soon after I started hearing the phrases "Ya Fucken Wog" or "Ya Fucken Skip" a lot more in the playground. Yep the racial politics had started but my black book had no colour line!

STRAIGHT OUTTA MALVERN

One of my favourite classes throughout high school was English coz I had the opportunity to write and express myself. One of my favourite books that I read in Year 7 was, *The Outsiders* by S.E. Hinton (1967). My English teacher was an older Jewish lady. She didn't give me very nice school reports but I'm glad she taught me all about the colourful characters who lived in the pages of that book. I could relate to them, and in a way, felt like I lived a lot of what they went through over my teenage years, just in a different time and place. She also asked us to write poetry one day, so I decided to write three short raps. I called the group 'WAC' (Wankers and Cunts). My English teacher posted my raps and my bubble style font LP cover up high on the classroom wall for all the other kids to see. An older Year 8 kid who was African American approached me and laughingly said, "Hey man, those raps you did in the English classroom are wicked!" He also said he liked how I named the group WAC, and said, "That cracked me up man, I loved it." I was like thanks, then to myself I was like, shit, I called my group WAC. I wasn't thinking straight coz we used the word 'toy' more often than 'wack', but the Wankers and Cunts acronym was a joke so I guess I was kinda taking the piss outta my English teacher.

Shortly after that I asked Daf if he wanted to form a rap group and with a big "Fuck Yehhh!!" he was down. I called myself Pussy D and he was FagBox. I wrote most of the lyrics, but Daf wrote some too. We met in the local park on a coupla sunny Saturday afternoons and began recording demos on a Panasonic double cassette recorder. We called our first track *One Hundred Aisles & Running,* which fittingly paid homage to all the mischief we were getting up to in shopping centres. We'd just lay down our raps over the top of the NWA tracks or the drum beat and melodies on a Casio portable keyboard. It was great fun, but Daf wasn't as pumped about it as me and the routine faded pretty quickly. But now I had a taste for it, which went well with my other favourite hobby, makeshift weaponry.

One day all the Year 7s had to sit a compulsory maths exam

in the school hall. Our maths teacher's name was Mr. Tossa. He was an older, sterner type of teacher, but he did have a bit of understanding when it came to mischievous young kids. He wore a grey suit to school every day, which I kinda felt deserved a certain degree of respect, but not too much coz a new outfit wouldn't have gone astray. We all sat at our desks individually, in single file, so no one could cheat. Back then, all my school mates had learnt how to make the most lethal pen guns you could think of. Certain brands of pens would be more lethal than others. We basically removed the metallic tip still attached to the plastic part with the ink, which would work as an arrow, so the longer and sharper the tip, the more damage it would inflict. We'd then tightly attach a thick rubber band and then attach that to one end of the pen shell, which worked as a barrel.

During the math's exam everyone was busy writing with their heads down over their exam papers. Jackson turned around and saw Medium's head facing him like a massive bullseye, the distance from Jackson's desk to Medium's was about 10 metres, but Jackson had modified his pen gun to shoot the projectile at least 20 metres. Now, as Mr. Tossa was walking down the aisles and making sure no one was cheating, Action Jackson turned around with a massive smile, pointed his pen gun at Medium's head and let fire. Bam! He hit the bullseye. The pen tip and plastic ink cartridge stuck right into Medium's head. The whole maths exam of 60 plus kids gasped, and Medium stood up with the pen sticking out of his head. He then said something I'll never forget, "Is there something in my head?" The whole room erupted into laughter. Medium firmly yanked the pen out of his head and broke down. Mr. Tossa shouted, "Who has done this?" Jackson owned up and was sent straight to the principal's office. Kids were re-enacting the scene by pulling their pens out of their heads and laughing while the teachers left the examination room. We had to re-sit the exam a week later.

On a fucked up darker note, there were rumours that some of the kids I knocked around with had been going around the neighbourhood hunting birds, possums, and cats with these pen guns, and killing them. I wasn't into being cruel to animals, so I avoided hanging out with those kids for a few months while they were doing that bullshit.

I sometimes used to crash at my friends' houses on weekends and we'd stay up late and watch movies. During this stage, we were into horror movies like *A Nightmare on Elm Street* series, *Friday the 13th*, Stephen King movies like the original *IT*, and anything else we could get our hands on in the video store, without being told we were too young to rent them. One night, I was at Ike's place and asked him where Medium got his name from. To this point it had been a nickname he'd mentioned to me in confidence. They'd both gone to the same school together before coming to Malvern and I said, "I've never really been close friends with him, so I was just wondering why?" He then went into a lengthy story, cracking up laughing along the way, about how when they were at his birthday slumber party, they were in a tent together and Medium was flashing his dick around saying, "Look how big it is! And this is only my *medium* boner!" Man did I laugh when I heard that and when I got to school on Monday, I told Memo and Jackson about it. Then they told more people and the story spread, and everyone that heard it cracked up laughing. So, when the kids at our school saw him, they started saying things like, "How you goin' Medium?" or just shouted, "Medium!" and waved their pinky finger at him.

I guess he didn't like this too much and one day as we were walking home through the park someone shouted out "Medium!" at him from a distance. I was honestly feeling sorry for him and had stopped saying things about it coz I could tell it had gone beyond a joke and he was getting upset. In actual fact, I felt a bit guilty about the whole thing coz I'd kinda let the worm outta the sack. However, instead of charging at the kid who'd shouted it, Medium saw red and charged like a wild bull towards me. I was a little shocked coz I thought he was going towards the kid who was actually taunting him, but no, I was the target. I was the shortest in the group, but he didn't know I could fight. I ended up beating him up pretty good in front of a large group of people and he started to cry. When I could see the tears fill his eyes I stopped, helped him to his feet, put my arm around him and said, "Are you alright man?" My friends teased me for doing this, but that was just me being me. I didn't want to have any enemies; I had enough issues at home with Mum and Wayno arguing all the time. It was simple, he charged at me, I defended myself, he got his ass kicked, and in my eyes, it was fair fight. I shook his hand, but he never spoke to me again and I never teased him after that. Shortly after that day, Medium changed schools. The Medium joke had gone far enough, I never intended on being a bully, but unfortunately the facts are that he thought I was, and he intended on letting me know it. And that wasn't the end of it; there was much more to come and on a grander scale too.

Towards the end of that year, I started writing songs again and spoke to Daf about forming another group. Daf was the guitarist, me and another kid were the singers. Daf was a big Chuck Berry fan and the best song he could play was *Johnny B. Good.* I loved that song, so we'd rehearse it together a lot. I told the South African music teacher about what we were doing, and she was impressed and asked us to perform in front of the school, while they were rehearsing for the end of year concert.

Some Year 8 girls I'd made out with throughout the year were there. The girls were laughing hysterically at our dance moves. The teacher liked our performance and asked us to perform as a solo act at the end-of-year concert. I was pumped. I knew we were going to kill it, and we did! On the night of the performance, we dressed in trench coats with berets, and at the end of the performance we got a standing ovation. I remember my Year 8 mates cheering and howling stuff out at us. That was a big compliment to me coz they were the cool kids of the year above us and it was great they showed their support. The small theatre was packed with at least 300 people, so when the applause started it felt like the roof was about to blow off.

A few weeks before the performance I'd seen the American Year 8 dude and his mate open up my front gate and fill up a water bottle with the hose in our front yard. They couldn't see me coz I was at the other end of my street on the way to school. Once they filled the bottle, they quickly ran off to the side alley around the corner. When I got to school, I went up to them on the ramp where they used to chill and said, "Hey

I saw you guys filling up water in my front yard this morning."
And the American dude just goes, "Oh man that's your front
yard, sorry dude we were just getting stoned before school." I
made a gesture with my hands, which suggested I thought they
were shooting up coz I'd recently seen someone mix smack with
water and inject it in their arm in a gangster movie. The other
dude said, "No way amigo, it's just weed, we were only filling
up the bong dude." At that point in my life, I'd only seen people
on TV smoking joints and didn't know about bongs. I was just
12 years old, but I still wanted to try it. My mate Farmer was
originally from South Australia, where it's always been legal to
grow a certain number of plants at your home. Farmer said he
could get some and had tried it before, so I asked if he could
bring some back from South Australia coz sometimes his family
would go back there for long weekends and school holidays.

A few weeks later he came back with some, but it was just
the dried leaves that we used to call kiff. Anyway, we met
up one night and we smoked it through his dry pipe. I guess
we got a little high, but we needed to smoke a lot of it to feel
anything. Farmer's dad brewed his own beer, so it was always
easy to get it when you were hanging out with him. One time,
he brought back some cocaine. Being a massive Scarface fan,
this was something I'd always wanted to try. It was cut pretty
heavily with sugar, but it still made my mouth numb and got
me high. Memo was there and had a line too. We left Farmer's
house that evening and jumped back on our BMXs to head
to John's Pinnies to hang out a little more and play pinball or
Final Fight, like we always did.

As we were riding towards John's Pinnies, Memo slowed

down and said to me, "Man we're going to Hell for taking that shit" I looked up into the stars and said, "God if we have done something wrong, give us a sign." We were riding our BMXs without helmets, which was against the law, but they'd only recently introduced on-the-spot fines for breaking this new law. As we approached the pinnies, a cop car pulled up behind us, and flashed its lights and siren. We were still high, looked at each other and took off from the cop car at high-speed peddling as fast as we could through alley ways, backstreets, and blocks of flats. They'd obviously called in for back up, so there were at least three cars chasing us. We eventually lost them completely and made our way back home. As I said goodbye to Memo that night, I said, "See, that was the sign." He just froze, turned around and looked at me. He was speechless, then his dad came to the door and let him in. Had it really been a sign from God? Well, the way I saw it, of course, it fucken was! Did I choose to listen? Hell No! So, we continued to terrorise the streets the best we could. Nevertheless, I did learn something that night. I should never test my faith and temptation has its consequences.

Jackson was also getting into the gear with Farmer and they were getting into more serious crime, although I'm sure smoking harmless leaf had nothing to do with it. They'd broken into one of the local Army Disposal stores by smashing a brick through the front shop window on a Saturday night. They didn't tell me about this: I found out from Memo, who was bragging about the new Swiss Army knife Jackson had given him. Jackson eventually told me and gave me one too. They'd gotten away with knocking off thousands of dollars of knives, tools and camping equipment. Jackson was still only 12 years old, Farmer barely 13. Not long after that Farmer's parents moved him to another neighbourhood in the outer east, far away from Malvern and he disappeared from my life, along with hundreds of other faces I've met along the way. As time went by, one day I randomly bumped into an old school friend she said, "Oh my God did you hear about Farmer?" I said, "No, you mean Farmer from school?" She said, "Yes, he killed himself about a year ago." And suddenly, I got this image of Farmer up in heaven smoking a massive bong, contemplating his next burg!

MENACE II YOUR SOCIETY

During the early '90s, there were some dope tracks released that made their mark in Melbourne and culturally helped shape a new generation through fashion and music. Songs by Naughty by Nature such as *OPP*, De La Soul's *Ring, Ring, Ring,* and Kris Kross's *Jump* started getting a lot of exposure on Australian commercial radio and TV video shows, like Rage and Video Hits. Or if you were into the underground scene rap groups like Public Enemy and Geto Boys were getting more popular and you could find their tapes or CDs in the independent stores like Central Station, where you could play on the decks if you wanted to try scratching and mixing.

My look was changing again to suit the music I loved the

most. Leading up towards the summer holidays, I started slicking my hair back with hair gel. It had grown pretty long by this stage and Opa used to do my undercut with hand clippers, into what we called a 'skin undercut'. He liked doing this, saying he used to have his own hair like this as a boy, just not so long on top. But damn it used to hurt coz the hand clippers would pinch the skin and draw blood. The first few times he did it I'd be going back to school with scabs all around my head, until the undercut grew back a little. I used to wear a black turtleneck skivvy, underneath a denim or sometimes checked shirt, buttoned all the way to the top, like I'd seen the Chicanos wear in the movies. My mates were starting to dress this way too. Initially, I'd wear Blundstone boots, that all the kids in school thought were lethal coz they had steel caps, or later some more stylish mustard-coloured Doc Martens, which looked more like Timberlands. I'd also been given a pair of Nike Air Max 180s by Bronzer, which I used to wear, but like the first Nike kicks he gave me, they were pretty worn out, but a hustler don't make a fuss ya, know what I'm sayin'? The pants I used to wear were Stussy. My mum loved these coz they were durable and would last a long time. She found no-brand imitation Stussy too, which were just as good, and you couldn't tell. It was an interesting time fashion-wise coz before then I'd say most kids our age would dress like surfies, but the scene was in transition and we started calling those people skegs. The introduction of hip hop to the mainstream, combined with the promotion of American sports, particularly NBA and NFL, led to more kids dressing like Americans.

The older writers back then in our neighbourhood seemed

to prefer the surfy look, but I noticed as the era progressed, they went onto dress more like 80's writers from New York with tighter jeans, shirts, parkas or puffer jackets. The skegs, retaliated by calling us homies, which was short for homeboys. To me the name felt derogatory, like being a wannabe. The term wog was used more often and in association with the word nigga. Crazily, it seemed white people suddenly thought it was socially acceptable or hip to use those words. I was never comfortable with it. I was part black, but obviously aware of the fact I looked more European, I couldn't help the fact, that the racial slurs caused conflict with in myself.

The full homeboy era kicked into Melbourne from about 1991. The look was assessed on how baggy your jeans were or by how bright your clothing was in general. Brands such as Starter, Nike, Adidas, Fila, Puma, Reebok, Cross Colors, and Australian designer clothes like Country Road were all massive during this time. The clothes were expensive, so if you couldn't afford them or manage to 'rack' them from somewhere, old suit pants, a flannel shirt, or a bandanna of the appropriate colour, would give you the look, without the price tag!

American sporting clothing from all the big teams across the codes were worn just for fashion and not as a sign of team support. Baseball caps were massive, and you also needed to wear them a certain way to distinguish you as a homie. They had to be worn high on your head, like the wind was gonna blow it off any second. You could wear it forwards or backwards and it looked best if your head was shaved underneath. Sometimes people would have a ponytail or braids sticking out the snap-back part. I remember my hat was so high, I walked into a music store in the city, placed a 12 pack of blank cassette tapes (which I used to make mix tapes with) under my hat and walked out again without the anti-theft sensor alarm being able to detect me in the doorway coz my hat was above it.

Most Fridays after school or Saturdays, we found ourselves on missions to play video games. *Street Fighter 2* was the biggest game out. In fact, big is an understatement – it was actually fucken massive! I'd first seen it played in a 7-Eleven in Malvern, while we were getting Slurpees. There were all these kids just standing around watching. I was mesmerised. One kid after another would pop dollar after dollar into the machine and challenge the winner. It was a video game Colosseum! There were a lot of Asian kids into this game, and I'd noticed way more Asian kids around the places we used to hang out. They were always in massive groups, dressed like homeboys too. They were mostly Vietnamese kids, or Filipino. There were Chinese, Korean, Malaysian and Indonesian kids too, but the Viet and Filo kids were more into gangs and usually rolled in big numbers. Sometimes they had their little brothers or sisters with them, who were younger than us at the time. We were younger than most kids around the traps.

The Viet kids were developing a bad reputation for being violent and using machetes in fights. They'd been involved in several stabbings and the term that was used was 'Chop'. They'd also swear a lot in Vietnamese. If they lost a challenge in *Street Fighter 2*, the word everyone got to know and would repeat was 'Do-Ma' which means 'Fuck your mother'. The Vietnamese gangs were from neighbourhoods like Springvale,

Richmond, Footscray and St. Albans. I'd always carry a blade with me and so did all my mates. Apart from Swiss Army knives, I also had a lethal long, thin, sharp-bladed flick knife I called Slither, and a mini butterfly knife. Jackson had a full-sized butterfly knife, which I used to carry and play with sometimes. I bought Slither from a local Chinese grocery store, no ID required or questions asked back then. It cost me seven dollars, after I'd hustled the store owner down from $10.

Memo and I had an after-school routine from Year 7 we called 'The Procedure'. He lived just two streets away from me, so we'd both go home have a snack, watch a bit of TV, especially if *Fresh Prince of Bel Air* was on. We couldn't miss that show and we'd rap out the Fresh Prince song on the way home. After the show Memo would come back up to my place with a soccer ball and go for a kick up at the local park or school. Sometimes we'd substitute the soccer ball for a basketball, football or play cricket instead. Other kids would join us too from time to time, but mostly it was just us. And that was officially 'The Procedure'. We always had a good time, hanging out having a laugh and playing sport, always competitive but more just for fun, to improve skills and keep fit. I think that's why we became good mates for such a long time. We started meeting other kids from around our neighbourhood, some of them went to other schools. It was during these times I also became mates with Devious, whose dad owned the local liquor store in the hood; a very good friend to have back in those days.

The day I met Devious he was riding a pink and black Mongoose BMX with long pegs on the wheels, and he was wearing an Adidas tracksuit with a Carlton Football Club scarf tightly wrapped around his neck, and a cap on backwards. I realised by the way he was dressed he was not from Malvern; he was from Doncaster and went to a high school about 15 kilometres away from our hood. Devious would help his dad after school and on weekends by working in the liquor store, stacking the cool room and shelves, and serving customers. In return, his dad would give him cash to splash down at the pinnies. Both Memo's and Devious's families were very good to me and treated me as family. They were always happy to bring me into their homes and provide food and warmth for me, especially when things were ruff at my family home, which was pretty constant. Memo and I would help Devious stack the cool room when his dad asked us too, which meant we could help ourselves to soft drinks, snacks like Burger Rings, Twisties, Samboy Chips and alcohol, long before we turned 18. These were some of the best days of my life but there would be turmoil on the horizon.

CiTY oF OMG

Throughout '92, I was spending most weekends with my mates hanging out in the city, or at random pinnie parlours around the traps. The problem was, I often didn't have a lot of money. I was getting $3 a day, 6 days a week on my paper round and Mum always encouraged me to save and not waste it all on video games. I tried to keep a coupla dollars aside each week for Maccas while we were out and about coz I thought that was a better way to spend my flow, and maybe keep some spare for a game or two of pool, which lasted longer than the video games. I also needed to buy a tram, train or bus tickets, coz of all the gumbys riding the train lines issuing fines for fair evasion. Gumby was the name we used to refer to the conductors or inspectors, coz they mostly all wore green back then I'd try and avoid buying tickets as much as I could, after all our crew was FTM, but I got stung a couple of times and the fines were steep.

Most of my mates seemed just as broke as me, but that was coz they were blowing all their dosh on video games. There was a lot of hustling going on to make extra cream and there was also 'rolling', when you'd stand over people for things they had that you wanted. Other crews would try and roll you too, so you had to be careful.

Yep, burgs, racking and basically steeling anything, anywhere, anytime, we did it all. Associates would pay good money for hot goods like bikes, car stereos, audio equipment, sports gear, Walkmans and TVs. There were other scams too, like windscreen washing at busy intersections. Sometimes we'd go door-to-door knocking asking for donations for random made-up charities, even giving out dodgy receipts. A favourite was nicking spark plugs we called clickers from people's backyard home hot water services, then use them to shock video game machines to get free credits. Then there were the dealers, coz a hood simply ain't a hood without them and it usually paid better than the other scams. But all the crime aside, on a really good day you just found some money in the street, or between a couch or seat on the train, or in a coin slot somewhere. I can't vouch for everyone, but the feeling of finding change always made me feel better about my life, like someone cared and was watching over me.

As our appetite for crime increased, so did the amount of tagging we did. "What the hell did the Met ever do to us?" Sometimes kids would ask, but they soon changed their opinion after coppen a coupla fines off the gumbys, but they had a good point.

I started finding entertainment in the stories Devious told us about the Doncaster Wogs and the crazy fights the fellas in his neighbourhood got into, and the infamous underage club, Existence, where all the young hot chicks use to go to. He hyped us up about it for months. Then one day he came down to the Tooronga Basketball court wearing a white bandanna and told us he'd joined a crew called Columbo. I was told 3174 had split up and evolved into smaller crews. The word on the street Columbo was one of them. If what I was told was true, it was odd Devious had joined Columbo, coz 3174 were from Noble Park, and Doncaster was in the opposite direction, by at least 30 kilometres. Anyway, we took his word for it, and it gave me a lot more confidence that one of my best friends had joined a crew with street cred like that. And now, I wanted in!

Devious loved fishing and sometimes, we'd ride our BMX's down to the Yarra River, with our fishing rods and chuck a line in. I caught an eel one time down there, but not much else. We had a few more successful trips down at station pier in Port Melbourne, where I caught some leather jackets and a flathead. Sometimes Devious's older brother would drive us to Rye, a place where a lot of immigrant Europeans had holiday homes, or sometimes Sorrento or Portsea. I caught squid a few times off the pier there, and an octopus. It was a rare catch. One random day, fishing down the Yarra with Devious, Memo and Li'l Memo, we were climbing the bridge with our fishing lines in the water. Outta nowhere my mates started throwing rocks at me, for a joke initially, but it was stupid coz the rocks were kinda big and would fuck you up if they hit you in the head. I said, "What the fuck are you doin'?" Lil' Memo, who was about a year or two younger than me, goes, "Fuck you, skip." I said, "I'm not a skip, dickhead, my mum's German." Devious and Memo saw that I was pissed off and for some reason decided they wanted to have a crack too. I was in shock; these were meant to be my close mates. "You're still an Aussie," said Memo. I said, "Fuck you, my mum was born in Europe like your mum." "Well, you look Aussie," said Devious.

I couldn't believe it. I was pissed off, ready to knock them all out. I felt like I was red in the face with anger. "Just coz I'm not Greek, you're gonna call me a fucken skip?" I packed up angrily and we left the fishing spot. The BMX ride home was cold and dead quiet. The three Greek boys rode ahead speaking the Greek words they knew but they didn't realise I was starting to understand their language and they were bitching. When we were pedalling down the last street en route to our houses, I called out to them, mad as hell; "Hey, wait there. If you ever disrespect me like that again we're no longer mates, or fight me now if you want to, coz I'm not backin' down. I'm as much a wog as you, coz if my mum didn't migrate here from Germany I wouldn't exist." But, the truth was being mixed heritage was a lot more complicated than that. It was a fight that only I could understand!

They never called me skip after that, but they had definitely challenged who I was and it sucked. I was getting really fed up with the Melbourne ethnic cultural habit of having to identify yourself as some kind of stereotype, then wearing it like a banner across ya chest, coz you're proud of who you are, or considered inferior. Things weren't like that in Primary School. But from the early '90s whenever I'd meet other ethnic kids it was very common to be asked, "What natio (nationality) are ya?" That question was never really straight forward for me. The easiest thing for me to say was that "I'm German." It made the most sense, especially having spent so much time growing up with my grandparents who had thick German accents. As I got older and I was in touch with my father a little more I would say that "I'm German and Australian part Pacific Islander," coz that's what he would tell me. To this day I still feel the need to reveal my ethnicity to people I first meet as an introduction to who I am and what values I represent, searching for a sense of familiarity in them and longing to have a connection with their ethnicity. I'm Australian coz that's what it says on my passport, but the reality is more complex than that in Melbourne. It's about acceptance and having that support network of people who understand who you are. Me? I'm mixed descent, my blood flows through the rivers of many lands, with every stream I grow stronger, more resilient and with time more empowered. Knowledge is wisdom, acceptance is bliss!

FRESH PRINCE OF MELBOURNE

I needed to find a new school. I'd gotten a low score on my entrance exam so I couldn't go to Melbourne High, and apart from that I was limited by the number of schools to choose from. In the vicinity of Malvern the majority of schools were private, and their fees were ridiculously expensive. For many parents the expensive school fees wouldn't have caused a dent in their finances, but in my situation there was no way my mum could afford it, and there was absolutely no way Wayno or my dad would be paying for it either. In a reckless and short-sighted move the state government shutdown 350 public schools in 8 years, crazily to save on costs, which forced me to travel into the outer suburbs to find a school that would enrol me.

I applied at a few public high schools, but I was told they were at capacity and that my behaviour reports were not acceptable. So, Mr. Tossa took it upon himself to try and locate a school that would accept me. Syndal High was more than 10 kilometres from my neighbourhood but was also set to close soon and was progressively being merged with Syndal Tech and then Glen Waverley High. Daf, Memo and coupla other kids from Malvern were in the same boat as me. On Mr. Tossa's advice our parents enrolled us in Syndal High. The penny had dropped, I'd lived in Malvern for almost four years and after mixing it with the rich privileged kids, the reality was, "It's back to the 'burbs where you belong, Benny Boy!"

Thanks for fucken up my education Premier Kennett. We began the Year 9 school year in 1993.

Mornings would start with my paper round, which meant waking up before 5 am, then after work get home, have breakfast and get ready for school. Pass by Memo's place by 7:15 am to make the 7:30 am train from Tooronga train station, where we would meet Daf, and then ride nine stops to Syndal station. It was then another 20 minutes walk from Syndal station to our school, and we needed to arrive before 8:45 am. Then repeat the process again on the way home. There were alternative routes, but we worked out this was the fastest. If we missed the 7:30 am train we'd always be late to school and needed to get a late pass from the office, for the purpose of God knows what? I often missed the 7:30 am train, it was a tight schedule and sometimes I could be late getting home from my paper round if there was heavy rain or some issues with my bike.

The first day at Syndal High is a bit of a blur coz I wasn't too excited about it, but at least I had some mates from Malvern with me. The other Year 9s immediately called us 'The Malverners' and once again the book, The Outsiders, spoke to me. There were a lot more girls at this school, and over the next few months I didn't waste any time in making out with some of the girls and getting phone numbers to organise weekend dates. Daf and Memo were doing well with the ladies too, something they'd held back on a little in the past. I'd never seen either of them even talk to a girl before we arrived at the new school. On the first day I rocked up to my first English class and a kid who had hair like mine, but was a little fairer and Aussie looking, called out to me and said, "Hey sick cunt, come sit here!" Some of the girls in the classroom started laughing. I initially thought, here we go I'm gonna have to fight this dude, first class, first day, first minute. But he was just looking to make a new mate and couldn't stop talking. The term 'sick cunt' was actually a compliment. The dude's name was Shane and based on what he was telling me he was a massive weed smoker and always up to no good. He also let on that his dad was a big drug dealer. I wasn't sure if this was legit or not, but Shane told me he could get his hands on any drugs I wanted. He had quite a lot of gold he would wear and flash around school.

On the make out front, within two weeks I'd had another one of those public events with a girl called Roslyn. The next day as I rocked up to school, Shane pulled me aside and whispered, "Hey man watch out, Wozza from the Forest Hill Wogs wants to bash ya for gettin' on with Roslyn." My first reaction was, "Yeh fucken good luck to him," but Shane was adamant the Forest Hill Wogs were big, and they were all in years 10-12 of the school. It seemed Year 9 was mostly Aussie's so I gathered I wasn't getting back up from them, and I didn't feel I could rely on Memo or Daf for back up either when it came to fights. "What the fuck is Forest Hill?" I asked Shane. "It's a shopping centre," he said. I was starting to think Wozza and the Forest Hill Wogs were sounding a bit like Robin Hood and his merry men.

I wasted no time in tryna work out what this Wozza mofo's problem was. If he thought I was a pussy, he had another thing coming. Deep down though I was a little shook and I had to be smart about how I handled the situation. I found refuge by assuring myself that if the fucker's wearing green tights I'll grab the nearest fire hydrant and spray the cunt. So, we met up in the school yard at the first recess in the perfect spot for a fight where the teachers wouldn't see anything. All the kids circling around us were Year 9s and 10s, so I was ready to do what I needed to do physically but it was a helluva lot easier than that and probably gained me the respect of the whole school.

Firstly, he got in my face a little bit asking, "Why did you get on with my girl?!" I just stayed cool, took a deep breath and said, "Mate she told me she was single." He didn't like that too much and said something threatening, which I can't remember, I just said, "Yeh well you lay a hand on me, you're gonna see half of Columbo up here by lunch time looking for you." He went white, shut the fuck up and backed down completely. His mates had heard of the crew I was talking about, and they all backed down and showed me respect after that. I didn't quite know what to make of this Sherwood Forest Ewok fucken crew at my new school, but some of them were okay on their own, I guess.

There was a lot of weed smoking going on at Syndal High, mainly with Shane and some of his year 10 mates. The other Malverners were in different classes, so had made other friends. The spot for smoking weed was called The Orchards, a small apple orchard at the back of the school, which we needed to pass through to get to school on time. We'd often seen Shane and the year 10's coming out stoned outta their minds making their way to classes.

"Hey sicko!" (short for sick cunt) Shane yelled out one morning and added, "Come smoke some cones with us at lunch time." You technically had to leave the school grounds to get to the apple orchards, so if you got caught, you'd be suspended or expelled. I had it in my mind I wanted to finish and pass year 12. Although I mucked around in class, I always did my schoolwork and never failed a subject. I felt like I had it ruff at home and I didn't wanna struggle my whole life. I pictured myself landing a decent job, but working 9-5 seemed boring AF, to me. The teachers used to say I was easily distracted, they were right, so I said, "Yeh, why not man."

Inside The Orchards the choofers had made a clearance with corrugated iron you could sit on or even use to make a shelter. Shane pulled out a bong from under a tree and packed me a cone. Man was that shit strong, I was seeing white ... It was nothing like the kiff I'd smoked around Malvern in the past. I remember sitting back in class and it looked like the walls were moving and the clock was melting, Shane was pissing himself laughing. He said the type of weed we were smoking was called Sinse and it was the best smoke going around.

The Malverners also liked sitting around The Orchards on the way home from school, but they'd sit on the other side to the choofers. Sometimes girls from the school would join us too. Daf and Memo weren't into weed at all but for some reason Daf used to bring a dry pipe along to school and we'd get our 'Huckleberry Finn' on and smoke acorns and leaves for the hell of it, light campfires, and also build huts from the corrugated iron, which was left in a big heap in the middle of The Orchard. One day we mustn't have put the campfire out, which TBH was more like a bonfire, coz the whole apple orchard erupted into flames. It was massive news that made the local papers and brought the whole school to an assembly the next morning. The principal spoke, "Those who are

responsible please come forward as this is now a police matter."
Was this dude crazy? No way in hell was I or my mates getting
pinned for some lame ass fire. Thankfully, everyone in the
school kept their mouths shut and the whole thing was quickly
forgotten. We were all back hanging out in The Orchards again
within weeks.

However, brushes with the law became harder to dodge. We
were hanging around the neighbourhood a lot more, especially
on weekends and almost every day after school till late. Cops
would drive by all the time and ask us what we were up to, tell
us to go home or take our names if they felt like it, probably just
to scare us into behaving. The first time I had my name written
down was when we were on one of our many adventurous
trips to the city. On this particular day it was summer and
very hot. After playing video games we decided to take a dip in
an old water fountain that used to be right in the middle of the
City Square. I thought the water was pretty gross, but I guess
it was one of those 'Huckleberry Finn' moments again. I was
with Devious, Jackson and Memo. Back then Swanston Street
was a busy main road but for many years now they've made it
a walkway, and for trams and bikes only.

On this day my mates were in a hurry to board the tram
home, which meant we had to cross the busy street. They ran
across first, I was soaking wet and hesitated before running
across the road. "Come on, hurry up you pussy!" Jackson
yelled. Yep he'd hit a soft spot, fuck you man I thought
and I just blindly ran onto the road. A big ass van suddenly
slammed on its brakes but was still heading towards me real
fast. In a split second, I reached my hand out and grabbed the

hand railing and pulled myself onto the tram. It was a miracle I survived. All the people on the tram were in shock, "You could have been killed love," an old lady said to me. God had my back that's fosho. I was glad to be alive and was feeling euphoric coz I instantly felt that spiritual feeling I'd felt in the past. It was short lived and when I heard a knock on the tram window behind me, a cop jumped on the tram, pointed his index finger in my direction and said, "Come with me boys." He told us we'd jay walked, and we'd all be fined. I wanted to say, "Seriously mate I pulled off one of the greatest stunts ever seen on Swanston Street and now your gonna piss on my bonfire and fine my ass... Dammn...Fuck tha Police!" But truthfully, I was stressing and thought it's best I told Mum. Surprisingly, she tried to ground me. I was pretty sure Mum had just seen or heard the term 'grounded' on a soapie or something, but I went along with it ... For a day, then I was back on the streets again and the fine never came!

On a slightly more serious occasion, one weekend with all the schools being closed, we got word that a High School, opposite to where Grimace was living, had been abandoned and it had some cool stuff inside. So, Bronzer, Grimace, Daf and me made our way down there with a basketball, so any witnesses thought we were just there to use the courts. We broke into the school and started looking around. It was a complete waste of time, but Daf was convinced he'd find some computers. I was honestly just there for the cheap thrill, with little regard to the fact that I was actually breaking the law. I was pissed off coz this was another school the state government had shut down. I just felt like I wanted to smash windows and rob whatever I could. We threw an answering machine and a phone out the window to Bronzer and Grimace. Suddenly we started to hear sirens in the background, but we didn't realise it was for us, we were very naive. As we casually left the building on our own accord, coz we were done snooping about, we were swarmed by two SWAT teams in vests with a police dog, closely followed by another six cops in three patrol cars. We were arrested and taken to the nearest police station in Camberwell. It was a massive overkill of law enforcement. The school had been shut down by the state government, I'm sure it was about to get demolished soon anyway. But the cops didn't give a shit, they had a sergeant to answer to, and that's all that concerned them. Oh, and quotas to achieve.

While we were waiting for our parents to pick us up, the cops told us they were going to charge us with breaking and entering but coz we were minors we'd only be put on a good behaviour bond. I still have no idea what that means coz I got a lot of those as a youngster, and nothing came of them. I can't remember getting in too much trouble from Mum or Wayno this time, but they mentioned that someone had broken out of jail that weekend and for some reason the cops thought it was them when the alarm went off at the school.

A JUVENILE THIEF I RAN WITH DECEIT, LIKE ROCKIN' UP TO BARBIES I CARRIED THE BEEF

Back in the Day, *King Hits* (2009)

Smooth Criminals

The Harold Holt Swimming Pool was a big hangout place over summer in our neighbourhood. I'd always liked that swimming pool and had good memories of going there. John's Pinnies wasn't too far away from there either. Over the summer holidays and weekends, I'd hang out at the pools a lot and got to know a few more kids in the neighbourhood, and heaps of private school girls around my age.

Everybody used to sit on a hill near the diving pool, smoke cigarettes or weed, make out, listen to music, sneak in booze, or chat up girls. There were a few dudes who were pretty good at doing tricks from the big 10 metre towers and diving boards. I would keep my tricks simple off the one or three metre board and drop bombs or another lame move we called a horsey. The scene was kind of like a cross between *Point Break* and *Dirty Dancing*, with a lot of Swayze-type characters lurking around who were older than us, like the lifeguards. Some were as old as 25, which was dodgy as fuck with all these young private school chicks hanging around them.

A lot of girls from my old school had moved onto private schools and those older Year 8 girls used to go to the pools as well. There was an Italian girl from that group, Bella, who was a couple years older than me but used to call me on my home phone all the time. We fooled around a little bit, but she was more like a friend, and she used to hook me up with her friends too. One day she was at the pool with one of her friends and they started messing around, treating me like their little cousin or something and asked, "Can we put make-up on you and dress you up like a girl?" At first, I was like, "No way." Then Bella said, "I'll give you $20 if you do it and walk a lap around the pool." That was great money, and I was just 13, and I just wanted to make these girls laugh ... But dammnn it was one of the most embarrassing things I've ever done! The whole fucken pool of like 1000 people right in the middle of summer, men, women, and children were cheering, chanting and laughing their asses off, even wolf whistling at me. I'd almost completed my lap when four *Point Break* looking motherfuckers who looked like Bodhi and the Dead Presidents tried to push me in the pool. They should have known not to mess with Johnny Utah...well I mean shouldn't have messed with mini Johnny Utah in a dress! I fought them off a bit, but the motherfuckers got me in the pool. Man I was pissed off, but I made sure the girls paid me my $20.

When the pool party came around a month or so later, Bella called me and asked me if I'd like to, "Rock up to the party with her and her friend." I was a bit hesitant, this time, but she convinced me, by saying "We're bringing a bottle of vodka." So, I said, "Cool, where u wanna meet?" It was the first time I'd ever tried vodka and it fucked me up big time. Like a teenage pimp I had one chick under either arm and we were fooling around in the park before we arrived at the pool party.

When I got there, the girls were out of control making out with everyone and I thought fuck it I'm gonna do the same. I was so smashed I never remembered entirely what happened after that, but the rumour was that I'd made out with 50 chicks and the Italian chick had ended up in an apartment banging one of those Swayze-looking dudes. I doubt it was true... I wasn't proud of my achievements, if it was; I'd gone too far and decided to keep my distance from those girls after that.

I felt like all those chicks I was fooling around with were getting me in trouble and I was getting a bad reputation. Especially if they were looking for a boyfriend, coz I was just having fun, and way too young to take anything seriously. One day one cocksucker rode down on his bike with his three mates to our neighbourhood right out front of Daf's place like a fucken hero and tried to stare me out. It was a bit like the *Boyz n the Hood* drive by scene when Ricky gets shot, but I was 13, they were on bicycles, no one had a gun, everybody was white (except for mixed race me) and nothing actually happened ... I did feel like knocking that cunt off his bike, but he rode off into the sunset with his mates like a pussy. Either way I knew I wasn't about to get any backup from these Malvern kids and the thing that troubled me the most was that Bronzer knew the dudes and I had a gut feeling he set me up. So I decided to keep my distance. Maybe he thought I had those clowns covered. Still, it was drama I didn't need. I definitely wasn't looking for enemies, especially over stupid troublemaking bitches!

The same shit was happening on train rides, we'd often see Mr. Medium Boner who was now dressing like a homie and thinking he was a sick cunt with all his new try-hard mates.

They would try and act tuff, but I'd just stare them down and they had no balls.

Suddenly it was like all our enemies had joined forces to try and jump us, although when it came to the crunch most of them were full of shit. Still, I was feeling the pressure as the targeted ringleader and they all knew my name coz my reputation had grown immensely. It was time to recruit new gang members, lose some dead weight, and re-name the crew. We settled on Tooronga Boyz.

Jackson's dad had sent him to an expensive all-boys' Private school to get him away from the rest of us coz we were a bad influence apparently. The man had no idea who is son was, he should have kept his 20k in school fees and bought himself a greyhound or two, a far better investment coz Jackson ended up getting on all kinds of gear and selling it to anyone and everyone at his new school, not that he needed the cash ...

While Jackson was at his new school, I met his mates and they were into their hip hop and homeboy culture just as much as us, only they were more privileged. There ended up being six of them that joined our crew, but I really didn't like the chances of getting backup from any of these privileged private school boys. There were a couple of Syndal High kids that showed potential, but I couldn't trust them as recruits just yet, mainly coz there was still a bit of us versus them. We got invited to all their parties, where we got pissed and stoned and had a laugh with them, but they were limited on street smarts, especially when it came to the inner-city suburbs. The best option was to recruit some of Devious's Doncaster mates that he was always talking about.

Just before I'd turned 14 and after much anticipation, Devious decided it was time for us to be shown around Doncaster in style. He'd arranged for me to crash at Ricks's house (who I hadn't met at that point) and Memo at his. I think there was still a little bit of the we're Greek you're not thing going on, and my dad knows Memo better and Ricks's parents are Aussie and not strict; they were actually stricter than all our parents combined. I was like yeh, "Fucken whatever," I couldn't give a shit at that point; I was just pumped and ready to rumble.

Devious had been preparing me for months with constant sparring, play fighting and stories about his new girlfriend, and how he was gonna set me up with her friends. The first thing I noticed in his neighbourhood was that all the houses were massive and the kids we met, who were mostly Greeks and Italians, seemed pretty spoiled. We spent the first part of the afternoon hanging out with the kids that lived closest to Devious's house. Devious had been building up our reputation for months across his neighbourhood on how crazy these Malvern guys were. Man, I completely relished it. Devious made me feel confident and unstoppable. It was like he saw something in me, and he knew I was destined to be a fighter. Looking back, he was a great mate!

That first night in Devious's neighbourhood he'd planned for us to go to Existence, an underage club that ran every Saturday night. We dressed in our best homeboy attire, and I slicked back my hair. Devious unloaded a can of hairspray into his hair and was dressed in all white, with his shirt open, strangely kinda going for a Michael Jackson look in the *Black or White* music video look. We met the rest of the crew before we lined up to get into the club. Everyone was talking about the punch ons from the week before, where someone had placed a billiard ball in a sock and belted a bouncer across the head with it. It got my heart racing, and I couldn't wait to get in.

When we got in, the music was pumping. It was a mix of hip hop and dance music. Most of the kids in there were wogs, who seemed to be embracing that whole thing with a minority of skips and nips which was the name the Asians started embracing in the same way. I felt like I was accepted as a wog and they made me feel right at home, but inside I still wasn't entirely comfortable with it. I drank a bit of the free soft drink and played pool with my mates. I sensed the spotlight was on me coz of the reputation Devious had built up. His mates were asking me heaps of questions about the stuff we use to get up to in Malvern. I started to showboat and began to chat up a few girls in the club. Memo did too, and we both made out with a couple. It was a dope night, and I loved this new place. I was just hanging for a fight.

I wanted to put to work all the sparring we'd been doing amongst ourselves. I don't know how it started but someone looked at someone the wrong way, or something stupid like that and it just kicked off. I came in out of nowhere and whacked the poor kid, and boom he went down. Then the bouncers came along, broke up the group and kicked some people out. Everyone was hugging me, telling me what a good punch it was and giving me high fives. Then something else started with another group of kids and boom! I'd whacked another kid. This time someone got his starter hat too. This routine went on at Existence for the next few months. I probably went there about 10 times all up until it finally got shutdown coz of all the violence. The first few times I went I stayed at Ricks's house, which was three stories high and massive. His dad had invested in a lot of property and his parents seemed to like me. We'd have a chat, and they'd sometimes make me food. They were a little bit older than my parents and Ricks had older brothers too. Ricks and I got on well, but there was just a slightly different vibe to my Greek mates and he didn't give a shit about all the racial banter, but it was easy for him coz he knew who he was.

On one of the night's, I crashed at Ricks's place after another successful night of violence and making out with chicks. I asked him, "How long you been in Columbo for?" Ricks said "What? Columbo? Oh man was Devious talking that shit with you too?" He then laughed. I was lost for words and pissed off. I said, "Yeh man, with his white bandanna and shit." Rick was pissing himself laughing and said, "That fucken white bandanna! Aren't Columbo from down your neighbourhood anyway?" I said, "Yeh kinda, but more like from where my grandparents are from. I kinda knew it was strange that people from this area would be in it." Fucken Devious ...

Devious's bullshit aside, I was in awe of Doncaster coz these kids all had big houses and were privileged compared to me, but still liked fighting, not like the pussy kids around Malvern. It fitted my personality like a glove. However, I constantly felt like my Euro heritage had to be on display proving I was a wog like most of Devious's crew. I also noticed that there weren't too many black kids in the neighbourhood, but they all dressed like Americans and listened to rap music and R'n'B.

So I felt it was best just to say proudly that I was German. It wasn't that I tried to hide it, but I felt that if I openly talked about my dad's heritage to some of these kids, I might not be accepted. The racial banter within the crew was constant. I hated it. I'd feel my face turning red and my blood boiling inside. I'd quickly change the subject if I was caught up in an uncomfortable racist conversation. Inside I was thinking, for fuck's sake, can't you people see that we all bleed red! We're calling ourselves wogs, which is a derogatory term the Anglo's used to oppress foreign migrants. Why the fuck are we oppressing ourselves! It made no sense, so I kept my thoughts to myself, and decided to vent my frustration through random acts of violence... It was a confusing time, but I guess things had reached a boiling point and most wogs were fed up with the racist antics of the Anglos. By embracing the derogatory term it diffused its power and took it away from the Aussies. The term inevitably became empowering. But not for me.

BLOOD IN BLEED OUT

ot long after I turned 14, I got laid for the first time. There was an older Year 11 Girl at Syndal High who had long dark hair. One day I saw her walk by my Year 9 class with her friend and she was smiling. Over the next week she walked by my classes more and more often and the smile had progressed to waves, then drawing love hearts and blowing kisses. Those air kisses hit me like a bullet right in the middle of class and said, "That chick wants to root you, sicko!" Or maybe it was Shane sitting next to me, punching my arm and saying that!

It didn't take long before she was walking my way home through The Orchards, which hadn't completely burnt down after the roaring blaze. We'd have these massive apple wars from time to time with the choofers, trying to nail each other with apples. But I had to put the fun juvenile stuff aside for a while coz this was an older woman. I felt like I had to act mature. Then one afternoon, she gave me her number and I just waited for the perfect opportunity to invite her to my place when nobody was home. And on that rainy Saturday afternoon, bam! We got it on, to da break of dawn! Dishes were done man! I'd been schooled by an older woman, and I was now a man, or so I thought at the time.

During the week after school, I spent most of my time hanging out at John's Pinnies, or the back of Devious's bottle shop. Devious's bottle shop would usually be closed by 9:00 pm and Johns Pinnies by 11:00 pm, if the owner wasn't playing cards out the back. The owner, John, took a liking to us, after all, Devious and Memo were his best customers. We'd call him Theios, which is Greek for Uncle. He used to make us coffees and give us free games of pool, and we'd play against him too. I got pretty good, so did my mates. He would speak Greek to me, even though I told him my mum was German, but I liked that he accepted me. I enjoyed learning the language too.

Memo's older sister had a new boyfriend who was Italian and drove a hotted up VH Commodore (Holden/GM). One Tuesday night they invited me to come along to 'The Lygon

Street Drags' and it became a regular thing for a few months. Memo and I would sit in the back seat while her boyfriend drove and played DJ, pumping out the latest techno and dance music going around at that time through his Kenwood system, decked out with a subwoofer, 6 by 9s, tweeters and an equaliser. Memo's sister always rode shotgun. His car also had tinted windows, Simmons alloy 18 inch, and was lowered. We'd usually arrive just before midnight. I was only 14 and not quite sure how I got out so late, but my mum was occupied with my baby brothers most nights, so I managed to sneak out. Memo and me were both still doing our paper rounds early mornings Monday-Saturday, so had to wake up before 5am but the drag racing action was too good to miss.

When we'd arrive, we'd meet some of their mates from another neighbourhood, Reservoir, which is on the northside of Melbourne. They were older than us, around 18-20 years old. One by one all the hotted-up cars would start rolling in. They ranged from Monaros and Calais (Holden/GM), to GTs and Mustangs (Ford) to even a few Lamborghinis and Ferraris. Basically, any hotted-up car or street drag car you could think of that was made pre '93. Sometimes people would roll up with cars looking like their old man's delivery truck just to take the piss. The music was always pumping, the motors were roaring, and some of the horns would play *The Godfather* or *Rocky* theme songs and stuff like that. We'd all be waiting in the Lygon Street Park. Sometimes the location would change a little if the jacks rocked up.

On cue, a coupla hoons would run out of a car with a container of motor oil and pour it over the road and one by

94

one each driver would take turns in showing off their cars and driving manoeuvres, doing burnouts and doughnuts in front of an animated crowd. The street would fill with smoke and the smell of burning rubber. Sometimes it would go on as long as an hour before the 'bacon' rolled up and dispersed the crowd. Sometimes, the crowd would retaliate by throwing bottles and projectiles at the cops, then run; that was the fun part.

The Doncaster crowd also loved Lygon Street, and coz a lot of the kids had money we'd eat out at pizza places on Friday or Saturday nights. Lygon Street is in Carlton and is known as Melbourne's 'Little Italy'. Some of the guys and girls would drink in the park before we met up, but I never drank too much around that crowd coz I felt if I got in a fight, I'd have to stay sharp. There were also some pinnie parlours where we'd play pool or video games, which were also underground gambling spots before the casino opened up.

Lil' Memo would take the train then ride his BMX down to our neighbourhood from Clayton. He did this all the time from a very young age. He was about two years younger than me. I'd been told his father had passed away and it had traumatised him. He'd break into factories and misappropriate all kinds of shit. No one taught him right from wrong. We'd play fight with the kid, to try and toughen him up. He'd laugh when you hit him, which made everyone go a little harder till he started crying, but he'd always come back for more. One day we were in Memo's room. I gave him a sidekick and he went airborne. His head went straight into a fish tank making a massive hole and completely flooded the room. We managed to save

Memo's fish, but I felt bad for Lil' Memo and I apologised. Thankfully, everyone was cool with it and didn't get pissed off.

One day, we were all on the train heading to Lil' Memo's place when suddenly I heard Memo say to Lil' Memo, "Hey malaka, what the fuck is this in your bag?" Lil' Memo had been at my house with all of us and he'd thieved me Sony Walkman and some other stuff. I was fucken pissed off. I didn't hit him though. I didn't need to, he broke down coz of the guilt and I guess I felt sorry for him. But, no doubt there were a couple extra punches in his arm the next day. But one thing was clear, doing over people in the crew was not on and later in life I saw some of the serious consequences associated with such a dog act.

While we were on school holidays in winter, the whole crew met up. There were about four kids from Doncaster, three kids from Jackson's school, and the Tooronga Boyz were rolling pretty deep, with about 12 kids all up. We were all dressed up in our best homie gear, including Starter Hats, beanies, baggy jeans, big-ass NBA style jackets, some kids were wearing overalls with the straps hanging out. We would even rip the hologram BK logo tags off the shoes in the stores and attach them to our jeans. Most of us were carrying our blades and were desperate for some action, so we decided to go racking down Chapel Street to find new clothes.

We went into a stores, where they sold the apparel we liked. Some of the crew distracted the retailer, while Jackson and other kids filled up their bags with clothes and 'dacked' shit. They'd gotten away with loads of hot stuff, but I guess we all got cocky and instead of leaving the area with the loot, we hung around looking for more shops to 'rack' from. We stood out and were making a lot of noise and play-fighting in the street, which caught the attention of the cops. They pulled us over and Action Jackson, being one of the taller kids, tried to stare them down and said stuff like, "Why ya hassling us? We haven't done anything wrong." The jacks didn't like this, so they grabbed him, checked his bag, and found all the racked clothes, with no receipts. Some of the crew were smart enough to run off, but when the cops noticed this, they started to grab the remaining 10 and chucked us in the back of the 'divvy' van. They'd already called for back-up to assist.

The jacks marched us into the Prahran cop shop, making each kid grab the back pocket of the person in front of him. Action Jackson was up the front in cuffs. I felt they did this to humiliate us due to our big baggy jeans. They strip searched Jackson and found his butterfly knife. He came out of the interrogation room with tears in his eyes. One of the bacon burgers came out after him shouting, "We got this kid's knife, so if you guys have weapons on you, hand them over now or we'll strip search the lot of ya.". Fuck that shit, I thought, and handed them my blade, Slither. To be honest, I was starting to feel immune to the pigs like I just didn't care anymore, they were just out to spoil the fun, and you got caught only if you were lazy and stupid. We'd been stupid by putting on a show on Chapel Street while carrying hot goods and blades. Good hustlers are cautious and cover their tracks. This was a technique that I refined over the years.

One by one parents of the kids in our crew came to collect us. Memo's Mum came in shouting in Greek and biting her finger. A couple of the other kids got whacks across the back of the head from their parents, and I was trying my best not to laugh but couldn't help it and had to bury my head into my arms so the jacks wouldn't see. I just kept waiting and waiting but no one came to pick me up. I was there an extra hour after everyone else was collected. I think the coppers were starting to feel sorry for me. Then finally Wayno arrived shaking his head saying, "What did you do this time?"

Mum was okay with what happened. In fact, she was actually annoyed the cops took my blade too coz she knew I loved it and we didn't have a lot of money. It was mine, to be used for self-defence purposes only. Opa had always said it was fine to retaliate if someone attacked you. Unfortunately, the Australian legal system sees this differently. I was 14 years old and could already see through the cracks.

Maybe it was racial? Just like what N.W.A. would rap about or that scene in *Boyz n the Hood* when Tre and Ricky get pulled over by the cops and the cop says, "You think you're tough?" The cops definitely had issues with the way we were dressed, humiliating us like that. I personally hadn't nicked anything, nor had I stabbed anybody; I found the whole situation ridiculous. I was getting used to the 'slap on the wrist' and I didn't care anymore. I thought I'd outsmarted them for a while, but I guess they always catch up with you eventually, at least that's what they want you to think!

No Retreat, No Pretender

The *House Party* movies with Kid and Play, and also *Beverly Hills 90210* was popular back then and all the characters in those shows wore their hair up high or in flattops. I decided to try and combine those kinda looks and I shaved it around the sides like a flattop and left a small strand of fringe hanging down. Sometimes I used a bronze kinda hairspray that made my hair a little lighter in colour. My mates thought this stuff was the bomb, and they'd borrow it from me. We all went for the same look with our hair, so Jackson stole some peroxide and tinted our fringes.

We started hanging out in a neighbourhood called Camberwell, where a lot of our private school mates and girls would hang out after school or on the weekends. Maccas was the initial hang out spot along with a pool hall down the road, on a busy junction. Two new pinnie parlours opened up and kids from other hoods started hanging out there too. Even though most of these kids were privileged, they were always dressed in the most expensive homie attire, making them soft targets for getting rolled by ruff less privileged kids. Prior to this period, Camberwell didn't seem that cool to me unless you were a private school kid.

During these days in Camberwell, Jackson's mates talked up a big private school fete, that a lot of kids said would be dope. They said it was on Saturday night and that there would be heaps of hot chicks there. The Tooronga Boyz decided to go down there in style, all dressed up, and we took a few beers along. When we arrived, I thought the fete was lame and just full of all these privileged kids dressed up in their expensive cool clothes. Suddenly, I just randomly flipped without explaining myself to anyone. I went up to three kids my age wearing the latest designer starter baseball caps, pulled out my beer bottle from under my jacket and said, "Give me your hats or I'm gonna crack this over your heads." They froze and gave me their hats. I'd scored three dope starter hats in one swipe, a hat trick! We also got a couple wallets and cash from two other kids. All in all, a successful haul. We went back to Jackson's to celebrate our success. I gave one of the hats to Memo and one to Jackson and we split the loot.

A few months later, on a Saturday night, I briefly became mates with a Lebanese kid, who I'd met in one of the new pinnie parlours playing pool. He told me he'd just gotten out of a youth detention centre interstate somewhere and that he'd found a shop that was easy to burg, close by. We took a stroll down to the shop in question and the Lebo kid showed me that the lock on the shop door was not very secure. Brazenly, and without a thought for consequences, I gave the door a solid front kick. The door flung open, and the kid broke in and raided the till, scoring at least $300; a lot of money back then. I asked him for my cut, and he handed me about twenty dollars in coins, and said he'd be back to give me the rest. I never saw him again.

My actions during that period in my life had been that of a *mad man*, but not in the crazy sense. I was angry. I couldn't make sense of why I had to be living so ruff at home. I didn't feel like I fitted in under Wayno's roof or anywhere else for that matter. Deep down, I was lonely. No one, and I mean no one, was like me. Not my mum, my dad, my stepdad, my brothers, my grandparents, my cousins, or any of my mates. My ethnicity made me unique and I had no full-blooded siblings to share that with. No one understood that but me. I've always wished my community here in Melbourne understood and accepted me for who I really was. I yearned to know more about my black heritage so I could properly embrace it. In my heart I felt that being black is not just about blood, but about a state of mind, a sense of solidarity. I just needed to be at one with my ethnicity.

Jackson's Dad, who was a successful businessman, was getting increasingly worried about his son coz we were getting into more and more trouble. Thing is, he seemed to be blaming everyone else but Jackson. In his dad's mind, I was always the bad influence and that wasn't true. Jackson was his own worst enemy. I always kept my own counsel and never asked anyone to get into fights or roll people. That's just what I did, coz at the time I liked it. Jackson had been stealing shit of his own free will for as long as I'd known him. It wasn't that I was especially bad – even though I liked fighting and violence – it was just that I had found something I was good at, so I stuck with it.

Jackson's dad had an idea to improve the situation with his son. He wanted us to enrol in karate classes, to teach us some discipline and reduce our need to carry knives. He thought it might even help keep us on the straight and narrow. Jackson's dad spoke with our parents about it, and they agreed. The problem was my parents were poor, so it was a bit of a hassle, especially for Wayno. He had recently sold his car to get some money towards renovating the house, and he was walking to his work at the furniture shop. The major construction stage of our renovations was scheduled to begin in 1994. Anytime I was at home, Mum and Wayno would ask if I could help with jobs. Most of the pension money Mum was getting was going straight to Wayno to help out with expenses. The renovation would end up taking another 5 years. Throughout this period, we didn't have any gas heating and I guess Wayno didn't want us wasting money on electricity. During the colder months, I would keep warm at night with hot water bottles and blankets. There was also no kitchen and Mum would cook all our meals out of an electric fry pan. Most nights she would cook two-minute noodles and make them more nutritious by mixing in vegetables. This was also to fill us up more, so we wouldn't go hungry. On pay days, or if we had seen my grandparents and they'd given us food, Mum would make some German specialities such as schnitzels, goulash or sausages.

I was excited about starting karate due to my passion for fighting and finally I had a place to formally train. I would have preferred to have started kickboxing, or boxing, if I could have found a gym close to where we lived, but karate was the next best thing. We were able to pay the first term fees in instalments, so Mum agreed to it. I was appreciative of that coz I understood the financial situation, and there were many arguments at home about it. All the other kids had proper karate gi's, but I was allowed to train in my tracksuit and t-shirt coz that's all we could afford. I enjoyed the training and got to spar with people of all ages. My punches and kicks become a lot cleaner and sharper, and my technique improved. After a few months, the Sensei announced we would be practicing kata for the upcoming gradings. This is the part where you proceed to the next level and start receiving your belts. The problem is, with each grading you needed to pay the karate school more money and then more money for the belt and gi, plus the ongoing training fees , which I still didn't have. There was no way I could afford to continue with this, so I had to stop training before the next set of fees were due. It was 'Peace Out' to Karate ... Kia!

THE MEDIUM BOILER RISES

Mum persuaded me to give away my paper round by offering to put the $20 a week my Dad paid in child support into my bank account. She didn't like that I would always work, no matter how cold or wet it was. She would say it's constantly making me sick. But I was used to dealing with asthma by then. I'd just push through and try not to let it bother me. I still took some medication to help but the meds were basically a mild steroid, there may have been side effects, who knows. Mum said she wanted me to look after myself with the money. I couldn't help feeling like my mum was tryna push me out of her life. I knew she cared deep down, but the age gap of my baby brothers with little kiddie issues and a teenage son who was constantly getting in trouble was a lot for her to deal with, let alone our fathers differences. I didn't know where I belonged, so I embraced my independence and avoided staying at home when I could.

When the school year started in 1994 there were a few new kids that joined our school. Some of them were from Syndal Tech, and other schools' that were getting shut down coz of the messed up government plan. What I didn't know at the time was that the Glen Waverley school didn't want me or my mates there. Apparently, they couldn't handle us. It bothered me. Again, I felt unwanted and rejected by another fucken shitty school. In reflection, I'm surprised I kept rocking up every week. I enjoyed hanging out with my mates but bottom line, I've always hated the feeling of failure, and at Syndal High I was prepared to lose the battle to win the war and pass year 12, unless a better opportunity came along.

While we were in drama class at Syndal High, my mates and me performed a dope cover version of the track *Colors* by Ice-T. We dressed like Bloods and Crips. I rapped out the track and we choreographed some fighting scenes with gang violence and fake weapons as props. The drama teacher and everyone in the class loved it. I felt like I was acting out what our lives were like at the time, but in reality, I was way off. Back then suburban Melbourne life was a little ruff sometimes, but no-one I hang out with had guns, apart from some kids parents, but no-one had ever been shot or anything like that. I also remember watching the movie and reading the book *To Kill a Mockingbird* in English class and I had to submit an essay about racial discrimination. My essay was called 'Black Blood'. I wrote about my black ancestry and although most people assumed I was white European, I could relate to what the characters in the book were going through; the feeling of not being accepted. In the essay I didn't mention where my ancestry came from, although my dad had told me he believed we were Pacific Islander decent, I simply couldn't write those words down. Then in geography class one day I realised how many Pacific Islands there actually fucken were. Something wasn't right and I knew there was more to our story.

My science teacher completely banned me from the class for the whole year coz he said I was distracting everyone. Truth was he just had it in for me. During that period, I would roam the schoolyard with nothing to do. On a couple of occasions, I snapped chair legs off the plastic and metal chairs, then went around breaking windows. Or I'd walk into empty classes and throw chairs, so they knocked all the other chairs over, like bowling pins, and I'd break and embezzle whatever I could find. One of my other favourite no-science-class-for-me activity was to get into the art supply storage room and grab carving knives, and practice my knife throwing skills into the art room door. I got really good at this, they'd stick right in the door and right on target, from long distances too. If anyone happened to be walking through the door on the other side they would have been seriously fucked up. I was pissed off at 'the system', it just kept letting me down, so I decided to wreak havoc on that school, and I seriously wanted to fuck up the science teacher too, for not giving me a chance to learn. I already held a certified PhD in vandalism and street smarts, maybe I could teach him how to throw a knife, I was kinda like the William Tell of Syndal High, after all ...

Everyone used to tilt the lockers at school, so when kids opened them all their books would fall out. We also used to raid the pay phone, tipping it upside down and shaking the fuck out of it, till the coins fell out. It was a battle to see which kid could get to it first, but on a good day you could score $50, so kids would punch on over it. Happy to say no one ever messed with me. At lunch times if I wasn't trying to scab more coins to buy stuff from the canteen or smoking cones at The Orchard's, I'd be play sparring with friends or playing soccer.

We blended fighting and soccer to create a new game called 'If ya kick the fucken ball over the fence everyone bashes ya'. For some stupid reason, we decided it was more fun playing soccer on the basketball court, even though there was a perfectly good grass soccer pitch with full sized goals. The numbers of players on each team was way more than regular soccer, at least 20 per side. The basketball court was surrounded by a big steel cage about 15 feet high. The goals were two poles which were parted almost regulation-size apart, both on each side of the court. All the normal soccer rules applied, without the offside rules except if you kicked the ball over the fence and out of the cage. If this happened, every player on the court of both teams 'would bash the fuck out of ya' and I don't mean a couple punches in the arm, this shit would get serious, black eyes, blood noses, the works! If you were smart, you'd just run. I took on the crowd a few times and I was always very hard to put down. I'd try and take as many down as I could before any kind of retreat, and it was best to just take on the main fighters in the group coz the rest would back off.

I ended up befriending a couple of Afghani brothers, who I met whilst hanging out in Balaclava playing pool with Memo, both of them were fully developed and physically strong dudes for their age. They'd often visit our school and hang out with us. Around about that time Medium started running his mouth again around the neighbourhood, claiming he was gonna jump me with his crew at the annual Harold Holt Pool party. He started thinking he was a gangster coz he befriended a coupla kids, who were apparently connected. I was seriously fed up with this cocksucker's bullshit, so I let the Afghani brothers know. "No problem," they said, "We'll be there, and we'll bring backup." This was the tipping point, the racial and socio-economic tension had hit a peak and it was finally about to boil over, putting an end to the Harold Holt Pool party forever.

The pool party was a massive event each year, with a bad reputation for lots of underage drinking. The scene was getting progressively more hostile as the homie fashion started getting more popular and the ethnic kids embraced many of its cultural elements. This was in contrast to the skegs who were predominantly Aussie or private school kids from affluent areas, and generally preferred rock music. There were many ethnic gangs that formed and prospered during this time, looking a lot different to the Aussies or wogs, including gangs made up of Asians, Islanders, Africans and Middle Easterners.

The Tooronga Boyz met in the park early afternoon before the '94 pool party. Dressed to kill, we knew there would be a massive punch on. There would be no making out with girls tonight and I was pumped and ready to take out as many of these Medium Boner try-hard-homeboys as possible. Initially, there were about eight of us, but we were waiting on the Afghani brothers and their crew to arrive. But the fuckers were late. We waited on a big hill looking down on thousands of kids running around, unaware of the impending doom. Being up on a hill, it wasn't long before we'd caught the attention of the Medium Boner crew. There were about 15 of them, and they thought they were tuff. Medium ran up to us with one of his crew and said, "This guy's brother is the leader of the Oakleigh Wogs." I just said, "I don't give a fuck," and let my hands go, throwing punches in his direction, smashing him, then I smashed another kid, and then another. Moments later I was throwing punches with both arms simultaneously like I was hitting speed balls and shouting, "Fuck off! Fuck off! Fuck off!" My violent and unpredictable reaction worked, and they all got scared. The rest of the crew were hitting people too. This lasted until a bouncer grabbed me and dragged me out of the place. During the fight Action Jackson copped a couple of cheap shots in the back of his head, but he later laughed it off, saying, "They hit like girls."

I tried to negotiate with the bouncer to let me stay. I said, "Man they started it." He must have been able to tell we were outnumbered and he let me back in. As soon as I was back in the Afghani brothers arrived with a crew of about 50 kids. "Where's this guy?" the older brother asked. "We've already taken care of them," I said.

I could still see Medium and the remainder of his try-hard crew hanging around. I was surprised coz I thought we'd touched them up pretty good. I knew our reinforcements would kill them if we went in for a second wave attack, so I let them go. Problem was that these 50 kids had also been pumped up for a fight. Any surfy-looking private school kid or try-hard looking homeboys that they ran into, or who looked at them funny, got bashed and rolled. The party was a complete riot. The Tooronga Boyz went on a looting rampage, and somehow someone got their hands on a backpack full of weed they had rolled off a kid, plus wallets, cash, CDs and walk-mans. With all the loot we decided to get the fuck outta there, before the place got burned to the ground. We managed to bring home a coupla ladies with us too.

We went back to Jackson's, smoked weed, drank alcohol and fooled around with the girls we'd picked up. We celebrated our win like we'd won the Super Bowl. I pulled an all nighter and I went home with a hangover the next day. When I got home I crashed out till 6 pm, while my mum and stepdad watched the Sunday night news in the lounge. "Harold Holt Pool party, is that where you went last night?" Mum asked when I got up and went through to the lounge. I said, "Yeh." "What the hell did you guys do?" Asked Wayno.

Our Riot at the party was all over the news coz after we left, the fighting spilled out onto the street and some kid had jumped on the bonnet of a Range Rover and smashed open the windscreen with his belt buckle, while the rest of his crew dragged the occupants out and bashed them. The word on the street was that the Tooronga Boyz were responsible, but I was never questioned by the jacks.

ONCE WERE FUCKEN WARRIORS

As much fun as it was getting up to all this crazy shit with my mates, the truth is I wasn't happy. I assumed I was depressed. I never took medication or had therapy or anything for it, but things just didn't feel right. I was drinking and smoking weed regularly, and I'd started sniffing glue, to try and get high. I did this on my own in my room at night, so it was pretty sad and stupid. I hated living in Malvern, in a house with no heating or a kitchen. It always looked a mess, with half finished work going on everywhere. Sometimes I didn't mind helping out with some of the jobs, but Wayno would annoy me. He was always talking up how good the house was gonna be when the renovations were finished and what a genius he thought he was for coming up with this idea. The truth was, we did without so many staple things that everyone else had, I felt that it just wasn't worth it.

The one thing in my life that felt normal was visiting Oma and Opa. It was a long journey to their home in Noble Park, but worth it, and I got to eat all the German food I loved. They would usually give me $5 to buy myself something when I left. I always refused coz I didn't want to take their pension money, but they always insisted I take it.

There was a big underage dance party at Melbourne Town Hall in the city centre on a Friday night. Memo came, along with the Afghani brothers and a couple of their crew, but the rest of the Tooronga Boyz didn't come along to this event. I think the Harold Holt riot must have freaked them out a little bit and rightly so, this new crew I was hanging with were a volatile bunch. As always, we dressed up in our usual homebody attire ready for a night of action. We started the night by playing games in one of the Asian-owned pinnie parlours we used to frequent in the city. I was hanging out the front when a Lebanese kid I knew came up to me and said,

"My friend wants to meet you." I went around to chat with him and there was an older Filo kid staring at me. He said, "I want one of your jackets..." WTF? I thought. Had I been set up? Even Memo was nowhere to be seen let alone the big bad Afghani brothers. I was wearing a dope electric red denim jacket over a Starter jacket. "Not gonna happen mate," I said.

The air was thick with tension. I was waiting for the cunt to make a move. I felt like I could take him out, he was sitting back standing at a distance. We were locked in a heated standoff for about 10 minutes, while his right hand was holding something in his pocket. Back then, the Asians had a real bad reputation for chopping kids, so I was ready for anything. I turned around and looked across the street to see Memo and my other mates entering the dance party. I was more pissed off at them than the fucker who wanted my jacket. My paranoid mind came to the conclusion that the assholes had fucken set me up. I immediately felt that familiar feeling of abandonment, like no one gave a fuck about me. I'd always been there for them.

Either way I had to think smart coz I'd stopped carrying a blade after the pigs confiscated Slither. The cocksucker was calculated and patient, more of a con man than a heavy. Had he swung a punch, I would have retaliated with violence like I'd always done, but his approach intimidated me. I was thinking, yep, this cunt's definitely got a shiv, coz he would have swung a punch by now. I was rolling people myself and that was my approach. So, I said, "Look, I'll tell ya what, you can borrow this jacket if you promise you'll give it back after the dance party." He said, "Yeh cool." I felt like I'd backed down and hated myself for doing so. I only assumed he had a weapon, but I hadn't actually seen one. I wished I'd fought him to save face. In my mind, I'd been a pussy and that just wasn't me. I always stood up for myself. Maybe, my gut instinct to backdown saved me from getting chopped. Regardless, to this very day I still regret not standing my ground. Rolling people wasn't right and I learnt a valuable lesson that day ... Always learn from your losses and move on!

I went into the dance party and pulled Memo aside, and said, "Where the fuck were you?" He said, "I thought you were just talking to that dude?" I think at that point in time Memo thought I had gone completely nuts coz he'd seen me do some fucked up shit. So I made excuses for his lack of loyalty and justified it in my mind that he probably thought I had what it takes to bash that cocksucker. I guess, it hurt me less to think that way. I'd seen Memo backdown a few times, he wasn't as aggressive as me, but in reality I was more vulnerable. I was 14 and uncomfortable in my own skin.

After the dance party, I thought I'd try and catch up with the guy and get my jacket back, but Memo said, "You're kiddin' yourself," and he was right. I took out my frustrations on a massive fight that erupted on the dance floor with the bouncers. They were surrounded by all the homies and getting hit in every direction with punches, kicks, and projectiles. The three bouncers took karate-style stances and moved to the back exit door to save their asses. I was ashamed I'd been rolled, so I didn't throw a cheap shot at the bouncers like the rest of the kids, as I genuinely felt I'd be a hypocrite. So, purely out of frustration I let go with a fly kick into the exit door as they had barricaded it closed. The venue switched the lights and music off, and we were all told over the PA system, "The night's over now, so get the fuck out of here."

Pathetically, a week later I got an apology from the Filo kid who heisted my jacket via the Afghani Brothers. It was just an excuse for them not standing by my side at the time. They told me they had tracked him down and had spoken to him, he said he was going to return my jacket coz he didn't realise who I was. Yeh right, what ever. I never bothered to follow it up. I was still mad at myself for not fighting him when I had the chance. I just went out and stole more shit to make myself feel better. Mum had bought that jacket for me. I told her I'd swapped it for the new clothes. The truth was, I was beginning to feel I couldn't rely on anybody for backup and I was always putting my ass on the line to fight for everyone else. But who was willing to put their ass on the line and fight for me?

The constant feeling of neglect was messing with my mind and driving my anger. Trust and loyalty are values that I hold close to my heart. So, I would doubt the values of the world when my family or mates let me down. I saw authority and the privileged as the enemy, coz I felt the privileged had everything that I didn't, including the protection of authority, hiding behind false values. I needed some stability, and family life at home was a mess. The arguing between my mum and Wayno was non stop and would often escalate into some kinda constant form of domestic violence. I couldn't rely on my mates, I just wanted to hang with people I could trust and count on. But all that was about to change, because of a girl.

Her name was Grace, my *Saving Grace*. She was originally from New Zealand, and she was Maori. She was a grade below me in school but almost a year older than me. Right at that stage in my life, when I needed some grounding, she came into my life. She looked pretty sexy back then and a little different to the other girls I was hooking up with. She dressed a bit like Left Eye from TLC and could have fitted straight into the BBD *Gangsta* music video. We both shared a passion for hip hop. I was interested in her stories about New Zealand, and she taught me a lot about Polynesian culture. She thought I looked part Samoan after I told her what my father had told me of our heritage, and she gave me a wooden Samoan bead, which I'd always wear.

We ended up making out one weekend and we became 'official'. Not too long into our relationship her girlfriend, who was staying at a 'care home', invited us both over to her accommodation coz her carers had gone away for the weekend. Saving Grace had planned this as the night we were going to take things further and she wrote that on a note she passed to me in the schoolyard. The classic track *Sexual Healing* by Marvin Gaye set the mood and we got it on while listening to Tevin Campbell and Bobby Brown. It was much better than anything else I'd experienced at that point in my life with a chick I liked. Just like Tevin sang, 'I'm ready....', we definitely had chemistry and with our teenage hormones going wild, we couldn't wait to hit it again, but the second time round didn't go as smoothly.

One Tuesday afternoon Grace, her stepsister Kiri, one of her friends and me were all wagging school, hanging around at Grace's place. Kiri and her friend were chilling in the lounge. Her friend had tea leafed a whole bunch of satin Looney Tunes boxer shorts and had given me some. Grace and me were getting it on, when Kiri came in running saying, "Oh my god, our parents are in the driveway!" Damn did I get up fast. I chucked on my jeans and shirt without shoes and jumped the back fence, in one leap and bam I brought down a fence rail with me. This all happened in a matter of seconds. I had an image in my head of her big-warrior Maori dad chasing me with a carving knife. The fence had sliced me open just under the rib cage, so I was bleeding a little bit. I had no idea how I was going to get home or get my shoes back; I also had no money. The girls figured I'd be at the closest park, and they grabbed my things for me and found me, clutching my ribs, glad to be alive!

BEAT STREET

A few months passed, and Saving Grace wanted me to meet her family. She told me that her dad had specifically asked her if he could meet me. I got the impression he knew something was up when he realised on that Tuesday afternoon that his fence was broken, but Grace assured me that she'd made something else up and he had no idea I'd been in his house, doing the deed. She lived in Glen Waverley with her dad, step mum and Kiri. She didn't like her step mum, and she had an up and down relationship with Kiri. She told me her dad had beaten her up a couple times and he'd also beaten up her step mum. He'd also punched a window, shattering it, and cutting his arm. I was told Grace's dad had left her mum for the step mum, when they'd started sleeping together after rugby games.

When I met Grace's dad for the first time, I was 15. He was a big Maori bloke, with a badass moustache. He was well built, a builder by trade and ran his own business. When I arrived at his house to meet him, he said, "So, you're Grace's boyfriend ay?" I said, "Yes, we've been going out a coupla months." He said, "You wanna beer, boy?" Hell, yeh I wanted a beer, "Yes, thanks," I said. We then had a lengthy conversation, and he went on to say, "If my Bub ever gives you a bit of lip don't be shy to her give her a bit of a touch up if you need to." I couldn't believe he was telling me to whack his daughter if she got out of line, I was lost for words...

I was getting hooked on a new drug, which was called 'getting busy with my new girl'. We'd fool around in the schoolyard, in parks, in public transport and cinemas, basically, anywhere and everywhere. There was an abandoned house in my street where we'd go to a lot. I'd broken in, smashed all the windows and tagged the walls. I even had three weed plants growing in the backyard. They almost got big enough to harvest, until the gardener showed up one day and whoever owned the house decided they were moving back in. Sometimes Grace and me would sleep in parks coz Mum didn't like her staying over at our place. At that stage I'd lost a lot of respect for Mum and Wayno with all their fighting, and the state of the house. It was embarrassing. I felt I was getting more love and stability from Grace's family.

One day Grace asked me a strange question, "Can I give you a smiley?" I said "Yeh cool." A smiley is a scar on the skin made from the heated-up metal hood on a cigarette lighter. Me and Jackson were high one night and gave each other smileys but it only lasted a week. Grace kept the lighter going until the metal was red hot. She then pressed it into my right hand near my thumb and held it there for about five minutes until my hand went numb from the pain. It didn't look good, just painful. I then burnt her back coz she wanted me to. Her burn didn't look good either. I gave her Mum and Dad's white gold wedding ring, Mum had given it to me a few weeks earlier, and Grace and I agreed we'd get married one day. Man, was I young and stupid. My scar was so bad, people would come up to me thinking I'd been shot. I was starting to look real fucking crazy. I still have the scar to this day.

As Grace's trust in me grew, she mentioned she'd been sexually abused by her cousin when she was a child back in New Zealand. This was the first time I'd ever heard of such a thing happening to somebody I knew, and it infuriated me. I wanted to do something about it. I talked about going over there, finding him, and beating him up. I was dead serious about it. Again, society's value had neglected the under privileged, it was a war worth fighting in my mind. The trauma had caused Grace to act rebellious and as our relationship went on, she also tried to resort to physical violence against me sometimes, or against any chicks who looked in my direction for more than a few seconds. I'd do my best to restrain her when I could. I felt compassion for what she was going through. She continued to rebel against societies values and eventually got too much for her dad to handle, so he kicked her out of home. I guess we were a bad influence on each other. She decided to move in with her brother Cal, in Dandenong.

Cal was a great bloke, much happier than his sister, and he

knew how to make us all laugh. He'd done well for himself, always paid his rent and bills on time, and rarely drank or smoked weed. He had a job as a manager at a takeaway chicken store called 'Chicken A-Go-Go', and he'd often bring home leftover food. We'd have massive feeds and play basketball in his backyard. He was like the big brother I never had and a good influence on Grace and me during the troubled period we were going through. He took the time to mentor us both as individuals. He couldn't care less if my ancestry was Islander or not. He just saw me as family and that was something that was more important to me than anything else. There were a lot of values I admired in him and my negative perspective of society began to change for the better. I felt like there *were* decent people around after all. Sometimes rumours would surface that certain enemy crews were looking for me, planning on making a move. He made me see that lots of people just 'talk a lot of shit'. I was a warrior just like him, we just dealt with things as they came, not worried about people who make threats. They did that coz they were scared. And I was too good to take the bait.

Occasionally we had a few Maori-style parties. They'd hire a keg of beer, put some old school music on, and everyone would sing together and end up so drunk you just passed out on the floor and woke up in the morning, thinking, 'what the hell happened last night?' One of the older uncles or aunties would be up making everyone breakfast and we'd all be cracking up laughing, reminiscing about all the fun stuff the night before. I'd stay at their place in Dandenong from after school on Friday afternoon, then make the long journey back to school from there Monday morning. I stayed longer during school holidays coz they never wanted me to leave.

Cal even paid for my plane ticket to visit Grace's mum in Brisbane. We had a great time visiting theme parks, playing basketball and rugby, swimming, and going to parties. One day we decided to jump off the end of the peer and swim back to the beach, we were told to wear t-shirts coz of the blue bottles, but the tentacles just ripped straight through our shirts, and we came up in painful stings all over our bodies. Grace's family friends assumed I was Maori too, and greeted me with 'Kiora, bro' (Hi, bro). Grace gave me her Bone (a whale bone), which her grandmother had given her and was sacred. There's a myth about Bones; if you ever lose a Bone someone has given you, it will always come back to you. Grace had lost hers in the alley that ran beside my house one day. We searched and searched for weeks but couldn't find it. Grace was devastated. Then months later we were walking down the alley and bam, under a leaf there it was! Myth confirmed!

Cal played competition basketball, which we'd go along to and watch. We'd also watch rugby games at a local club, that Cal and a coupla other family members had played for. He had a dope Sony stereo system in his lounge, with all the CDs of our favourite artists like Snoop Dogg, Blackstreet, 2Pac, Jodeci ... the list went on. You name it, he had, or if he didn't, he'd get it! We'd pump the tunes all weekend around the house or in his big old, gold Ford LTD.

There were a couple local Melbourne R'n'B groups getting big around this time and making it to the Top 40. One of the groups that got our attention was called Past 2 Present.

Four members of the group were Samoan and one of them was Maori. Cal and his girlfriend knew him. His name was Leigh, and we went to a large Polynesian festival one Sunday afternoon to watch his group perform. When they got off stage Leigh came over for a chat with us all. He had a cool vibe and I remember feeling like there was a strong spiritual connection and a certain energy between us. It's hard to explain, but I guess I thought that one day I'll meet the dude again and I imagined us rocking a show together up on stage.

Sadly, Saving Grace and I broke up, and I rarely saw Cal again. Although I did visit him once in his new apartment in Dandenong. He and his girlfriend had two kids by then. They were just as accommodating as ever, and we all missed each other. Grace had enrolled at a new school that year and with all the new influences she'd gone off the rails, even more, they said. She was dating a local up-and-coming rapper. It felt ironic coz after we broke up, I began to write lyrics again. I would freestyle at parties too. I guess it hurt a little still being my first serious relationship, but that's just who she was. When we were together, I felt she was just as protective of me as I was of her. She'd constantly tell me how much she loved me, and I told her that too. We were a little like Bonnie and Clyde sometimes. I remember she scared the shit out of the girl I hooked up with after the infamous pool party. I guess she made me pretty jealous too, but the truth eventually came out that she was cheating. I assume this was due to her insecurities and we were way too young for such a serious relationship. Before we broke up, I had such deep feelings for her I'd see her talking to dudes and just run up and whack them. My reputation as a troublemaker grew and I was banned from events and parties around certain neighbourhoods for a few years coz I behaved that way.

But the truth was what I missed most was my 'big brother' Cal. I've learnt that it's often the way it is in families, after a breakup it gets really hard to maintain the same bond and friendship with the people you once felt so close with. The influence Cal had on me during that time in my life was something I never forgot; we had crossed paths for a reason. I don't believe in coincidence; our friendship was more than that. I never imagined he had any weaknesses or vulnerabilities, but we're all human and when our values are betrayed our actions can be out of character. One Sunday morning, years later three Maori guys I'd gotten to know through the scene past me in the street around 7 am. One of them said, "We're off to play rugby now bro!" They mentioned they'd been partying all night. I said, 'Shit, without sleep, you guys are crazy, who do you play for?' They mentioned they played for the same club we use to watch. So, I asked, "Do you know a guy called Cal?" They said, "Oh shit bro, yeah we do, do you know him well? Did you hear what happened?" I said, "No, I haven't seen him in years, but he was like my big brother to me when I was younger." One of the guys leaned over to me compassionately and said, "Sorry to tell you this bro, last year he went on a long drive towards Canberra and never came back ... He took his own life"

I was in shock; I hadn't seen him in years but immediately felt a strong pain in my heart. Would have been great to see him one more time. I stopped what ever it was I was doing that morning after hearing the news and headed home. I had so many questions, running through my head. That night, I lay in bed awake for hours feeling sad and abandoned. The system had let Cal down, he had supported his family all those years, but who was there to support him. I wish I could have been there. I know you're with me Big Bro, your positivity, kindness, generosity and mentoring will never be forgotten. The path you laid out will continue to grow with every step!

MY WORDS ARE IMPECCABLE TIME TO RECOGNISE FLOW AND HEARTS BE INSEPARABLE

Warriors Fight, *The Impeccable Word (2017)*

Boyz Get Outta the Hood

Towards the end of '94 the teachers told all the kids at Syndal High, who were not allowed into Glen Waverley High (when the two schools merged in '95), that they would need to find new schools. My behaviour wasn't good, but I hadn't been caught for most of the bad shit I'd done at the school. I'd passed all my subjects too, coz I've never believed in failing at anything I did. They offered me a spot, but I would need to repeat Year 10. Fuck that, I thought, and I was more than happy to get the hell outta that school for good. Most of my mates were in the same boat.

During the summer my dad wanted to catch up with me again to see if I'd got myself on track with my behaviour and schoolwork. I told him I wanted to drop out of school and become a builder. I'd still been occasionally helping out with labouring work on the home in Malvern, and the builders who had started working on the major construction mentioned the money was good. Dad told me that I'd regret it if I did, coz being a builder was a tuff physically demanding job. He wanted me to finish school and see if another career came to mind, and then if I still wanted to be a builder, go for it then. I thought about it then I agreed with him and mentioned a school called

Swinburne that the other Syndal kids would be going too. Dad agreed to me going there but had one more request that made sense to me. He said, "Son it's time for you to embrace your name Benjamin Sinclair, no more of this Ben Kaul or Douglas bullshit. It's not who you are, your mum should never have changed your name to begin with. Every kid has their dad's last name. I've only seen my dad twice since I was three years old. If I'm a Sinclair, you're a Sinclair too".

I'd actually never really thought about it too much. I'd just gone along with what Mum wanted. My dad was right. So, for my last two years of schooling I enrolled at Swinburne as Benjamin (Benny) Sinclair. For the first time in a long time, I felt that my dad did care about me! Right, at that moment I decided I would never be a name dropper, Benny Sinclair would be the name people dropped ...

The new school was dope and a lot closer to Malvern. I just had to jump on a tram or train and be at school in 20 minutes. The teachers were very understanding about all the problems I was facing. They were like trained counsellors. We addressed all the teachers with their first names, and we didn't have to wear a uniform. A lot of people had enrolled at Swinburne coz they'd either dropped out or were kicked out of other schools. Or private school kids who didn't fit into the bubble. There were also mature aged students there too.

There were heaps of kids I gotten to know over the years at Swinburne from all the different schools I'd been and the crews I mucked around with including good ol' Memo. The majority of the students were into the Arts, which is the reason why there were heaps of writers at our school or from other places that just wanted to come down and hang out coz it was a cool place to be. Some of the students at the school were musicians, actors, models, and a couple pro skaters. There was a lot of weed smoking going on and harder drugs like speed, ecstasy, acid and smack. We weren't confined to the school grounds at Swinburne, we were given a lot of freedom and accountability for our own actions. There were kids that would pretty much spend all their time smoking bongs in 'rocket park' that was right near our school. They would sometimes be in large groups, some of them were basically hippies and play guitars and games like hacky sack, if they weren't choofing.

A new scene was growing in Melbourne as techno, house and dance music got bigger, so did the underground rave parties, festivals and nightclubs. This scene also had its own fashion and greatly contributed to people taking all kinds of party drugs, getting all fucked up and trippin' out on the laser shows and shit like that. Those party people were known as 'ravers'. The original homeboy scene was starting to fade, I guess a lot of kids now had criminal records and decided to dress in an inconspicuous way. I'd been lucky I'd gotten away with so much petty crime and random acts of violence with no serious charges, just slaps on the wrists. I still disliked cops, but I was a little smarter. I realised I needed to respect what they did. If I didn't show a certain amount of respect for them and they ever questioned me, I knew I'd get in more trouble.

At the new school, I wanted to improve my reputation and turn over a new leaf. My friends now knew me as a Sinclair and I wanted to fully embrace who I was. My priority was finishing school and getting myself out of the mess I was in. I wanted to be successful. I didn't want to struggle financially like my mum. I also started to dress a little more on the conservative side. Over the summer holidays that year I'd gotten right into the movies *Beat Street* and also *Krush Grove*. Yep, I was as passionate as ever about my Hip Hop, so no doubt it continued to influence the style I liked. My jeans were now tighter, I'd wear big parkers and lots of Adidas, or Nike clothing and kicks. I still wore baseball caps, just not as high up on my head. I also had a dope New York Yankees leather jacket that Cal had given me that became infamous.

A lot of the homeboy kids were getting into a fad called chroming, which was inhaling spray paint or fly spray fumes from aerosol cans through a plastic bag. It would get you high real quick, then fade out. I tried it once and straight up it was wack. Some of my Viet mates progressed onto heroine and selling it on a big scale. This led to a lot of drug-related deaths in Melbourne. The drug dealing was organised via larger gangs who had their foot soldiers, often kids around our age or random junkies tryna support the habit, pushing on the street, in the inner-city projects or out of the pinnie parlours. You'd walk down certain streets in those days and people would frequently ask "Are you chasing?" or just "You chasing?" The phrase sometimes sounded like they were asking "Are you Jason?", so, for a joke amongst our mates sometimes we would say "Yeh, I'm Jason!" and watch the looks on the pushers faces and crack up laughing. But we still needed to be careful, some of these pushers were making big bucks and if one of them flipped, you could find yourself getting chopped or stabbed with a fucken syringe!

I enjoyed being low key at school, I didn't want to attract

attention or have more distractions. I also shaved my head for the first time. This was a look I began to prefer and I grew a moustache. I'd play table tennis with some new mates I'd met at school, like Brando who was Italian and had just got out of the infamous juvenile detention centre Turana. He was older than me and had been busted after he committed a violent home invasion trying to heist weed plants and loot. Brando was trying to get his life back on track too.

The first day of school I remember walking into English class and seeing a couple kids I recognised from around the neighbourhood. I didn't really know them too well before then and my gut instinct told me we had some beef in the past and it was best to keep my guard up, in case things kicked off. Not the start I was hoping for on my first day. But, to my surprise they were cool, we let bygones be bygones and ended up becoming mates. Cal's mentoring had made a significant impact on how I wanted to live my life, but as time went on and after the breakup with Grace, some of his advice began to fade and from time to time, my menacing behaviour would come out.

My mates Budge, Dids and Jake from the crew EMB (East Malvern Boys) would often rock dope legal burners not far from school. Peeps would be hanging out drinking beer, jamming out to New York hip hop like KRS-One, NAS or A Tribe Called Quest through a boombox. We'd hang out on our lunch break, at a certain spots in the schoolyard or down by the train station. It wasn't long before I got the bug back for tagging. Again, I knew I had to re-invent the crew and stick with a traditional three letter type gang, as it was better for notoriety. Especially if you wanted to be taken seriously among the other crews. After school one day on a tram home, it hit me ... RSH (Raising Some Hell), coz that's exactly what I'd been doing all these years! My tag became Bugzie, once and for all. Everyone was down for the change, and we recruited new members.

Ricks and Devious were heavily into 'breaking' during this time and would often rock the moves at the parties we were going too. This was a good way for them to impress the girls and also made our crew look dope. I'd practice with them occasionally, but they had me covered with their advanced moves, they were training flat out and had it all down pat, so I'd just rock the turtle, backspin or a bit of up rock from time to time. But, as a matter of fact, I was enjoying fighting more.

One Friday night I was at a party in the suburbs with the crew and I ran into a gang of assholes that I didn't liked too much. I guess it would have been wiser just to let things go, but on this particular night, I couldn't get over it and I wanted to fight them all. I'd been drinking and smoking heavily throughout that day. I approached the group and started on them, saying shit like, "What the fuck you cunts looking at? You wanna fucken go?" They just stared at me and said nothing. One of my mates pulled me away saying, "What the fuck you doin' man? There's more of these guys here than us." I just said, "Fuck them."

We ended up leaving the party early coz I'd killed the vibe for everyone. I felt my mates were getting frustrated coz I was always starting shit and they had no time to meet chicks. I had a hangover the next day and I was feeling down on myself coz I'd ruined everyone's night, and yeh, maybe we could have enjoyed it and met some girls and had a laugh. I decided I didn't want to go out on the Saturday night. I just wanted to stay home and watch TV, which was strange for me back then. I turned the channel dial on my portable TV, which was so old it came from an era before remote controls were invented, and stopped on Channel SBS, as the dial wouldn't move any further.

I watched a documentary about Mike Tyson and his trainer Cus D'Amato who had been introduced to him when he was in a reform school and how boxing had turned his life around completely. Tyson went from being a troubled young kid to the youngest heavy weight champion of all time, aged just 20. It showed some early footage of Tyson that I'd never seen before and I felt I could relate to the things he was telling the reporters, like about the trouble with the law and the feeling of not fitting in, and not being accepted. I knew then and there I needed to find a boxing gym to change the person I was becoming, turn my passion for fighting into something positive, find some direction.

I started thinking about the bigger picture at last. With boxing, I could perform in front of crowds, get paid and achieve all I hoped I would in life. I'd just need to train hard and show the world what I can do. This would finally give me some focus and provide some discipline to help me get through school. I was no angel, but I had experienced an epiphany.

BLOODSPORT

It wasn't easy finding a boxing gym coz back then the sport wasn't that popular in Melbourne, and it didn't help living in a posh neighbourhood. Traditionally there weren't too many fighters coming out of places like Malvern. We didn't have internet at home or anything, so I called up the telephone directory service and asked if there were boxing gyms in the area. They mentioned a place called Malvern Martial Arts that had just opened up and it wasn't far from my house. I wasn't interested in doing anything like karate where you needed to buy a gi or sit gradings, but I thought I'd walk down and take a look as soon as I could. One Monday evening I wandered down to check it out.

The set up was good. They had plenty of space, lots of bags and a boxing ring. There were several classes taking place at the same time, the atmosphere was good, and you could just hear the sounds of people hitting pads, bags, kick shields or each other. I was sweating a little as the adrenaline kicked in. There was a guy who looked like he ran the place called The Doctor. He was dressed in a kung fu gi and was about to start a class. I'd seen him recently at the local park taking kung fu classes. I thought it looked cool, so I asked him if they had boxing at this gym. He said, "No, but we have kickboxing, come with me and I'll introduce you to Nick."

Nick came over and introduced himself, he would have been about 40 at the time, and I'd just turned 16. I liked Nick straight away; calm easy-going guy, very humble, and he always wore a diamond stud earring like I had, but mine were fake back then! He said he was happy to get me to come on board and train with him and his team. He mentioned 16 was a good age to start. He didn't seem interested in the money; I could tell he was doing this for the love of Martial Arts. He explained he was an ex-kickboxer and had also trained in kung fu. The fees weren't much at all. I still preferred the idea of straight boxing, but kickboxing in Melbourne in the '90s was at its peak and popular amongst my mates. Plenty of local promoters were putting on quality shows, although sometimes the decisions were questionable.

I was pumped about starting kickboxing and I told Memo about it on the way to school. He ended up coming along too. We'd train three times a week, and each training session was at least two hours. I bought my first set of gloves, wraps, Muay Thai style kickboxing shorts, anklets, and a mouth guard. Nick didn't believe in wearing shin guards. When we practiced our kicks and leg checks it would be shin to shin and no holding back on power, so we'd get conditioned to the pain. Same with elbows and forearms, and we'd strike each other in the guts and thighs for conditioning too. I was the youngest in the class of about 10 people. Most of the students were in their 20's or 30's. There were some girls that would join the group from time to time, but it was mostly dudes.

When we started sparring, I was giving most people in the class a run for their money, easily landing kicks and punches on everyone. I just needed to improve on my defence coz I got a few black eyes, and my mum would get worried. Plus, it wasn't a great look when rocking up to school. It was a little frustrating coz I'd never feel any pain at the time while I was in the ring, but the bruises were a reminder that I was getting hit. It became a bit awkward when sparring with Memo coz the next day on the way to school together, he took the hits a lot more personally than me and whined about the bruises. The sport wasn't really for him. He dropped out after a while and wasn't showing a lot of commitment anyway. But I loved it!

I began to run at the local park on the days I wasn't training and would watch kickboxing or boxing as often as I could on video, as well as any other martial arts movies from my favourite martial artists like Bruce Lee (I bought a massive Bruce Lee Poster for my room), Van Damme, Jackie Chan, and anything to do with the Shaolin Monks. I also practiced some basic Tai chi moves that I had found on an instructional video. At that time, I was listening to Wu-tang Clan *36 Chambers*, and GZA *Liquid Swords* a lot.

I started having dreams about becoming a professional fighter and a future world champ. In fact, I had a dream around about this time that I'll never forget. I was training in an exotic tropical jungle with my trainer Nick and all my training buddies, when a brightly coloured exotic creature came floating down from the treetops and asked me to follow it. I followed the creature up a massive tree and onto the jungle canopy. The creature told me that this was my path, and to keep following it. For weeks I thought about the creature in my dream and wondered exactly what the path was that it wanted me to follow. I wished it would come back to me in some way, but it never did. I convinced myself, coz my trainer and buddies were in the dream, that I should continue training until I became a champion and that was all the creature was really tryna tell me. Well, that kinda made sense at the time.

But in my heart, I was torn. If that was my path, then why did I leave my training buddies to follow the creature up onto the jungle canopy? There was something I wanted even more than becoming a world champion fighter, something I had never told anyone and hadn't completely come to terms with myself, especially as I'd been focussing on building such a staunch reputation the past few years. The truth was that what I wanted, more than anything else, was for the world to accept me for who I really was. I needed to find my way on my own. Was it possible the brightly coloured creature knew this, before I'd admitted the truth to myself? Regardless, I continued to train.

Through my commitment to training I started to understand the difference between street fighting and professional fighting. Street fighting is dangerous and should only ever be used as self-defence, you could end up killing someone or getting locked up. Training in a professional way and sticking with it teaches strength, discipline and focus. It provides many opportunities to better your life, and society respects that, coz you're an athlete, not a thug! There would be no turning back for me, but as it happened, that was easier said than done ...

THE UNUSUAL SUSPECTS

During '95 Devious and our Doncaster mates started hitting the clubs. They were a little older than me and legally you needed to be 18 to get into clubs, buy alcohol or cigarettes or drive in Melbourne. Devious was driving and clubbing before he was 18, coz he could use his brothers ID and his dad would lend him his car, a VL commodore. Before then I was just drinking with friends on weekends or at parties, but I never had to worry too much about ID coz Devious would sneak bottles of liquor out when his dad wasn't looking. Each weekend he'd grab something different for us to try and this usually meant we would drink straight from the bottle like scotch, tequila or vodka, and combined with smoking bongs, I'd get pretty wasted. Every time I'd smoke weed with my mates the pressure was on to 'pull a cone', which meant you had to pack the cone to the rim with weed and tobacco, then finish it in one hit without coughing or gagging. It's a fact that most smokers in Melbourne mix weed with tobacco when 'mulling up' to stretch it out. I got to the point where I could pull a cone and hold the smoke in my lungs, then pull another cone straight after, then breathe all the smoke out at once through my nose. This party trick earned me the nickname, The Dragon, when I smoked with our crew ... I loved it!

A few weeks later, Devious was telling us about a club called Razers that he'd been going to on Sunday nights with his Doncaster mates and some other mates from the Richmond neighbourhood. It was '80s night, so they played that kinda music and everyone would dress up in '80s clothes too. One Sunday night he convinced us to come along. We raided my stepdad's wardrobe and found some old suits and shirts. I slicked my hair back and wore my shirt open so you could see my gold chain, like I was in the movie *Saturday Night Fever*.

We caught a taxi in coz we thought it looked slicker rocking up to the club that way. I was 16 and so was Memo, and we didn't have any ID on us. We lined up nervously for a little while and watched a few people get 'knocked back'. Later in life, I learned that the rule 'Management reserves the right to refuse entry' means a few things; Like: no ID, if you look pissed, don't fit the dress code, don't fit the look of the crowd they want, for example too old/too young, too muscular/too fat, you look like trouble, you have previously been known to cause trouble, you're of a particular ethnicity the management don't want in the club, or there are already too many males in the venue. It's a slippery can of worms when it comes to discrimination, and a grey area when it comes to legislation.

When we arrived at the front of the cue the 'door bitch' said, "Straight in, boys." I was pumped and wasted no time getting inside before she changed her mind. I can't remember drinking too much that night, but I briefly met some of the crew from Richmond and a few of the Doncaster guys I'd met before. I was probably inside for about an hour when it seemed everyone around me was looking pretty smashed. I went to the gents to drain the main vein, and right next to me at the urinal was one of the AFL's biggest stars. A couple guys on the other side of him were hangin' shit on him, calling him names and all that. He turned to me and said, "Hey mate have you seen *Dumb and Dumber*?" He was of course referring to the two blokes who were taunting him. I was at a urinal, so it wasn't really a place I wanna start a conversation and I didn't want to get involved. I just put my head down, finished my business, and got out of there.

Right after I left the urinal, a fight erupted on the dance floor. One of the Richmond boys had been hit bad and got his eye opened up and there was blood streaming down his face. He'd been jumped by a group of Turkish blokes who were much older than us. The head bouncer, who was Greek, came along and kicked everyone involved out of the club, which meant, by association, Devious, Memo and I were chucked out too. The fight continued out on the street and the head bouncer was fighting some of the Turks coz they resisted leaving the club. I was comfortable fighting grown men coz I was sparring with them all the time in the gym. As the scuffle continued onto the road I jumped across and round house kicked one of the Turks in the thigh dropping him to the ground. Then another guy charged at me, and I gave him a front kick and he went down, rolling across the road into the path of an oncoming taxi, which quickly slammed on its breaks and narrowly missed his head. After that the Turks started to retreat and one guy shouted, "I'm going to my car and coming back with my fucken shotgun!" We heard that and ran out of there as fast as we could, and jumped in a cab back to Malvern, celebrating our great night on the way home!

At home, the house was starting to look better. They'd built the second storey, with two bedrooms and a bathroom, so I now had my own room downstairs, which made it easy for me to sneak in and out of my room as I pleased. I'd look after my brothers when I could, and I loved being a big brother to them. I felt I could once again embrace that part of my life, and it brought me a lot of joy. However, randomly one night, Mum came down into my room and completely wigged out, telling me to, "Get out of the house and don't come back," coz apparently, I'd woken her and my brothers up late at night when I'd snuck in and been too loud. I was shocked that she'd said this, as I felt at the time things were finally getting better between us. I chose not to argue with her and I stayed at

Memo's house for a week until things cooled down. Mum was having some issues and I later found out she had depression. She had even taken some funds from my room and lost it gambling on the horses. But she did confess and paid me back. Either way I knew in my heart if she did get that big win the first thing she would have done was taken us all on a much needed holiday and cooked us up a big plate of schnitzel!

Back at Swinburne, I continued to keep things to myself, but my mates could tell my home life wasn't great. I felt my friends at school had embraced me and were all pretty compassionate. A lot of them were going through similar things, but most of them were a little older than me so had worked through the system to find accommodation and certain financial benefits, which were sometimes lucrative. Occasionally some kids would show me some generosity, by buying me food or soft drink. I liked that feeling and I knew when I had more coin, I'd do the same. But nothing compared to how Cal had taken me in. I still missed how things had once been.

Smack was everywhere when I was at Swinburne and a kid from one of my classes at school, Joseph who was different from the other Viet kids I knew, very articulate and would often recite poetry, OD'd on the drug, right towards the end of the year. The day he died he'd been out with the Italian kid, Brando. They'd both asked me to come along to the city and join them that Friday night. We were going to play video games and hang out, but I already had plans. They ended up scoring some gear from a pinnie parlour we called the Red House. Then they went to Brando's place and shot up in his room. Joseph just lay in the bed next to Brando and quite simply never woke up. Strangely, Brando arrived at school on the Monday and told me what happened, as if he was telling me the story in the third person or something like he was completely removed from the fact they had taken that shit together. It was fucken warped. He just coldly said, "Joseph, the idiot, never woke up, I shook him in the morning and the cunt was blue."

A lot of kids from school went to the funeral. They were surprised I didn't go but I was tryna keep a low profile. I said my own prayers for Joseph and ultimately paid him my respects in my own way. Looking back as an adult, Brando was obviously in a state of shock, I'm sure he deeply regrets what happened, we were all good mates, and I could tell it greatly affected him. I hardly saw him at school after that. Joseph's death was a reminder that life is short, and our life journeys can be very unpredictable. It's important that each decision we make has a purpose and that the purpose doesn't lead us into something negative or harmful. We are human beings, and throughout history our race has dealt with tragedy. We adapt, rebuild, evolve and ultimately survive. That's just what we do. There is no greater sacrifice than death, so never take life for granted!

During that time around the neighbourhood and along the train lines and carriages, I started to see the Tags from a new crew getting up around the spots. A few weeks passed and someone had tagged my back fence with *BDM* (*Bring Da Machete*), the new crew I'd noticed, along with the tags, *Blaze* and *Showdown*. Who were these clowns? I was thinking, damn, everybody knows me in this neighbourhood, who'd have the balls to tag my fence around here? They're all soft cocks. Little did I know, just a few days later, we'd all become mates and our crew was about to get bigger ...

COLORS OR COLOURS

First day back at school in '96, I noticed a kid on our morning tram that looked about my age. He got off at the same stop and walked in our direction towards the school ground. Memo was with me and said, "I've seen that dude down at John's Pinnies before." But I didn't recognise him. It was always good to see everyone after the holidays, so I was busy the rest of the day catching up with all my mates and hearing what they got up to over the Christmas break.

The next day we saw the same kid on the tram. I started a conversation with him, and he said he was Greek and that he lived in the milk bar right next door to John's Pinnies. I was surprised I'd never met this dude before, he said he skated, smoked weed, and was into east coast hip hop. We become mates straight away and started talking about graff and he said he tagged *Blaze*. I was like, "You're the dude that tagged my fence!" He apologised and because we didn't know each other there was no drama. I was running around throwing up heaps of tags everywhere myself, my fence just got caught in the friendly fire.

A few more dudes from his crew had started out at our school too, like Chorlito, who was Peruvian, and a boxer. Pez, who was a massive stoner and use to live in a church coz his mum had shacked up with a minister. Also the other dude that tagged my fence Showdown and his younger brother; they were Timorese. Either after school or if we were ditching, we'd catch up and smoke weed in Blaze's room on the top storey of the milk bar. If his parents were downstairs working, Blaze would grab us munchies, like Doritos or Monaco bars, which where my favourite. We'd listen to rappers like Wu-tang, Biggie and Gang Starr. This inspired me to go harder on writing lyrics, and Blaze (aka Jonny Blaze) started writing lyrics too.

I recorded a ruff mess-around-demo over the *Hey Lover* instrumental by L.L Cool J. It sounded fresh, but raw AF because we just used tape recorders and live vocal. The track was about my ex, Grace, I guess it hadn't really been all that long since we'd broken up when I wrote it. I kept writing and I'd bust lyrics out to my friends at parties or basically any opportunity I had. However, Blaze lacked the hunger and passion for music because he preferred to skate, smoke weed and chase his girlfriends around. My confidence was growing when rapping out to crowds, but I'd usually be high, which helped me flow freestyle. Sometimes I'd rap over techno or trance beats, which was generally the more popular style of music in Melbourne back then.

Blaze's dad caught us "choofing" in his bedroom several times. He wasn't a happy man and screamed at us in Greek. That meant it was time to go home or back down to John's Pinnies. We found some chill spots in our neighbourhood where we could hang or smoke uninterrupted, like under a tree near one of our local stations. This was a good spot coz there was a level train crossing there, which meant trains always needed to wait there longer than normal, giving us the perfect opportunity to run onto the tracks with our cans and paint 'throw ups' on the panels. Or 'back ons' which meant we'd tag the back carriage, then hang onto the outside window rail and stand on the ledge once the train started moving, until we got to the next station. Other writers would meet us there to hang out like Diskreet, an Aussie Jewish dude, but it was Chorlito who I resonated with the most coz he was a fighter.

It was cool having another fighter in the crew. It felt like we had a big advantage over anyone who wanted to mess with us. Chorlito was committed to his training. When he chilled with us he never drank or smoked weed. I'm not sure if he felt he was missing out, but he made up for it with crime. Any given opportunity he would be tagging, breaking into stuff, racking shit or going on joyrides; we called that 'getting a hottie'. I liked the dude, he felt like a long-lost cousin for a little while. When it came to graff and fighting, I felt that the guy 'stood up'. After getting to know him better he told me that his older brothers were previously in 3174, coz they all lived not far from that neighbourhood, so we had stuff in common.

Chorlito and his brothers had grown up together in the Richmond commission flats, when they were young kids, but their mum had got them out of the flats and bought a house in Doveton. One Saturday afternoon Chorlito and me were walking in the city down near Flinders Street station when a big, tall dude about 35, wearing a North Melbourne FC beanie and a long grey trench coat, stepped out in front of me and said, "Who won the footy mate?" I noticed he barracked for North Melbourne, like me, coz of the beanie he was wearing, so I took the time to stop and then said, "I don't know." He said, "Well what fucken good are ya?" I immediately shaped up and went to hit him. Chorlito grabbed me and pulled me away, he said, "What the fuck you doin' man? You hit him all that crew are gonna jump in." There were about 10 older, homeless looking people standing behind him. But I still didn't care and said, "Fuck him." Then Chorlito said words to me that I'll never forget, "Mate be a warrior not a worrier. Don't let shit like that get to you, ya can't fight everyone. Be smart. If they cross your path and you have to fight, do what you need to do and take care of business." They were deep words. I listened, and we caught a train to Richmond and hanged out. Like I did a lot back in those days on trains, I drifted into deep thought. I didn't want to take shit from anyone, but my filter hadn't worked out how to sift through it when I needed to. I was a warrior, but I needed to grow up and own it!

KiDS WiTH ATTiTUDE

A car wash opened-up in my neighbourhood and while it was under construction, one of the owners had become a regular customer at Devious's liquor store. He mentioned that they were looking for workers and Devious gave them my name and got his phone number, coz he knew I needed some dosh. I called the guy because it seemed like a cool job, and I ended up working there every Saturday for about three weeks. The boss was a stress head, telling me to wash faster, when I already was going as quick

as I could. On the last shift, I opened up the ashtray of an old
ladies Mercedes Benz to clean it out and found a couple grams
of weed. The uptight boss, who kept looking over my shoulder
the whole shift, came over and I showed him the bud and said,
"What should I do with this?" He snapped back at me saying,
"Just throw it in the bin." I was like, "You serious?" And threw
it in the bin. But before I finished my shift, I quickly grabbed
it out of the trash, while he was counting my pay for the day,
which was about $30.

I then headed down to John's Pinnies and met up with Blaze
n' the crew. The boys asked me how the shift was, and I pulled
out the stash and showed them. Blaze said, "I'll buy it off you
man, how much you want for it?" He would get cha-ching from
his dad, who was working next door in the milk bar, pretty
much whenever he asked him, so it was a done deal. I asked him
how much he thought I had, and he said it looked like more than
a gram. I said, "Ok bro, give me $30." I'd made exactly what I'd
made in my six hours of washing cars for that pushy, ungrateful
prick at the car wash. I was thinking the boss was expecting to
grab the hooch himself and smoke a couple joints after work,
that's why he'd told me to throw it in the bin and not leave it in
the car ashtray. I never heard from the guy again to work there,
so I assume what I thought was true. But, more importantly, I'd
now discovered a more efficient way to earn a dollar without
bustin' my ass for six hours.

I never had money to blow on weed; mates would just shout
me, unless I managed to find or nab the shit from somewhere.
As Chorlito started hanging out in our hood more, he told us
that his older brothers had a hook up; an old Russian lady,

named Genie, they'd score ganja from. I was like, "No fucken way, how old is she?" And he said, "She's like a grandma, at least 50." I couldn't believe it; it just didn't seem realistic. So, I said, "Get the address man." Chorlito called up his brother and got the address. Blaze grabbed some bread from his dad, and we all waited in the alley way, while Chorlito knocked on her ground floor balcony window and bought the dope for Blaze. I didn't see her at first, but Chorlito assured me she was legit, and he'd scored some really nice smoke too.

Blaze was getting hooked. He'd go through at least a couple grams per day, so he asked Chorlito to introduce him to Genie so he could score anytime he wanted. Genie's problem was she was greedy and would pretty much sell to anyone who'd knock on her window. I guess she figured that they must be friends with her customers if they knew where to get it from. She'd also give out 'tick' and I never understood why she had so much trust in little hood rats like us. Greed was the only explanation that made sense. Blaze would rack up bills of credit with her, but he'd always pay her coz he wanted more pot. Sometimes if he owed her too much she stopped giving more credit, he'd send me or Memo up there to buy another gram, so Genie wouldn't hit him up for what was owed and he could still smoke.

That's how I got to know Genie. After doing this for Blaze a few times I thought, fuck this, rather than smoking this shit with my mates I should try and buy a larger quantity and sell it myself. The next time I went up to Genie's I asked her, "How much for a quarter?" In her thick Russian accent she said, "I no have. You must see my son Drago, I call him for you." She called him to check if it was okay, then she gave me his number and I called him and arranged to meet him at his place near the Highett public housing. There wasn't a lot of profit in it at all if I think about all the trouble I used to go to. I'd need to catch a tram and bus to Drago's and the same back home, weigh it up, bag it, and then sell seven bags to seven different dudes, who most of the time would ask for "tick". I also had to buy plastic bags and scales, but Genie used to wrap her weed in foil, so eventually I figured it was cheaper and more convenient this way.

I'd try and stretch it out to make eight bags from the seven, to push up the profit. After a while Drago dropped the price, which meant I could double my money on the eight bags if I didn't smoke any myself. I didn't think Drago really looked Russian. He was a tall white guy, but with dreadlocks and no Russian accent. Blaze was one of my first customers and it didn't take him long before he was using our friendship to get tick. I started noticing he was a little shifty and would avoid me by telling his dad to tell me he wasn't home at times when he owed me bills. I started to lose trust in the guy, but he eventually paid back what he owed.

Most of the crew would hang out at the back of Devious's liquor store playing a Viet card game called thirteen, especially on Sunday afternoons when his parents had the day off. Devious would grab us a packet of cigarettes and cans of beer or UDLs off the shelves and we'd play all day in between him serving customers or helping him stack the cool room. Sometimes we'd mix it up with a game of blackjack but most of us preferred thirteen. John, who ran the pinnies, trusted Memo and asked him if he could work the Saturday morning shift for him, coz he had something else he needed to do. I'm not sure what he got paid, but it was a good job, coz all of us would hang out the back and play cards, just like we'd seen all the old Greek men do for so many years, but we'd choof too.

The problem was that from the time the first Melbourne casino opened up in '94, a lot of the underground gambling dens died in the ass, which would have cost John a great deal of his profits. I think he was using the free time on Saturday mornings to look into other businesses, coz things weren't looking good for him, especially with the much larger casino set to open up in '97. Of course, he never told any of us his business, we just knew. We had some close calls when John nearly caught us mid-session at the back of his shop. He was like an old strict uncle, and he would have got pissed off had he known, so we had to jump the back fence a coupla times. Perhaps the fumes mellowed him out, coz in reflection he actually never said anything about it at all ... Yasou Theios!

ENTER THE DRAGON SMOKER

As all my mates left school, I wasn't gonna be a follower and fail what I'd set out to finish, but tryna handwrite all my school assignments was getting hard. As the school was adapting to the internet and computers were introduced into our schooling, I managed to buy a 'hot' laptop for $50 from a junky. The screen didn't have colour, but it did the job, and I could get through my work a lot faster and didn't have to use white out and wait for it to dry if I made a mistake. I was also getting more efficient with how to get our tags up on trains, with what we used to call 'loops'. We'd basically jump on the trains at one of our regular stations, on off-peak times, bomb the fuck out of the inside of the carriages with our felt tip markers – the fatter the tip the better – then jump off at the very next station and do the same thing on the way back. When we first started doing this, we thought it was great coz our tags would stay on the carriages for a day or two before they got cleaned off; all the other writers would see them. But it didn't last long enough for the risks we were taking.

We started noticing other tags were staining the carriages longer term, so we started to ask around and work out how this was done. It was like top secret information among other writers, like boxers giving out in-house info about how they were winning fights. If you let people know your tricks, you're gonna get exposed! But we cracked the code. It was acetone, the chemical used in paint thinner and nail polish remover. If we unscrewed the tip of our marker and mixed a certain amount of acetone in the marker, it would make a bad-ass stain, and your tag would last forever, unless they replaced the whole fibreglass panel in the carriage. Our crew absolutely smashed it for a couple months, to the point where other writers and crews were getting envious. Diskreet and others in the crew had started rocking pieces by this stage too. As much as I thought I was bombing, the rest of the crew were bombing 10 times more, coz they'd dropped out of school, and apart from smoking weed, hooking up with their ladies or skating, bombing was like their full-time job. Until they got busted …

I guess graff life catches up with ya sooner or later. Pez and Memo got complacent, doing loops at the same time and the same stations every day. They racked up a massive cleaning and repairs bill for the Met, like $30k in damage each. The BLTs set up an undercover operation and detectives arrested them one morning. They were asked questions about the rest of the RSH crew, but they kept their mouths shut and went to court a few months later, copping fines and convictions for vandalism. Most of us kept a low profile for a short time after that, just bombing occasionally.

As the crew grew tighter we'd hang out almost every day and when the weekend came around it would be time to go out to parties, meet girls and mingle with other peeps too. Thing was though, everyone in the crew was completely wild, there was constant action, and we were always seeking that next big thrill. Bombing was always a rush and when Ricks or Devious would bring the cars we could just stop wherever we wanted, bomb and take off quick with less chance of getting busted, then continue onto the party. The driver would usually smoke weed while the rest of us drank liquor too. But there would be times when we didn't have enough cars to transport us all across to where we wanted to go. This led to the phrase, 'Let's get a hottie'.

There were a couple of girls at our school that used to hang around the schoolyard with us too, but I ignored them most of the time. Then one afternoon one of the girls invited me to her birthday party in a neighbourhood called Williamstown, which is on the other side of the Westgate Bridge. It was a kind gesture so I said that I'd try and make it across. I let some of the crew know about the party and most of them wanted to go, only problem was on the night of the party we had transport issues...

I never really needed to resort to it coz, Devious or Ricks would usually be driving, they were always happy to pick me up or drop me off from wherever I was. They were like a free taxi service for a while. On this particular night it was just Devious that came along, so there was no way we could all squeeze into his VL commodore and the potential cab ride there and back was more than most of us could afford, so Pez yelled out, "Let's get a hottie!" We just all started cheering and laughing. I got caught up in the hype and said, "I'll get it with ya, bro!" Apart from just the pure thrill of the joyride, it was me who invited all my mates along, so I felt I should be responsible for making sure we all got there. We made a few failed attempts before we broke into an old early 1970s model Datsun 180B and got it started with a screwdriver. We then headed off across the Westgate dropping burnouts along the way. Blaze was driving, with me riding shotgun, while Devious and the rest of the crew were in his VL laughing and driving in the lane next to us. We saw a couple of bike riders peddling along the road beside us, so Blaze put his foot on the gas and swerved a little, and they panicked and fell off their bikes, while we all cracked up laughing and beeping our horns with the golden oldies AM radio music pumping to represent our retro ride.

We finally made it over the bridge, and we were at the lights making a lot of noise and messing about. Some dudes on the street must have thought, shit these guys look like they're having a great time, they yelled out, "Where you guys from?"

In reply, Blaze dropped a massive burnout at the lights right at that moment, while I was hanging out of the window yelling, "South Eastern Suburbbbbbszzz!" As the car sped off down the road, leaving a trail of smoke behind us. We must have looked fucken crazy!

When we finally arrived at the party after all the hype it was really lame, with more dudes there than chicks. The dudes were alright with us, so there was no point making trouble with them and ruining the birthday party. I wasn't sure why I'd been invited TBH, in the back of my mind I thought maybe I had a chance of getting to know the birthday girl a little better, she was cute but really shy and didn't talk that much. At the party, she wasn't talking at all, so we decided to leave. I was feeling disappointed we'd gone to all that trouble of getting a hottie and then the birthday girl didn't even want to give us the time of day.

It was a cold night and it had been raining. We all got in the same cars for the drive home, and as we got near Chapel Street, Devious pulled up beside us and said they wanted to stop and grab some Hungry Jacks before they headed home. I didn't feel like going into Hungry Jacks, so I stayed in the car on my own. When they all left, I started feeling edgy. The night had been a letdown, so much fun getting the hottie, then so flat after getting to the party. When Blaze jumped back into the car with his Whopper meal, I said, "I wanna drive man." Instead of talking me out of it, Blaze said, "Yeh man go for it ... Ahh wait a minute, can you drive?" I said, "Yeh," but I was very reckless behind the wheel, and I hadn't mastered driving manual. The Datsun 180B had a bit of grunt too. It took a little while for me to get the ignition turned over, again with the screwdriver, then suddenly, the engine began to roar like "Brahhh bra bra bra brahhhh". I put my foot down hard and the rubber started to burn. I was driving like a maniac, behind a supermarket in a big car park. I almost took out some pedestrians along the way. I had made a lot of noise and attracted a lot of attention before I crookedly parked the car in the same spot again.

Someone must have called the Bacon Deluxe coz two minutes later they pulled up next to me and asked for my license. I told them I left it at home, but they knew I was lying. It literally took six coppers to restrain me and throw me in the divvy van. What a fucken joke! Two more jacks grabbed Blaze, and right as we were thrown into the van, I saw the rest of the crew eating Hungry Jacks, just watching the scene, while we were being set upon by these desperate and hungry fucken jacks in blue uniforms. Man was I pissed off! As we sat in the van, I looked through the back window and noticed a crowd had formed around the vehicle. I could hear a group of drunken bogan Aussie larrikins chanting "You're going home in the back of a divvy van!" like they use to say at the infamously rowdy Bay 13 at the cricket at the MCG back in the '80s. The coppers flashed their flashlights in their faces and said "Move on, move on, or you'll end up like them." The bogan larrikins responded in another chant, "What's the colour of a two-cent coin? Copper, copper!" Then dispersed into the night. I was again taken back to Prahran cop shop and interviewed. I just played dumb, like I had a learning disability and couldn't understand their questions. I told them, "We were just on our way to put it back from where we got it from," which, amongst all the other bullshit, was actually the truth. It was a ninja-style trick my mates used, so that it almost seemed like nobody had committed a crime at all.

Besides we had no contacts in the auto rebirthing game back then. My lame alibi had obviously missed the mark and made no difference. We were charged with theft of a motor vehicle, and Blaze and me both ended up going to court. I got a fine and an admission of guilt without a conviction, and I think Blaze got a conviction and a fine coz he had priors. Now, that would have been the end of the auto theft story – just some plain old stupid juvenile shit – but unfortunately this story would come back to haunt me for a very long time. I was young, had acted dumb and took a stolen car for a joy ride to get to a party. I never thought such a lame ass, immature, adolescent and impulsive crime would cause me so many problems later on in life. Every action has a consequence, it took me a long time to realise that!

KRUSH GROVEN'

A couple of weekends later, on a Friday night, Chorlito called me up at home and said, "Hey man, come down to my girl's mum's place, in Prahran near the skate park. We're hanging out here. The girls have weed and booze and shit like that!" I was like, "Dope, see you soon, I'll tell Devious and the crew." We rocked up after 9 pm when Devious finished his shift at the liquor store, and he grabbed us a bottle of Chivas Regal and we were off. I was wearing my New York Yankees jacket and a white Raiders Starter cap with a black logo.

When we arrived we met Chorlito and he took us inside. We met the chick, he'd been hooking up with, and a couple of her friends. We all started drinking and listening to music together. After a couple of hours, a girl from school asked if I wanted to smoke some weed with her. I said, "Cool." I was already pretty drunk by this stage, so when I pulled a cone, I just flaked it on a mattress on the floor. Next thing I knew, the lights were off, and she was on top of me, and we went for it. All I saw were flashes and people giggling in the background. I was completely out of it and felt sick. I eventually just passed out.

When I woke up, they turned on the lights saying, "It's time to go!" I woke up remembering I'd hooked up with a girl but had no idea of the details. When I got to school the Monday after I acted like everything was normal. I shyly said "Hi," to the girl, and just made it clear that I liked her more as a friend and that I was really wasted on Friday night. She said she was cool with that. So, everything was sweet, until after school.

What I didn't know was that Chorlito had rocked up to school that day on a mission. I rarely saw him in the schoolyard and just assumed he'd dropped out like the rest of the crew. His mission was to develop the photos he'd taken from the Friday night in the school's darkroom. The flashes I'd seen on the Friday night were Chorlito taking pornographic photos, FML! ... Man, it was like he showed those photos to every fucken writer in Melbourne. Except, as he put it, out of respect he cut my head out and only left her face and naked body in the photos. It didn't look good, and I wasn't too happy about it, although you couldn't see my face, you could clearly see my trademark New York Yankees jacket, which I was wearing the whole time. I immediately thought about what the expression on Cal's face would have been like, seeing his jacket worn in that way. I have no doubt he would have wanted to smash Chorlito for disgracing all of us. But I hadn't seen him in a long time, I'd gotten too wasted and let it happen. I questioned if I should get Benny Blanco on Chorlito's ass and take him out. But my crew convinced me I was king and Chorlito was like family, so I let it go.

For the next three months I had so many dudes in the graff scene just randomly coming up to me whenever I was wearing the infamous jacket at parties or places like Richmond station, which was a massive hang out spot for writers coz of the interconnecting train lines saying, "Hey man you're the dude in the photo! Love your work, bro!" And giving me hi-fives and shaking my hand and wanting to throw up tags with me. I'd gone viral before viral was invented. But that was about all I had to deal with regarding the photos. The girl from school was left to deal with a whole lot more. I felt for her, thankfully she was mentally strong, and she didn't let it get her down. It should never have happened; she deserved a lot more respect. She ended up reporting Chorlito to the principal and he was officially kicked outta the school, not that he ever showed up much anyway.

Looking back, Chorlito and some of the others in my crew who I considered to be family, didn't behave the way true mates should. It just took me some time before I woke up to the facts. I wasn't sure what values I stood for anymore, what Raising Some Hell stood for. What the fuck was it all about? What was the fucken point of being in a crew anyway? Was it just simply to raise hell and inflict punishment on anyone who dared run the gauntlet. That's certainly how it seemed, coz I wanted to fuck up any cunt on the street that messed with my crew, and if ladies got caught up in the crossfire, I wasn't about to show them my nicer side either. But this wasn't truly who I was. I'd always had faith in spirituality, yet I came up with the name Raising Some Hell. The greatest trick the devil ever pulled is convincing the world he didn't exist, right? What had I manifested? I was starting to realise, I'd lost myself a little, forgotten some of the stuff Cal taught me. But I knew I was tuff and like always I was gonna keep on fighting through. Just like the quote, "They tried to bury us. They didn't know we were seeds."

Amongst all the 'hell raising' there were definitely some lighter moments, which made kickin' it with the crew worthwhile. Some days we'd all head out for a skate. I personally wasn't the most passionate of skaters, I preferred rapping, tagging and yeh, of course fighting, but someone would usually lend me their deck to mess around on and I enjoyed chillin' with the crew more than anything else. Blaze and some of our mates would pull off some dope tricks which lifted everyone's spirits on the day, forming a strong sense of comradeship between us all. It would suddenly make life seem so positive with all the other negative shit going on in my life.

One day the crew wanted to skate around the city, so we'd stop at different locations until the Five-O or security come along and kicked us out. We ended up at Melbourne Exhibition Centre which was newly built back then. On this Saturday afternoon, we'd knocked off a slab of beer from somewhere and I was drinking and tagging while the others were skating. I'd learnt a trick where I could open the bottle without a bottle opener by quickly and swiftly hitting the lid against a bench or concrete step. I was on to opening my sixth beer when, 'swoosh' I'd missed the lid and broken the bottle slicing my thumb open deeply. I couldn't feel any pain, but there was a lot of blood, and my thumb was wide open. Blaze grabbed some tissues out of the car and put pressure on my thumb with tape.

I was beyond tipsy, I simply brushed it off like I didn't give a fuck, I just kept drinking and running amuck. It was bad cut though. I still have the scar. As we walked back to the cars, I heard a loud knock on the Exhibition Centre windows. I turned around and saw Deni Hines, she looked beautiful. Deni was a certified and successful pop star in Australia during this time. She is best known for the hits she had with her band Rockmelons in the early '90s *L.O.V.E (Love)* and *Ain't No Sunshine*. She's also the daughter of an African American singer, Marcia Hines, who migrated to Australia as an artist and had much success as a singer and on a TV show called *Hey Hey It's Saturday*. Deni was saying something to me that I couldn't hear, so she started using sign language and kinda flirting, smiling, and laughing a lot. She looked really cute; she would have been at least 10 years older than me. I pointed towards the door, so she could come over and talk to me. And she did. She said, "Don't drink, you're too young." I said, "I'm not that young, I'm 17." She laughed and said, "You don't need it, be healthy."

Honestly, it was like she was my musical angel. guiding me towards a better path. I said, "Okay," and threw the beer out in the bin in front of her, and we kept talking. The rest of the crew had come over by this stage. They had their decks out and fat markers in hand saying, "Can you please autograph my deck?" And "You're beautiful,"... She blushed a little and was very gracious, she wrote her autograph on their decks and she said, "Don't write on things, you will get in trouble."

The rest of her band was waiting for her inside the building, they'd been rehearsing for an upcoming gig. She said, "I better go now, they're waiting." I said, "Bye," and my mates were yelling out stupid shit like, "We love you!" She went back inside and, no word of a lie, she turned around from behind the glass door, gave me a smile and drew a love heart in the air and said thank you. I walked away thinking, Damnnn should have got her number ... It was a priceless moment.

RAGING TORO

There were a lot of distractions during that time, but I never lost my focus. I was still rocking up to kickboxing training three times per week and I'd never miss a session no matter what, I just loved it. Fighting was my thing, I'd always been good at it, now I was using it as a sport, it was a much more positive outlet and I knew it would stop me from completely going off the rails. My reputation grew and I became known for it. My coach, Nick, was impressed with my sparring and asked me if I wanted to have an exhibition fight in an upcoming tournament being held at our gym. We didn't have to wear shin guards or headgear, but just a mouthguard and groin guards, same rules as a pro fight. I was honoured and immediately said yes. I couldn't wait.

Nick told me I'd needed to be under 160 lb. Another member of the club, Mick, was also asked to fight in the tournament but in the weight class below, which was under 154 lb. Mick asked me if I wanted to start training with him for an hour every Wednesday and Friday morning, in addition to our regular training days. I agreed, meaning I was now getting in five solid training sessions per week. Mick was about 25 at the time and worked for his dad in the furniture business, so he drove a big old white truck, and even though the park was just down the road from my house, he'd pick me up about 5:30 am and drop me off home again about 6:30 am, so we kept to our routine.

Before he'd pick me up, I'd wrap my torso in cling wrap and he'd do the same, so we'd sweat more while we trained, and lose more weight. Sometimes I'd cut holes in a garbage bag and wear it like a singlet under my thick tracksuit. We'd run laps for 20 minutes and practice our leg checks and combinations. It was always cold in the morning, so I'd feel every strike we blocked or checked. In the gym it was bag work, combination drills and sparring, and mostly with Mick coz we were both fighting on the same day. I'd grown my hair long, which I'd slick back with a ponytail, and I always wore caps back then, except when I was training. Amongst the crew we had made a pact to not cut our hair or the whole crew would jump you, and you had to pay every crew member $100. People started cheating and getting trims and tryna to weasel their way out of the bashings and having to pay up. But if I say I'm gonna do something, I always stick to my word.

On the morning of the fight, I weighed in and made weight. There were a lot of fighters having their first fight on this card, who went onto have good fight careers. Some professional fighters I recognised were in the audience too, like the legendary kickboxing icon 'Stan the Man' and a rising star named Sammy Soliman, so I wanted to put on a good show to impress them. Wayno came down and most of the crew got a seat in the front row. Inside I was nervous, but excited about getting in the ring in front of a crowd.

My fight flew by pretty quickly. I was young and had lots of energy. I felt like I hurt him more than he hurt me, but as it was an exhibition there was no result, just both our hands raised at the end of the fight. I thought perhaps the way we were training in the gym had lacked a bit of explosiveness, that I could have benefited from during the fight. It was a little more towards a kung fu class sometimes, where we'd practice things that you couldn't use in the ring, more just for self-defence. I loved it; but I realised I needed to train like a professional fighter and my true passion was traditional boxing. Chorlito came down with the rest of the crew to watch my fight that day, so I asked him where he was training and he said, "Yeh man, at Leo's Gym, come down whenever you like." The first thing that came to mind was yes, no more sore legs! However, I felt a little bad leaving my trainer Nick straight after a fight, so I stuck with him until the end of the year.

SHOTGUN ASSASSIN

owards the end of '96 the routine of rocking up to parties on the weekends continued, sometimes we crashed and sometimes we were invited. Our crew still had a bad reputation and were still barred from most parties within extended friends' circles. Somehow, most weekends we fell through the cracks and ended up getting into more trouble. I didn't intentionally set out to ruin anyone's party. At the time, I just felt everyone else was so fucken privileged compared to the dysfunctional environment I was living in. I was struggling with my identity and felt different to everyone else, it was a battle just to fit in. I guess I'd developed a complex over the whole thing, or perhaps a chip on my shoulder and an excuse to un leash. My crew and my friends' circle was very multicultural, but unlike me, most were not of mixed heritage. I felt that anyone who disrespected me, particularly in public, would need to be shown a lesson not to fuck with me. I always had something to prove. I had a short fuse and at times I'd flip. But deep down I knew that acting in this way wasn't right, I needed to be more disciplined. It was a recipe for disaster, something needed to change.

One night we decided to go to an 18th birthday party in East Malvern. I'd been there about five minutes, when some dickhead grabbed a helium-filled birthday balloon and rubbed it in my face for no reason. I've always hated people getting in my face and this triggered a violent reaction in me. I instantly went to hit him, but my mates had a few more brains and pulled me back, saying, "The guy's drunk don't worry about it." But I was smashed and fucken pissed off that the guy had been so disrespectful. He started walking off about 10 steps in front of me. I just saw red and in one action I picked up a plastic chair with steel legs and threw it at the guy, but I missed and hit someone else in the head, knocking them to the ground. I quickly picked up another chair and it missed again, hurting another person. I picked up a third chair and 'bang' it hit him right in the head knocking him to the ground. I ran over and started beating him. Suddenly I felt people trying to pull me off him; it was the birthday girl's parents and the security who were looking after the party. I began fighting with them and picking up things like beer cans off the ground and smashing them into their heads. I'd gone completely wild. There were six adults I was fighting with and still I had enough energy to keep fighting. One of the adults eventually took the calm approach and said, "Mate, please would you just leave, you've ruined my daughters party." His words hit me, and I started to feel really bad. I apologised to him, and we left the party and drove home. Everyone was talking about how crazy I was. But the victory celebration had stopped, I'd gone too far this time. It was time to focus on my fighting career, which would hopefully earn me coin I needed to have a better life.

Not long after the party I was struck by another lightning bolt, that reminded me I needed to convert to boxing. It was the Mike Tyson vs. Evander Holyfield fight. I had snuck into a pub down the road from home. None of my friends were interested in coming along, but it was a fight I was never gonna miss. I was convinced Mike Tyson would get the job done easy and continue his reign as heavyweight champ. The pub was packed, and I was the youngest dude in there. I didn't feel like drinking, I felt nervous and was sweating due to the adrenaline. As the fight started, I found myself yelling out at the TV screen, supporting Tyson. His timing seemed out, he just couldn't land anything clean and the ref wasn't stopping Holyfield from head butting, it wasn't fair. It was a great fight, but also a great disappointment. I felt Tyson was robbed by all the head clashes because he was unfairly cut and damaged from this. Holyfield had fought strategically, but I felt his style was kinda dirty and boring compared to my boxing idol Tyson, a better ref might have DQ'd him. Tyson had only gotten out of prison in '95 and I'd forgotten about that already. I wasn't too concerned about his personal life, after all I'd never met the man, I just loved what he did in the boxing ring and had a strong sense the system had also let him down many times. Tyson made me feel that I could fight my way through all the bullshit too.

I couldn't wait any longer, I let Chorlito know I was ready to start boxing. He suggested starting in the New Year of '97 after the Christmas close-down period. I was still only 17, too young to drive by myself but Chorlito had turned 18 and bought himself a Holden Torana. I'd catch a couple trams and Chorlito would drop me home after training. I remember the first time I walked into Leo's Gym. There was an old man sitting down behind a desk. It was Leo. He was very well known back then, especially within the boxing community, which has always attracted a lot of gangsters in Melbourne. Leo had also trained with Wayno's father (who died of a heart attack in the '70s), a fighter who went under the alias 'Red Murphy'.

When I approached the desk, Leo said, "How can I help you, son?" I said, "I'm here to do some boxing, my mate Chorlito said to come down." He said, "Ahhhh...okay mate, have you been here before?" I said, "No." He asked, "Are you working or still at school?" I said, "Not working, but just finished year 12." Leo nodded, then said, "Alright son, write your name in the book and when you start working, place $2 in the ice cream container if you want to train casual, or $5 for the week. Training times are 3-6 pm Monday-Thursday and 8-9.30 am Sunday mornings." Leo then pointed in the direction of the change rooms. The gym reminded me of the gyms I'd seen in the movies. I thought to myself, This is *it* ... You're gonna be a boxer now.

SOMETIMES I CROSSED THE LINE AND YEH I MESSED THINGS UP, SO I GOT TO THE GYM & TRAINED IN WHAT I LOVE

This City, *Assumptions (2019)*

Eye of the Tiger

My final high school exam results were average. I didn't care, the main thing was I'd passed, stuck it out and finished no matter what was going on in my life. My Business Management and Psychology teacher had awarded me with two certificates of merit for my studies; she wanted to present these to me at a graduation ceremony. I didn't attend coz all my mates had dropped out and I felt like I'd be a geek if I rocked up. My teacher knew about all the issues I was going through at home and elsewhere. I had no desire to attend university and just study something lousy for the sake of it ... I wanted to chase that paper.

I signed up for the dole until I found full-time work. I used the welfare money to go to the Casino with Devious and the crew, using a fake ID coz I was still 17. As we'd played card games like 13 and Blackjack so often out the back of Devious's bottle shop, it seemed natural to start playing for money on the big stage under the casino lights. The movie *Casino* with Joe Pesci and Robert Di Nero had been released earlier in the year and had me pumped about going to our casino here in Melbourne.

Roulette was the first game I played. Blaze and Devious had gotten in before me and met me at the table. I watched Devious play a couple of rounds first to see how it was done. He was placing his five dollar casino chips on black or red, he'd won $200 real quick. Blaze joined in, then I did as well. I won $100 by basically doing the same thing as them and I was happy. We hit a strip club right after to celebrate. Devious got himself a lap dance. It seemed like a rip off to me, coz it was just a tease and he'd just blown the cash he'd won on the roulette table, in like two minutes. We continued on at the casino almost every night, and we all got a bit hooked on the buzz. It seemed okay at the time coz I never lost. But I wasn't greedy, which helped, I was just happy with winning $100, sometimes $200 or $300. I'd know when to stop and when to leave and most of the crew would listen if we told each other to pull up and get outta there. Over time it wouldn't be so easy to walk away.

Apart from Boxing, rapping was legitimately all I wanted to do and at the time I seriously considered how I could turn my passion into a career. But, it just seemed impossible to make money from it back then. I had no idea of how to produce beats and I had no cash behind me, or even understand the process of how to officially record a track in a studio. I was going to need to put a lot of work in if I was ever gonna make it. So, I attended a hip hop event with my crew and met up with some other writers in the city one night. We were on that 'let's run amuck' type vibe. I managed to get behind the bar and grab a bottle of liquor, so I got pretty smashed. A couple of older writers got up on stage and started rapping. It sounded pretty raw, but I respected them for giving it a crack and they rapped in strong Aussie accents, which was authentic and a new concept to me. I really wanted to get up there and rock the mic, but they were running the event, so I just sat back and watched. That night definitely gave me some inspiration that just maybe it was possible that Melbourne rappers could be taken seriously, I was just gonna have to figure out how to get there myself.

I was enjoying my life out of school. I didn't feel the same weight on my shoulders anymore, family life was getting better too. I was on the right path to living a more rewarding life and my family and friends respected me more for the person I was becoming. Mum had mentioned she might be able to get me a job. She'd heard they needed workers at a cafe which was just a short tram ride away from where we lived. I said yes and started working straight away. It was three hours work early mornings Monday to Friday. I was washing dishes, peeling potatoes, making coffees, and grilling bacon 'n' eggs.

I'd head home after work, watch cooking shows and imagine myself becoming a TV chef, then I'd take a siesta, eat and get ready to go to boxing training. There were a few occasions still when I got rowdy on weekends after drinking, but definitely not as often as before. Boxing training was making a big difference. I also got some great news that my grandparents wanted me to come on a holiday to Germany with them to meet family, I couldn't wait. I'd been waiting to see where my family had come from my whole life and put all of the stories I'd heard into context. We were set to fly out just after my 18th Birthday. I'd be old enough to drive, get into clubs, and buy alcohol.

In the meantime, back at the gym, Leo had a bunch of old lace up boxing gloves and bandages around his upright boxing ring. After I'd place my bag in the change room, I'd come out to grab a set of those bandages, roll them up and wait for Leo to wrap my hands. It was a good time to chat with him and find out how my progress was going with training. Initially, my knuckles would get bruised and cut up. I used to hit the bags as hard as I could and my bandages would be soaked in blood after every training session. Leo explained I had protruding knuckles so he would place a strip of rubber over my knuckles to help stop the damage. They were like that from all the street fighting. The skin around my knuckles eventually hardened up and the bleeding stopped. However, I noticed when I'd rock up to the gym the next day, my blood was still stained on the bandages. I don't think they were getting washed often, they were just hung out to dry from the sweat on the turnbuckle. I tried to make sure I matched the blood-stained bandages coz I knew they were mine and back then everybody was terrified of getting AIDS.

I'd brought in a photo Wayno had to give to Leo of his dad, Red Murphy, with other boxers from the 1950s, all standing in a row next to Leo. They looked like old school gangsters. It was a great photo and Leo loved it. Leo said they were close, and he was very sad Red had passed away so young, and that he'd gone to the funeral.

It wasn't long before Leo let me spar with Chorlito and an older guy who was a plumber by trade. Chorlito had a coupla fights before, but I'd never asked him what his record was. He was good. He landed some nice shots, but I never got too rattled, and I'd continue to trade punches, landing back on him. Somehow, one day during sparring, he'd managed to cut me over the eyebrow on my right side, it had gotten through the 16oz gloves and my head guard. Leo picked up on it right away and immediately stopped the sparring and cleaned my cut with Betadine and cotton wool. He was shocked that it had happened, "Did he have something inside his glove?" he asked. I didn't answer... I felt I shouldn't have got hit regardless. A reminder to move my head and work on defence when throwing punches. The objective is to hit and most importantly not get hit!

The layout of Leo's gym was great. The round-timer was consistently counting three-minute rounds with 60 second breaks, just like a pro fight. During a standard training session, I'd make sure I got a solid 15 rounds in on the circuit, my workout would consist of skipping, shadow boxing, speed ball, heavy bag, floor to ceiling, then finish with exercises like sit ups, medicine ball drills or light weights. If I had more time and energy, I'd put more rounds in. I'd get a couple rounds on the pads with Leo from time to time but he was getting old, so other dudes around the gym would volunteer to hold pads for me too. I'd also run laps of the footy field behind the gym before or after training a couple times a week too. If I was sparring, the routine would be a little different.

The 400 metre Olympic gold medallist, Cathy Freeman, would practice her running drills behind Leo's Gym too. I'd say 'Hey, wassup," and she was always friendly. World champ Kostya Tszyu had also trained at Leo's in the past when he had fights scheduled in Melbourne, and there were photos of him on bulletin board training at the gym. Leo was good mates with Kostya's trainer Johnny, who had a gym in Newtown, Sydney, and had trained other world champs like Jeff Fenech and Jeff

Harding there. Leo hooked me up with a week of training in the Newtown gym, after the week was done Johnny said he was impressed with me that he wanted to line up some fights for me in Sydney, but I decided to return to Melbourne.

It might sound crazy but in '97 I didn't really know a great deal about Muhammad Ali, or that he'd fought George Foreman in Africa in 1974, billed as 'The Rumble in the Jungle'. I'd heard Ali's name many times but never watched his fights and didn't know his story. George Foreman was still a heavy weight champ during this time, so I knew about him and about his famous grill, which was advertised on TV. As long as I could remember, Mike Tyson's name had dominated any conversation regarding heavy weight boxing, and he was my favourite fighter. Back then I'd watch fights on VCR, or read books about fighters. I feel that the documentary *When We Were Kings* (1996) revived Muhammed Ali's household name status, especially amongst my generation. Wayno's sister asked if I'd like to watch the film on the big screen; she said she heard it was good. I couldn't wait and she picked me up after training one night.

I loved every minute of the film. I had no idea how charismatic Ali was, or that he rhymed and used his words in such a moving and powerful way that it seemed like the whole world would listen and pay attention. I felt it was another sign telling me this was my path. He was a great entertainer with a big heart and loved to make people laugh. I was in awe of his spirit. I'd been focusing on being so aggressive and intimidating over the past few years, I'd nearly lost myself. Ali was the greatest, I wanted to be the greatest ... Inspire people, change people's lives for the better, make a difference in the world. I was done with all the negativity; it was time to embrace being positive!

NOTORIOUS

It was a cold May night in Melbourne when I flew overseas for the first time in my life with my grandparents. Wayno dropped us off at the airport. Devious and Blaze also drove out to the airport to say goodbye coz they knew I'd be gone awhile. Part of me was thinking I might never come back. We were flying with Louda Air and our first stop was Vienna, Austria. The food on the flight was unbelievable, like all the German stuff I'd grown up with, but never eaten outside of being with my family. My opa enjoyed me having a couple of beers with him, and it was all legal now I was 18. He also liked Jägermeister, which he would drink out of a small hip flask.

I remember when we got off the plane that for some reason my opa thought he was speaking German to a taxi driver, but he was speaking English. He'd got himself all confused after the long 20 plus hour journey, but he was getting old. I was cracking up laughing with Oma. When we arrived at the hotel, I remember the streets of Vienna smelling like a big bakery. It made me hungry, and we got out and got some food and beer almost straight away. We stayed in Vienna for about a week, and we kept going back to the same restaurant because my opa started a conversation with the owner, and we got to know him. Opa told him I was his grandson, also a boxer and a chef. The owner asked if I was qualified, he was speaking German to me, I couldn't understand every single word he was saying, so Opa and Oma would translate. He said if I had my qualifications as a chef, he'd give me a job in his restaurant. It was a great idea, I decided at that moment that's exactly what I would do as soon as I arrived back in Australia, I'd get a job as an apprentice chef, get my qualifications and come back and work in Europe. The restaurant owner also mentioned that he had to pay protection money to Russian gangsters to operate his business, and it was the same in all the restaurants in his neighbourhood. Before then I'd only ever known about the Italian Mob and some other gangs back home. I was fascinated by this new wing of organised crime, and I asked the owner a lot of questions. I meant well but I'm not sure if he was too enthusiastic about talking about them. After all, they were shaking him down.

I asked my grandparents to keep speaking German to me for the rest of the holiday and I would ask them about any new words I didn't understand. I felt like a little kid again getting around with my grandparents, but I didn't care because I cared for them a great deal. Plus, I needed time away from Melbourne, to reflect, change my ways, think about a career and keep training. Since I'd been training at Leo's, my life was changing for the better.

After leaving Vienna, we visited Salzburg, where Mozart was from and we walked past the house he'd lived in as a child. After a few days in Salzburg, we caught a train to Munich. On the way through we passed Bad Endorf which isn't far from the Austrian border. Opa was cursing as the train stopped at the station, but he insisted we get off at the next stop and see a house his father had owned as a holiday retreat. Oma reflected on how opa's father called her "Zigeuner", and how derogatory that was and I guess contributed to why she kept her true heritage to herself during such horrific times during the war.

We got off at the train station and my grandparents bought us beer, bread and sausage, all of which tasted a lot better than what I was use to in Australia and we walked for about an hour until we came to a beautiful farmhouse in the middle of a field. My opa had been hoping the house had somehow been abandoned, but it hadn't. Opa walked up to the steps, sat down, reached into his bag opened up a beer and began to drink. He then passed me a beer, some bread too, and sliced off a piece of blood sausage with a knife and ate it. The owner of the house opened his front door and spoke in German, "Can I help you?" Opa said, "Can I help you? Can you help me? This is my house".

The owner of the house was in shock, he didn't know what to say. Oma jumped in and apologised and began to explain the situation. Opa shouted at her for interrupting his conversation, so I tried to keep everyone calm and let the man who owned the house speak. The man said he had inherited the home from his parents, who had bought it from Opa's sister, who had inherited everything. As much as the situation broke Opa's heart there was nothing he could do. The house legally belonged to the man. The man then went inside leaving us sitting on his doorstep drinking beer and eating bread.

The walk back to the train station seemed longer this time as we hung our heads and dragged our feet. When we arrived at the station, there were lots of Polizei on our platform, including the heavy-duty, special operations police they have in Germany. Oma asked the train station manager what had happened? He told us there had been a large group of neo-Nazis, making trouble and starting fights and rioting at the station. They'd boarded the train just before we arrived.

In Munich, we stayed in Opa's childhood neighbourhood, Forstenreid. I really liked it there. I had a great time seeing the sights and taking the short train ride into the city centre. Our accommodation was near a large forest, so I started going for long runs, shadow boxing and skipping. When I ran through the forest, I saw wild pigs for the first time. The smell of the forest was amazing, so refreshing, it was really good for my asthma. There was also a plant in the forest that killed warts, which Oma showed me, and it destroyed one I had on my finger almost straight away.

My hair was very long at this point, and I decided I needed to get it cut. I visited the hairdresser and he cut it short on top and left a long rat's tail at the back. People would say I looked like Kostya Tszyu because he had a similar hairstyle, except his tail was in a different spot, slightly higher than mine. Oma met with her best friend from her childhood, Ula, who now lived in Munich after fleeing from Breslau after the war, like Oma had done. She was a very funny, nice old lady, and she taught me how to play 'schapfkopf', a popular card game in Bavaria. She had a brother and husband, who both passed away a few years after the holiday. She also had grandchildren who I became friends with, they felt like cousins. Her grandson, Klaus, who was my age and spoke a bit of English, took me out to see the nightlife around Munich.

On my first night out with Klaus, he was driving a red convertible BMW, and he asked me if I'd heard the latest track by Puff Daddy. I hadn't heard it yet; it was *I'll Be Missing You*, the tribute track to Notorious B.I.G. This track instantly triggered emotion with in me. It was a tragedy what had happened to Biggie and same with 2pac. I had a gut feeling there was something very fishy going on considering both shooters hadn't been caught. I couldn't help but wonder, maybe the jacks were in on it? We pumped that track driving around the streets of Munich, and he knew where everything was. He showed me the red-light district, and I practiced my German on a few 'working girls', who were waiting in their cars on the side of the road. Klaus was in tears laughing and we quickly drove off.

Another night Klaus said, "We are going to a rave on a tram." Huh? I had to ask him if he translated that correctly, but It ended up being a great night. There was a DJ inside a tram playing house music and break beats from turntables and you could buy beer and other drinks on the tram too, while it travelled around Munich. Some of Klaus's friends joined us. After a few beers I started rapping to the break beats. The crowd on the tram formed a circle around me, whilst I free-styled. I felt the crowd just thought it was cool coz I was rapping in English, and they had no idea what I was actually saying, so I decided to rap in German instead. I was going pretty well, until I dropped a line in German which ended with in English translation 'Hitler has just spoken' and everybody around me gasped in shock ... I could hear a pin drop at that moment. In Germany it's a crime to speak of Adolf Hitler or Nazis in public and you can be arrested and jailed for it. Particularly, if it's in a supportive pro-Hitler way. I hate Nazis and what they stand for, it was just a line that rhymed in German with whatever line I'd said before that and, in my mind, I was making fun of Hitler. But I thought quick and shouted out in German, "Sorry I meant Mussolini," and everyone around me started cracking up laughing and all was forgiven. But after they stopped laughing Klaus's friends pulled me aside and said in English, "Oh man, be careful, you can't say those kinds of things, it can be taken the wrong way." I felt bad, but the fact everyone was laughing about it helped me to get over it pretty quick.

TRIUMPH

The next destination was Nuremberg, where my mum and her siblings were born, and the city Oma's family had found refuge in after the war. They'd all found very good jobs and made a comfortable living, being able to build big two storey homes with basements underneath that could be used as entertainment areas. One uncle and aunt had a sauna in theirs and another had a fish farm on their land, where they would farm freshwater trout and sell them at the markets. We stayed at all their houses over the next three months. I got to meet a lot of family I'd never met before, and they made me feel that I was German just like them.

I started to feel a lot more comfortable with who I was. They'd ask about my dad's side of the family and I'd say, he's Australian and of Scottish and black descent, possibly Pacific Islander. Apart from family, most people we would meet around Germany and Austria would assume I was Turkish or Italian due to my darker features and complexion. I have green eyes which Oma said her mother had, so I realised that must be an Eastern European gene. One afternoon my Great Uncle Manfred, who was extremely generous, gave me 100 Deutschmark and said, "Go and buy yourself something," so we went for a trip to the mall.

I went straight to the music store and my uncle showed me a CD on the shelves that was by one of my cousins. He was a musician in a children's music group and was well known in Germany. I then went to the hip hop aisle. I couldn't believe what I found; it was the *Wu-tang Forever* LP. It had just been released and coz I was busy sight-seeing around Germany, I hadn't even realised. Without hesitation I bought it and picked up a coupla other CDs while I was there. It is fair to say it was a banger of an album but I preferred *36 Chambers*. Then like a message directly from the rap gods, the most amazing thing happened. I just couldn't believe it. I saw a poster right at the end of my uncle's street advertising that Wu-tang were on tour in Germany and would be playing in Nuremberg. Unbelievable! I could hardly contain myself. I bought my ticket right away. It was the first big gig I had ever been too. Wu-Tang Clan in my mum's hometown, there's no doubt in my mind it was a sign. I felt blessed ...

The gig was at the Serenadenhof Nurnberg and it was packed with people. I was checked for weapons before we entered the venue. There were a few Germans of African descent in the crowd and I think I heard some American accents. It felt like there wasn't as much of an African community in Australia back then, as there was in Germany.

There was a small merchandise store in the foyer as we walked in and a DJ played a set before Wu-tang got on stage. With all the hype around the gig, a big brawl erupted around me, but I fended off anything that came my way, until Security came along and kicked out the troublemakers. I knew all the tracks and I rapped along with them. At one point Method Man pointed me out in the crowd and held the mic in my direction, so I could finish the line. I was hyped, I felt like I was up on stage with them. He closed out the show by rocking a 'windmill'; like a true B-Boy! They then held a 'lighters in the air', tribute to 2pac and Biggie. It was inspirational, and that moment when Meth pointed the mic in my direction was epic, I knew I could mix it with the best! I just needed to work hard and find the opportunities and that would be me up there, touring the world, pointing the mic at my fans.

About a week later Tyson fought Holyfield for the second time. With the time difference from USA, it was fought early Sunday morning in Germany. I overslept and woke up shortly after the fight to Uncle Manfred, who was watching the TV and yelling in German, "Benny! Benny! Tyson hat Holyfield gebissen," I was like, "Huh?" I couldn't believe it. It just didn't make sense, he had totally lost his cool and lashed out. My favourite fighter in the world had become a *biter*... WTF! I felt he'd just given up on the world and I felt my idol's pain. I wasn't too concerned about Holyfield who had lost part of his ear. I told myself, don't worry Mike will bounce back, besides think of the pay cheque he was gonna get. Maybe this boxing game was all about business and the whole thing had been planned for another rematch. Either way I didn't care, I was still gonna fight no matter what people thought about the sport. I quickly remembered the values I respected in Muhammad Ali and he became the driving influence in what I aspired to be.

We visited one more country on our holiday, Poland, primarily to see Oma's original hometown, Breslau; in the historical region of Silesia. We drove across the border with my Great Aunt Inge and her husband. When we arrived at the border the guards assumed we all had German passports and waived our car through, had they known my grandparents and I had Australian passports we would not have been let through without a visa. We stayed in Swidnica and checked in at a Polish Gasthaus. Opa wasn't happy about having to visit Poland, he felt that Bavaria and Austria were better than anywhere else in Europe, but he came along anyway.

When we arrived in the city, our car was immediately set upon by young kids, saying we needed to pay them protection money to watch that our car doesn't get damaged. There were about 50 of these little hoodlums jumping all over the cars in the parking lot like a swarm of bees, but we shewed those tiny hustlers away. It was very different from Germany. Things in Poland were a lot more run down, old men would be walking in the middle of the road and stare at you rather than just cross the street. The freeways were just one lane, so if you were stuck behind a truck, you couldn't pass them coz you couldn't see if the other lane was free. I saw several cars flipped along the side of the road because of this. My uncle said up until a couple months before the fall of the Berlin Wall, Poland had been communist, and people had lost the will to look after their houses because they didn't own them, the government did.

As we got out of the car and walked around the city, I noticed two things; good looking girls and the young Romani kids hitting us up for coins. I remember I bought a pair of Levis in a store and a hot girl put her hand right down the front of my jeans to check if I had enough room. Man, it was embarrassing because it was right in front of my grandparents. When we left the store, Oma surprised me by saying, I should have gotten her number.

The Romani kids would see us every day and follow us around because I'd given them some change the first time they'd asked me. They couldn't have been older than six. On the last day I decided to buy them apples, but the kids just wanted the cake. My uncle said, "See they want the money, so they can give it to the people they work for, they are professionals."

I enjoyed Poland, it was different, but Opa was growing more and more agitated. He could speak Russian because of his time in the war; he'd try and speak to the Polish people in Russian and they didn't like it at all, mainly coz they had been occupied by the Russians during the war and it brought back trauma for them. We visited Oma's childhood family home in Breslau. Unlike the home in Bavaria, the occupants invited us inside for coffee. Oma's family had lost the home completely when the Russians invaded, and the house had been assigned to the family who lived there since this time. There was nothing my oma's family could do about it but let it go, and they kept a good friendly relationship with the owners, so they could visit whenever they liked.

Opa continued to speak Russian and my Aunty Inge told him off. Opa completely lost the plot and cursed at Aunty Inge and her husband. Opa announced he would be leaving Poland. He got back to the Gasthaus in Swidnica, jumped in a taxi and headed for the German boarder en route to Nuremberg which was about 5 hours away, a very expensive cab ride. Apparently, he was almost arrested at the border coz Border Control had questioned his Australian passport. But somehow, he got through.

Meanwhile, back at the Gasthaus, I'd met a girl my age whose grandparents were also from Silesia originally. We played cards and I taught her how to play thirteen. We ended up making out and her opa caught us. He came storming into the kitchen, where we were hanging, and told her to go to bed. I never saw her again because we left Silesia for Germany early the next morning. It had been quite a trip, for several reasons. Unfortunately, just like the fallout he'd had with his family many years before, Opa had now fallen out with his in-laws, avoiding them for the rest of the holiday and this really hurt my poor oma. Just like with his own family, the relationship was never repaired. Apart from with Uncle Manfred, who was everybody's favourite, always understanding and generous.

After over four months away from Melbourne, I was ready to come home and see my friends and family. I felt I'd matured a lot in Germany and had completely kept myself out of trouble for the longest time in many years. But I was really looking forward to getting back and seeing my crew and also meeting some girls, coz it had been a bit awkward to do that in Europe, not having my own transport and being around family all the time. I had bought myself a dope switchblade from a small army disposal shop in one of the towns we'd visited. They're illegal in Australia, but I managed to smuggle it in undetected. For whatever reason, Mum or my stepdad couldn't pick us up from the airport, so I rang Devious, and he came to collect us. I gave him the switchblade to say thanks and filled him in on all the stories from the holiday with one addition. I'd met an older Austrian woman on the plane trip home, and she'd given me her number. She was 34 and wanted me to take her out ...

CHORLITO'S WAYWARD

Things had changed a bit when I got back to Melbourne. Everyone was hitting the Casino hard out, sometimes as often as two or three times a day. I started to play blackjack, winning quick but loosing faster and would usually end up right where I started. The crew had pretty much split but Devious had recruited some younger kids that used to hang around John's Pinnies. Most of us older generation were done with the tagging, but the new recruits kicked on with it for a while, then when they were done, they recruited the generation under them and the pattern repeated itself.

I got back to training at Leo's a few days after being back in Melbourne.

"Hello son, how was Germany? Did you find some boxing gyms over there?" Leo asked.

I said, "We weren't close to any boxing gyms, so I just ran, skipped, shadow boxed whenever I could." He was happy I did this, and when he watched me workout, he noticed my fitness hadn't been affected that much. After the session I asked Leo, "Where's Chorlito?" He grumpily said, "He hasn't got it in him mate, he lost his last fight and I told him to give it away." I was shocked. I went home and tried to call Chorlito, but when he answered I couldn't make sense of what he was saying, he sounded fucken smashed. I asked Blaze if he knew what had happened to Chorlito, he was like, "Oh shit didn't you know?" I was like, "Bro, I've been in Germany for months, I don't know anything about what's been going on here." Blaze explained, "He's quit boxing altogether, he's graffen flat out, also started drinking and doing drugs, the harder shit too." I said, "Shit, all those times we'd been drinking and smoking he always turned it down, now he's flipped, that's fucked up man." At the time I just couldn't see the sense in it all, I just knew I needed to focus on my training, and I was dreaming of winning a world title.

The truth is, it's hard to adapt to normal life after boxing, with little to aspire to in comparison to the dream of winning a world title, the fame and the fortune. The energy gained from boxing training can turn into a loaded gun, especially if you never got the opportunity to achieve all you wanted in the sport. The facts are a lot of talented fighters are mismanaged, or simply get damaged along the journey. Most will never be good enough to make it all the way to the top and some resort to drugs, alcohol and excuses. For many reasons it can seem like there's a missing void in your life, without boxing. That's why it's important to channel your energy into something positive and never let go of keeping healthy and in shape. That's not always easy, but if you have fought in the ring before you know about discipline and commitment. Excuses don't cut it, there's no exception to this rule!

I had a vision of being a people's champ like Ali, but ruthless like Tyson in his prime. I wanted to be a heavyweight but the more weight I put on, the lazier I got. I needed to stay at middleweight to feel sharp. I continued to train harder than ever before and only sparred with serious boxers. I also made some more friends at the gym, like Trevor, an older Aussie dude in his 40s who'd hold pads for me. He was covered head to toe in tattoos and looked ruff as hell. I noticed when we were in the shower one time, he had an eye tattooed on each butt cheek. I wasn't about to ask the guy any questions about it. He took an interest in my boxing and would give me tips here and there, like a lot of the older guys used to. But later on, down the track I noticed Trevor had not been at Leo's gym in a long time, I'd been missing his pad work. I asked Leo "Where's Trevor been?" Leo said angrily, "Mate didn't ya fucken know?" I said, "Huh? What happened to him?" Leo said, "He fucken set himself on fire one day and he's dead mate." I was in shock, but I could tell he had some issues, he was one of those dudes that looked crazy on the outside, but on the inside he was a nice guy. A lot of people drifted in and out of my life while I trained at Leo's.

Something that surprised me about Leo's gym was that girls

were not allowed to train there. It seems so strange now, but Leo was from another era. I was used to training with girls at the kickboxing gym, so it didn't faze me if they trained or not, but Leo would get furious with them. They'd come in all politely, "Excuse me can I train here please?" And Leo would say, "No, get out!" Then if they said stuff like, "That's very sexist," he'd scream louder, "I told you to get the hell outta here," and stuff like that. Thankfully it's different these days, we all have the right to defend ourselves.

At the end of '97, at the very last boxing session before the Christmas break up, I saw people coming into the gym dressed up nicely while I continued to punch the bags. What's going on? I thought. Is there some kind of event going on here tonight? And there was. It was presentation night, and I had no idea it was on or that there was such a thing as presentation night at the gym. Leo said, "Hurry up Ben, go take a shower we're about to start." Fucken hell, I just wanted to keep training. When I came out of the shower, Leo was presenting trophies to all the volunteers who'd helped throughout the year and gave a speech while everyone cheered. Then he said, "And the award for the best training for the year goes to Benny Sinclair!" I couldn't believe it. I had no idea that was about to happen. I would have preferred for Leo to finally organise me a fight, but I accepted my trophy with pride and gave a short and sweet thank you speech. I'm pretty sure I was a little red in the face, but I was now more motivated than ever to compete as a boxer!

SLIGHTLY BETTAFELLAS

omething else changed in '97. I got a full-time job as an apprentice chef at a restaurant not far from where we lived in Malvern. It was one of the busiest and most popular restaurants in Melbourne at the time, and on the weekends or events like Valentine's Day, Mother's Day, and New Year's Eve, the restaurant would turn over thousands of customers. During summertime and busy periods, service didn't stop between 6 am and midnight, seven days a week. I got the job through the manager, Norm, who knew Wayno. Norm was the backbone of the restaurant and was always good to me. The restaurant was setup in sections. So, you had some female staff behind the bagel bar, servicing fresh sandwiches, bagels and focaccia, cakes, fruit salads, and ice cream or gelato. The girls were usually a mix of ethnicities but mostly Romanian and Ukranian. There was a bar, which was usually staffed by a couple of guys that would make drinks, cocktails and coffees, they were a mix of heritages too, like Maltese, French or Mauritian.

There was a wood fired pizza section, that would make pizzas, calzones and bake bread. The pizza makers were Moroccan and Tunisian. Then there was the kitchen where I worked, and it was also split up into sections. Firstly, the kitchen hands, who were either Bosnian or Pakistani and Sri Lankan. Then the sections where the first year and some second year apprentice chefs worked was called cold larder, which looked after salads, desserts, and small menu items. Then the rest of the apprentices were located in a section called stoves, which had the grill, pans, deep fryer, along with cooks, the second chef and the head chef. The kitchen was split between predominantly Greek and Aussie staff. The waiters were also a mix of ethnicities, and the owners were Lebanese.

It felt like an extremely volatile place most days. When I first started the head chef: Jimmy, who was Greek Cyprian and extremely feisty, said to me, "Ah, another Aussie boy, huh?" I was thinking these bloody arrogant Greeks are gonna call me 'Aussie' because they can't work out my heritage, so I said, "Mate, I'm half German and my Dad's Australian, part black, I'm not Aussie." Some of the Bosnian kitchen hands would speak German to me, so that shut up his bullshit pretty quick. He was a bit of an asshole at first, but I was never one to put up with his shit, and he ended up liking me because I worked my fucken ass off. We also had another thing in common we both supported North Melbourne. But Jimmy had a bad reputation for screaming his head off at everyone. He brought many people to tears, including a Greek apprentice chef, who started out the same time as me. Jimmy would smash plates and throw shit against the wall and was really out of line a lot of the time. I didn't let his shit get to me, and he could see that.

My pay rate was about $5 per hour as a first-year apprentice chef, even less after tax, and most weeks I would work at least 70 hours, which would bring me home about $330 per week, and out of that Wayno asked me to chip in $50 per week board money. Initially, I used to walk to and from work but started getting driving lessons and passed my test, getting my license a few months later. I had somehow managed to save some money and bought myself a small no thrills kinda car to get myself from A to B in, from one of the Bosnian kitchen hands for a cheap price. It was a silver and white Holden (GM) Astra.

When I first started, I was under the guidance of three other first year apprentices. I figured out pretty quick that none of them were working half as hard as I was. I got obsessed with trying to pump out as much prep work as I could in the fastest time. They would say I was slow at first, but I knew this was bullshit. I wanted to prove everyone wrong and become the best chef in the restaurant. The staff on shift before me would write a big 'prep list' and I would tick things off as I went. I always tried to do more work than was on my list, then by the time the next shift would come on I'd make sure there were hardly any jobs for them to do. When I got good at it, I got real good at it, and I'd have six crepe pans going at once and flipping them over in the pan to a rhythm. I also became the best at making choux pastry. My profiteroles would come out light, fluffy and with the perfect amount of crispness. It's an art form getting them right, and none of the other apprentices could nail them like me. Jimmy would use my profiteroles to make croquembouche for weddings and other larger functions, because they were the best.

RUMBLE FiSH

When I fucked up in my first year, I really fucked up, but somehow I always kept my job and took my mistakes on the chin. One memorable, almost unforgivable, mistake was when I was making a batch of sticky date pudding dough. Our prep kitchen was downstairs, and our service kitchen was upstairs. I'd grabbed everything I needed to make the sticky date puddings, but I'd forgotten a metal perforated spoon to scoop the dates into the mixture, which was spinning in a large industrial mixing bowl. I looked above me on top of the sink and saw a small ceramic dish. I thought, fuck it I'll use this. Big mistake! As I scooped up the dates and attempted to add them to the mixture, I made contact with the spinning beater and the ceramic dish split and fell into the dough. I'd worked my ass off all day and was tired. I looked into the dough and presumed the dish had split perfectly in two because it seemed to fit together again without any bits missing. So, I chucked the mixture in the cool room, wrote my prep list for the oncoming team and signed off for the weekend.

When I got back to work on Monday, there was a massive investigation taking place. Norm came charging into the kitchen red in the face and said, "Jimmy, it's happened again. Who the fuck has put porcelain in the sticky date puddings?" Oh shit, I thought, I'm screwed here. There goes my job. The ceramic dish must have chipped and splintered right through the dough. A lady had apparently chipped her tooth on Saturday night. And six people had come across the ceramic chips like a fucken 'sticky date pudding surprise'.

The thing was though, everyone was getting blamed except me. The reason I didn't get blamed was because no one realised how much work I was doing. It was almost impossible for most of them to comprehend, as they were too busy talking shit, smoking or trying to pick up the waitresses. Meanwhile,

I was doing the prep work of three apprentices. I was that far ahead that there was no way they would have thought I made it on Friday morning. They thought it must have been someone on a Saturday afternoon shift. My prep was four services in advance (dinner Friday, breakfast, lunch, dinner Saturday).

I went home and although I was off the hook, I felt really bad and couldn't sleep. I decided I'd tell Jimmy what had happened. When I was making the mixture, I had a young 16-year-old private school kid that had dropped out of school beside me who I had to train up. He hadn't seen me drop the ceramic dish in the mixture, coz he was fucken away with the fairies and completely useless. The kid didn't wanna be there. I had the feeling his mum had got him the job as a wake-up call to the real world. Anyway, I'd asked him to watch the mixture and place it in the bucket, while I cleaned up, then I stored it in the cool room. I ended up telling Jimmy the story minus the actual part about me breaking the dish in the mixture and he sacked the young private school kid straight away. Hard work always pays off!

On another busy Saturday afternoon, the apprentice chefs before my shift had not properly prepared enough lasagna trays for the dinner service, so we'd completely run out. My shift started at 3 pm, leaving me the task of preparing and baking 10 massive trays (as much as I could) of lasagna before the 6 pm service. What I didn't realise at the time, was that if you cut into lasagna when it's still hot, it looks sloppy on the plate. George, the boss, didn't like the way this looked at all. He wanted the lasagnas to have height and look three dimensional. So, in order to do this, you need to let them set, cut the piece when they are cold and reheat them in a ceramic bowl in the microwave with Napoli sauce and cling wrap on the top to warm them through. In my mind, I didn't really care about presentation, I was thinking the customer is getting fresh lasagna, straight out of the oven.

During that dinner service we got absolutely slammed and God knows why but every second table wanted lasagna. We must have sold around 100 portions, and given the variety on the menu it was crazy that so many people wanted it. My lasagna must have been fucken amazing, but the boss didn't see it this way, as it didn't conform with his height and dimension demands. George used to sit at the pass and clap his hands and shout at us to work faster. He'd scream out things like 'bastardo' and curse in Italian, Arabic or Greek. It was an international melting pot of a restaurant, so any swear word in any language would do the trick. I didn't like George's cocky attitude, but he was the boss, and I was an 18-year-old first year apprentice chef. It wasn't about losing the $5 an hour job. It was about not wanting to fail. I wanted to show them how good a chef I actually was.

On this particular night, there was no proving George wrong. I attempted to tell George the lasagna 'just came out of the oven', but I was quickly dismissed with screaming and shouting in addition to Jimmy, the head chef, and other more experienced chefs putting in five cents worth of criticism. I felt like shit, but I thought, fuck them, and kept my mouth shut and kept working. My mind was rattled, and my ego had taken a big hit, so my productivity slowed down and we fell behind. I packed up my shit and got the hell outta the kitchen at the end of my shift, thinking that I might have lost my job.

The next day was Sunday morning. I woke up early and headed down to Leo's. After a good work out at the gym, I was feeling a lot more positive, and started thinking about looking for another job and finding a restaurant where my hard work would be appreciated. I was waiting at the tram stop on the corner of Chapel Street when a dope, brand new convertible silver 1997 SL 500 Mercedes pulled up right next to me at the lights. I couldn't believe my eyes, it was George, my boss, wearing Versace shades and an Armani shirt. He looked at me and said, "Hey, where you going?" I said, "I'm just heading home after boxing training." He said, "Huh, you're a boxer? Jump in. I'll drive you home."

I quickly got in before the lights changed. I couldn't believe my luck; it was a fresh ride and George had really shown his gratitude there and then. We had a great conversation about boxing on the way home and he dropped me off right at my front door. I didn't bring up the lasagna drama from the night before, neither did he, coz I understood it wasn't personal, it was just business, and this guy was riding the freshest whip going around for a good reason. I don't believe in luck; I believe in hard work and George was the same. You don't own one of the best restaurants in Melbourne because you serve people slop on a plate, you have the best restaurant because you run a tight ship and if things ain't right you fix them. After all, second best in business is never good enough. It wasn't the greatest food from a fine dining perspective, but it did very well because of these principles and just at the right time, George knew exactly how to make you feel valued. In my heart boxing and becoming a rapper were what I wanted more than anything in the world, but at that point I needed George and George need me, synchronicity brought us together that morning.

From then on everyone in the restaurant knew me as 'the boxer' or 'Benny the boxer'. I'd kept boxing quiet before then, but I was glad I told the boss before anyone else. I decided to cut off my rat's tail because I wanted a change and was getting a little tired of being compared to Kostya Tszyu. I wanted to be a known as my own kind of fighter, not a look alike, so I shaved my head again. I'd work a lot of split shifts at the restaurant and that's why I was working so many hours. A split shift meant you'd start midmorning to help with prep and lunch service, then clock off for about two hours from say 3 to 5 pm, then come back and help prep up for dinner, then work the dinner service, getting out around midnight most nights.

On my break I'd head down to Leo's, workout, shower then head back to work. Sometimes I'd get back to the kitchen a little banged up from sparring, with marks and scratches or black eyes. Smart-ass managers or waiters would say, "What happened mate? Forget to duck?" Or if I made a mistake in the kitchen, "Too much boxing Benny, you're punch drunk!" I'd get a little embarrassed and try and laugh it off, but deep down it would piss me off. I wouldn't feel the punches while sparring, I just used to mark up after it sometimes. I'd get hit heaps but that's just what happens, it doesn't mean I just stopped throwing punches or ever got knocked down, coz I never did. People outside of boxing just don't understand that.

There were many staff that came and went at the time I was at the restaurant in Malvern, and it wasn't a job for the feint hearted. One of the bar guys used to say, "Stress is for the weak, fuck stress." He was right. And then as I was frying away having the time of my life, I heard a massive scream coming from outside the kitchen door 'Aaaaahhhhhh!!!' it was Jimmy. He'd poured cleaning acid down an outside drain to unblock it and like a volcano it exploded up into his face, burning his skin and eyes. All the apprentice chefs were in the process of doing trade school, and most of us were in the first year of a three-year course to get our qualifications, so we'd learnt somewhere that vinegar neutralises acid. Unfortunately, this doesn't work if cleaning acid makes contact with your skin, in fact, it makes it worse.

One of the apprentices, thinking about what he'd learnt in trade school and forgetting that factor, yelled out, "Vinegar neutralises acid, pour vinegar on him!" Oh man, people started doing this and Jimmy started screaming even louder, they were basically cooking the head chef alive, and no one realised it. I just stuck to throwing twenty litre buckets of water on Jimmy, who by this stage had his shirt off too and it was a cold night. Apprentice chefs were slipping and sliding on the floor, falling over each other and tripping down the stairs during the ordeal, coz people were spilling water all over the place. Finally, an ambulance arrived, and Jimmy was taken to hospital. We were told he almost died and was off work for the next six months. A doctor later told me what we should have done was wipe the acid off with a towel; the liquid made the burning much worse. It was a case of the blind leading the blind. With Jimmy gone, the kitchen ran a lot smoother, and the bonds between the chefs, male and female grew stronger.

LUDOS MAGNUS

I slugged out a big year at Leo's Boxing Gym in '98, and was really hoping to get a couple of fights in during that year having finished '97 with 'The Best Training' trophy. I thought this would make me a certainty, but it was not to be. No doubt I improved my boxing skills and sparring, and I also got in even better shape, but there were weeks, sometimes months, when I felt that Leo wasn't interested in getting me fights at all, although he kept saying he was looking into it. After a couple of hopefuls from the gym lost their fights, I didn't see them at the gym much, and a few other regulars dropped off too. There was about a three-month period towards the end of the year that I didn't spar at all. This is a long time when you're 19 years old and hungry as hell. I kept thinking of how Mike Tyson had won the heavyweight title at 20 years of age. Boxing was once commonly known as the king of sports, but over the '90s leading into 2000s in Australia, apart from occasional media reports about Kostya Tszyu's career, the sport seemed to almost fade out. It was considered a sport for thugs and I was becoming a bit disillusioned with it all.

Between training and working at the restaurant I was also attending Chef School, one day a week during term. Memo and Devious had also decided to become chefs. During term two at chef school, Memo and I were in the same class. This would officially be the fourth school we attended together and as usual we got up to a bit of mischief from time to time. The first term's class sucked, I didn't think much of the teacher and the kids in the class would suck up his ass and it was boring AF. The chef teacher had a couple lame catch phrases he'd say in class. One of them was a reference to McDonald's and their success, "It's because it's the same time, all the time, any time, every time … Or it's for free." Good one dickhead, I use to think to myself, why didn't he go and work for Maccas? Obviously, he didn't cut it as a chef in the real world, so the next best thing was to be a teacher. Those who can't do, teach, and those who can't teach, teach gym. He also failed me once on a practical test. I felt like slapping him across the side of the head, because a fail meant you had to re-sit the test at your own expense and buy the food you needed to cook. The next term's teacher was much better, easy going and I learnt a lot more, I got good marks too, even if we messed around a little bit.

Towards the last term, the word had gotten out that I was a boxer training up for a fight. A tall, skinny apprentice chef I hadn't seen before approached me one day and said, "You're boxing down at Leo's, yeh?" I said, "Yeh, how do you know?" He said, "I used to train down there in '95, when Chorlito was boxing out of there." It was before I arrived and I wondered why he still wasn't down there, so I asked him, "What happened?" He said, "Be careful training at that gym mate! I got shafted. I was flat out sparring with Chorlito and some of the other fighters, getting them ready for fights, and never got any respect from Leo at all. I would hold my own and all I wanted to do was fight, he just never gave me a chance, I felt used. Don't trust him, he'll use you up for sparring, then even if he gets you a fight and you lose, he'll tell you to leave the gym, just like he did Chorlito when he lost his fight!"

Now I didn't really know this dude from a bar of soap, let alone see him throw a punch to see if he was any good, but somehow he did know a lot of inside information, particularly about the circumstances of Chorlito no longer training at Leo's. I didn't entirely trust what he was saying. The facts were though, I was growing more and more hungry to fight as the months rolled on and I'd been promised fights that year but hadn't sparred in months because all the attention had been on a famous ex-footy player who surely has had more than his fair share of spotlight in his life. I was starting to feel neglected and that a fight through Leo would never happen.

When the end-of-year presentation came around again, I showed up this time stupidly expecting to get the award. Absolutely nothing came through, there wasn't even an announcement of 'Best Training Award'. Just trophies for volunteers and a couple younger kids that would come in and train with their dads. It just didn't feel right. Reflecting on the year, the awards night, and on what the skinny apprentice chef had told me, I decided to call the telephone directory number again to find boxing gyms close to me like I'd done a few years back. The directory operator mentioned Malvern Martial Arts. "Anything Else?" I asked. She said, "Oh wait a minute, how about this Boxercise at the Harold Holt Swimming pool?" I paused and thought, Hmmmm, Harold Holt Swimming Pool, that brings back some memories. Boxercise is more aerobics, and sounded a bit soft, but I thought a bit of summer fitness training might help. I said, "Sure, why not, thank you," and she gave me the number.

I called right away and was put straight through to the

trainer, Kel. I explained my background in kickboxing, how I was feeling at Leo's gym, and how much I wanted to fight. Kel said, "No worries, mate, I think you'll like training with me, and I have another boxer Andy, a Kiwi who's your age, but a little bit lighter. He's had one fight, a loss but it was a bad decision. You guys can spar, and we'll see how you go."

I went down to the Boxercise class on the Monday. It was a lot different to Leo's and there were women training with us too. I was beginning to feel that I wasn't sure if the aerobics class was quite what I needed to become a fighter, but before the class ended Kel turned to me and said, "Would you like to spar a couple rounds with Andy?" There was no ring in the room, so I was a bit surprised. I thought maybe what he'd said on the phone was just to get me to come along to the class. "In here?" I asked, confused. Kel replied, "Yeh just here, you'll be fine, I'll tell you if you're going outside of the boundaries." He then placed witches hats down on the floor in the shape of a boxing ring. Andy and me sparred three or four rounds and it was great, I hadn't sparred in so long and I was really enjoying myself. Although he was a lot quicker than I expected, and a little harder to catch, I caught him with some nice shots, and he landed some good ones on me. After the sparring, Kel looked at me and said, "That was great! We'll get you a fight at the Reggio Calabria Club in February." I couldn't believe I was finally gonna fight, and I couldn't wait to get in there. Andy, my new sparring partner, was very supportive and positively complemented my boxing style. That day, I decided to leave Leo's Gym and join my new team under the guidance of Kel. Things were starting to look up on the boxing front again.

Oh, but before I forget and we jump into 1999, one of the highlights of '98 was going to see Snoop Dogg play at Melbourne's iconic Festival Hall. I went with most of the original RSH crew, and we met some rowdy Islanders in the car park that Ricks knew. They wanted to form a big crew and start some shit. But we were all pretty lit and there was no way I was gonna miss out on seeing Snoop Dogg live by getting in a fight for a stupid reason. I kinda tried to lose everyone when we got inside and just found a nice quiet spot where I could see everything. The gig itself was dope, not quite as dope as seeing Wu-Tang in Germany, but that was coz it was my first gig, and they were all up on stage including ODB and Cappadonna. Snoop had his crew with him too and blazed up a fat ass joint and passed it around the crowd, and I took a hit. It felt like we were smoking together so it was sick! The rowdy motherfuckers we met in the car park all got kicked out for fighting, so I was glad I'd chosen to lose them and enjoy the gig on my terms.

I'VE TRAINED TOO MANY HOURS RAISED MY GLOVE IN EVERY DREAM

My Moment, *Impeccable Word* (2017)

Sopranos Pizzeria

started '99 with focus. I had a new trainer, and a new job opportunity came up too. A mate was working as a duty manager in a Greek cake shop on Lonsdale Street in the city. I'd visit him sometimes after knocking off work and he would give me free cakes and coffee. I had to watch which cakes I ate, coz I didn't want to blow up in weight for boxing. He mentioned that a new Greek restaurant, a few doors down, were looking for a chef and they were paying $10 an hour flat, which was a lot better than the $6 second-year apprentice rate I was getting at the time.

The restaurant was right next door to a tavern where some of my mates from Doncaster worked. Lonsdale Street is known as the Greek precinct in Melbourne and once a year they have a festival to celebrate Independence Day. These days the Hellenic community seem to prefer the suburb of Oakleigh. I walked into the restaurant and introduced myself to one of the owners: Kirky, who introduced me to the head chef. When I told them about my previous cheffing experience, and that I was a boxer with German heritage, they thought I was a good fit, and I pretty much got the job on the spot. I mentioned that I had my first amateur boxing fight coming up in a few weeks and would just work a couple shifts until I'd had the fight. I was on holiday leave from the restaurant in Malvern during this time. When I officially resigned, they offered to match the $10 an hour, but my mind was made up. I did one or two shifts just to help them out, but that was it, it was time to move on.

There was something going on at the new restaurant that quickly got my attention. There was an underground 'hot goods' racket running on the side. Lonsdale Street crosses over Russell Street and in the '90s Russell Street was one of the biggest drug hotspots in Melbourne, predominantly for smack dealers and their loyal customers. With so much horse around, the junkies would be knocking off a ridiculous amount of stuff to pay for their habit. Most of the time they were so desperate that you could buy stuff for next to nothing. Stuff like mobile phones, car stereos, alcohol, TVs, designer clothes and just about anything on earth you could think of. It was fucken crazy!

Different junkies would bring in different items. You had a liquor junkie, a power tools junkie, a laptop junkie, all these specialist junkies, and some of them just got whatever they could, whenever they could. I told the crew about this, and everyone started placing orders, from fishing equipment to Rolex watches and diamond rings, we could get it all. Everyone I knew caught on and were asking for stuff, along with people I trained with, people from chef school, even customers at the restaurant who I'd gotten to know. And from there it extended to the bouncers working security in the clubs close by, along with other cafe or restaurant owners and workers.

I had a lot of free time on my hands as a chef at this new restaurant because it was a lot smaller and nowhere near as busy as the old one. On quiet days we'd be lucky to feed 50 people for dinner and lunch, compared to a quiet shift at the old place where there would still be at least 1000 people.

The junkies would hang out in the back alley behind our kitchen, and they'd call out to us to get our attention and show us what they'd scored. I was a natural hustler and could haggle with the junkies until I got the best price. The scheme was incredibly profitable. When the larger items would come in like TVs or bikes, computers, or stereos, I'd call Devious who'd drive to the city in his dad's liquor delivery van, meet me in the back alley where we'd load up all the goods. He'd get a cut too or get to keep the goods he wanted.

On a Sunday afternoon in February 1999, I was locked in for my first Amateur fight at the Reggio Calabria Club in West Brunswick. The venue is a large soccer club with poker machines and a big reception area, which could fit thousands of people. The ring used to sit in the middle of the largest room surrounded by tables. There was also a kitchen that serves pizza, pasta, cans of beer and soft drink. It's run by the Italian Calabrian community who are often associated with the 'Ndrangheta and there may be some direct ties to Italy, but I didn't see any of this, as I didn't get too involved with the community beyond boxing. The promoters who ran the shows kinda reminded me of the Stucci brothers, outta *White Men Can't Jump*. The weigh in for the fights was a couple hours before the bout.

I got up early that morning after a good night's rest and drove out to Andy's place. We'd planned to also pick up Kel on the way, so we could all drive in together. When I arrived at Andy's, he said, "Come upstairs mate, we should watch some of these fights before we see Kel, for inspiration." He put on 'Hearns v Haggler'. Wow what a war! I couldn't believe I'd never watched it before. It only lasted three rounds, so I had plenty of time to make the weigh in. Watching that fight really took the edge off and made me even more hungry to get into that ring at 2 pm. Plus, Hearns and Haggler were also middleweights like me. We had a little bit of time to watch another fight, so we watched 'Duran v Leonard', which pumped me up even more.

We then drove out to Kel's place, and he drove us to the fight. On the drive in I had butterflies and was a little nervous, but I was really looking forward to getting in the ring in front of a crowd. Kel did a good job of keeping us both calm. We were the first two fighters he'd ever coached. We arrived at the venue, and I needed to be under 160 lbs on the scales. I made weight without a problem and so did Andy. As it was my first fight, I was the first fight up on the card, which I was happy about coz I didn't have to wait around. Most of RSH made it down and got there early for front row seats. None of my family members made the effort to rock up, deep down that brought back those old feelings of not being accepted for who I was, but fuck it, I had a job to do!

The ring announcer, Howard Lee, introduced me to the crowd as I shadow boxed and kept loose. The venue was packed out with punters given there was around 20 fights scheduled for the day. When the bell rang out, I started the fight confidently and was landing my jab cleanly. I felt light on my feet and was moving well. The fighter backed up towards the rope and I pressed forward with a jab, cross, left hook combination and caught him with the left hook. His legs lifted-up underneath him and he hit the canvas hard. The referee gestured for me to go to the neutral corner, but I had no idea what that was, so I ran back to Kel in the blue corner. Kel quickly said, "No Benny. Neutral corner. The white one." By the time I made it to the neutral corner, the fighter's trainer had thrown in the towel. He'd made it to his feet, but he was in bad shape, and very wobbly. I'd won my first fight via TKO, about one minute into round one. It was a great feeling! My win impressed the promoters, the Stucci brothers, and other trainers and I was advanced straight through to the Novice Victorian Title fight in two weeks' time. In this fight I again dropped my opponent in the first minute of round one with a straight right. He also hit the canvas hard, but this time unexpectedly he got up and wanted to brawl. He was tougher than the first guy I fought. In round two I moved a little better, and I decided to circle around my opponent then I strategically got inside and KO'd him with a short right uppercut, winning my first state title after my second fight in under three rounds of boxing all up! Andy also won the novice state title in the welterweight division, via points decision, he'd made a comeback after being dropped in round one. Kel was very proud of our achievements, and we showed up at his boxercise classes wearing our winning medals and being introduced as the new Victorian State Champions.

RONNIE KRAY

I wouldn't say I let the victories get to my head, I'd say it was more the people around me that got a buzz from it. I just wanted to keep fighting. It was the greatest rush I'd experienced in my life. Nothing really came close to that feeling. Andy would compare me to Mike Tyson, which was exactly what I'd hoped to hear. When we sparred, I never used to unload my punches. I realised I had knockout power and Andy was a weight division below me. Sparring is about keeping sharp, increasing fitness and learning. There's no need to spar egotistically, no one wins a spar – it's just training. Sometimes you have bad days, so you gotta make sure you have more good days than bad in the gym, or you'll stop enjoying it!

I continued training hard and the following month I had another fight lined up at the Calabria Club. Only something happened before this fight that I didn't expect, right after I jumped off the scales. The trainer of the fighter I was lined up to fight had looked through my fight record book and noticed I had two KO's victories, so he turned the fight down. Man, I was pissed off, all that training and no action! I watched most of the fights on the day and kicked back and ate pizza with Andy and Kel, but I was flat. Back then, people smoked inside the venue, drank a lot and shouted loudly in their bogan slang, which gave me a headache.

The next month's fight came around and you wouldn't believe it, the exact same thing happened again. Kel needed to devise another plan in order to keep me active. Kel took us to a place called the Australian Academy of Boxing, which was run by an old English trainer who I thought looked like Ronnie Kray from the movie *The Krays*. He ran white collar boxing tournaments from this establishment and would also referee. There was just one judge. They'd award medals after the fight. On a busy day you could draw a crowd of 200 people, but sometimes it was a lot quieter. The fights were filmed, so you could review your performance if you wanted to. There were also no KO's allowed. When Kel told me the rules I was like, "What am I supposed to do? That's what I do best." But Kel said it would be good for me to improve my boxing skills in front of a crowd and a judge. He said I'd become more well-rounded as a boxer, so when I came across better fighters; who actually went the distance, I'd be more comfortable. The fact I couldn't knock out my opponents wasn't very motivating, but I didn't want to let Kel down and I understood what he was saying. I just didn't prepare myself as well as I did for the other fights.

The first time I competed, I was introduced to the crowd as the 'Middleweight State Champ' and that they would be watching closely to ensure I wasn't intentionally trying to knock out my opponent. He made it clear the tournament was based on skills. During the fight, as he was refereeing, he took points off me continuously and I felt a little scrutinised, but Kel said to treat it as a training drill, so I did. I continued with the bouts and ended up fighting almost every month over the next few years, winning about half of them. You were allowed to fight multiple times and some days I got three fights in; which was a solid 9 rounds. I'd mix it with fighters as young as 16 right up to mid-40s. I'd keep cool to avoid embarrassing

DQ's and as frustrated as I was by the rules sometimes, I still ended up with a stack of medals.

After missing out on two fights at the Calabria Club, I finally got a third fight lined up with an amateur fighter called Paul, who had a good clean record of eight wins and zero losses. I thought I had him covered but there was something that I wasn't told about or had trained for: Paul was a southpaw. Kel had devised a strategy of throwing punches and then circling to my right, to avoid an orthodox fighter's right hand. This had become instinctive, coz I'd practice the strategy constantly while sparring. The problem was when you fight a southpaw and circle the right, you walk straight into their left hand, which is exactly what happened to me during that fight. I didn't get banged up or anything, but he was a slick fighter and I lost on points. I was disappointed, and shocked that I hadn't knocked him out. Maybe I was expecting it too much.

Paul and me were a semi main event and the promoters handed us the microphone to say a few words after the fight. Paul refused the microphone. I felt I should wear the loss on the chin and keep the reason I lost to myself, so I turned the microphone away too. Later, I joked with Andy that I should have 'busted a freestyle'. Truth be told, I was devastated I had lost and self-doubt started to sneak in like a vindictive evil spirit possessing my mind. But, I never should have taken my loss to heart, it was all experience, just like on the street, I always learnt something. Besides, I didn't get injured or knocked out. I still dreamed of winning a world title and becoming a household name back then. I thought world champs never lost fights. I was wrong, a lot do, especially when they're just starting out!

My fourth fight that year at the Calabria Club was another state title bout, but this time it was the Intermediate Middleweight Title, which I won on points. I fought an older dude that was also a kickboxer. He was from Malvern Martial Arts. The place had changed since I trained there, and I didn't recognise the fighter's trainers or his team members at the time. The fight was on a Saturday night, which I enjoyed more than fighting on a Sunday afternoon. The atmosphere was better and the crowds were bigger, with thousands of supporters, jam packed inside. I felt like a pro that night and it was good to get another state title medal under my belt. Although I didn't speak to my opponent after the fight, a Vietnamese fighter from his gym came up and congratulated me. He'd also won the title in his weight division. I came to know him as Dragon and we became good mates.

I finished off '99 with one more fight, again at the Calabria Club against a more experienced fighter, who'd recently fought for the Australian title and lost. He'd had about 60 fights in the past, but I felt he was a little scrappy. The fight was meant to be an exhibition, but I got screwed because he came out blazing trying to knock me out. I had to regroup in the corner and after round one, Kel said, "Mate you better move a little better, I think we've been fucked over and this is no exhibition, it's a proper fight." I responded in the next round by keeping him on the end of my jab and right-hand coz he was a little awkward on the inside. Then I split him open above his left eye with my right hand and the referee stopped the fight calling it a technical draw. Kel showed me the newspaper the next day and it had been officially recorded as a draw on my record. He said not to worry because a draw wasn't a bad result considering we were misled and under prepared.

Surprisingly my dad turned up to that fight to see me in action for the first time. It felt strange having them there. I didn't feel myself. I could hear his voice in my head and it distracted me thinking is that really his voice or was it the voice of abandonment telling me I didn't have what it takes. I'd never lived with him, he'd never seen how hard I trained or watched me win my state title fights, even though he lived just down the road from the Calabria club. I couldn't help wondering if he had just turned up to see me lose. But what did it matter? I'd drawn, not won. I had let too much emotion creep into my head.

Down Casino

By 1999 my mum and Wayno's problems had boiled over the pot. The house was finally complete after 10 years of renovations. Unfortunately for Wayno the years of stress had taken its toll. Mum wanted out of the marriage. She would drink with friends on weekends at the casino getting home later... And later... And later. Then one weekend she didn't come home at all. She eventually came home one Monday evening but Wayno didn't yell and scream at her like he'd done in the past, he was lost for words. It was an awkward moment for me as his step kid, as I was always going to side with my mum. I felt like saying "see mate, this is why I never wanted to live here, couldn't you see how miserable we all were, what was the fucken point in living in this fucked up neighbourhood?" But I didn't. I just comforted Wayno by putting my arm on his shoulder, embracing him while he broke down. It was an intense moment and extremely difficult to deal with; I was 20 years old, he was a middle aged man. From that day on their marriage was over. It also meant I was going to need somewhere else to live because they were getting a divorce and planned to sell the house. All that stress and hard work over the years was a complete waste of our lives. There was nothing anyone could do but put it all behind us and move on. Living with Wayno in Malvern was never right for us, it was strange it took mum so long to see it that way, but eventually she did and that's just life.

Just like when my parents broke up as a kid, I moved back in with my grandparents. They were now renting a unit in a suburb called Mentone, near the beach. I was happy to move in with them, coz I didn't want to be out living by myself just yet. Opa was like my best mate, and Oma was the loving caring mother figure that I was missing in my life. She was also an amazing cook. I had to stop her from cooking me too much food, especially when I was a few weeks out from a fight.

My day off was usually Sunday and I was still going to chef school once a week. My schedule was full on. I was training six days a week and on three of those days that meant twice a day. I'd also have to make time for track work. It was getting extremely challenging maintaining all of that, especially with the chaos of another family breakdown in the background, which I shrugged off the best I could.

All that aside, work was going well. I guess all the drama had kept me driven to succeed with my career in search of some much needed stability for my future life. Shortly after I started, the other chefs resigned and a new head chef was appointed, who we nicknamed Dude because he was a massive stoner. He'd smoke huge joints in the back alley, before lunch or dinner service started, and he was constantly calling everyone dude, even his girlfriend, which he'd say was a term of endearment. Never found out what she thought about it. I'd sometimes organise his weed for him and have a few puffs with him every so often and we'd be cracking up laughing, while we cooked. We ended up becoming good mates and he was cool with me running the hot goods business on the side, as long as he got to keep what he wanted.

Dude promoted me to the second chef position, which put me on more dough than most apprentices and Kirky was happy enough because we got a lot of work done. We hired a couple of kitchen hands, one of them was my old mate Diskreet who we taught how to cook and prep a little. Outside of working with us he was now going hard graffen' with the crew SDM (Sleep Deprived Maniacs). After less than a year of working together, Dude started up a chef clothing business. He thought this was an easier way to make money. He was burnt out and always steamed up over little things, so he resigned from the restaurant. Kirky asked me if I wanted his job and I accepted, becoming the head chef of the restaurant aged 20, but not world fucken champ!

Becoming head chef meant another pay rise for me. For my first official management decision I hired Devious as my second chef, gotta look after the homies after all! The restaurant was starting to get busier coz we were doing a great job. The locals had embraced our food and I introduced new things to the menu. I took the head chef role seriously, reading cookbooks, visiting other restaurants and cooking traditional specials. Having the locals come into the kitchen and tell me in Greek how much they liked it was a massive boost to my confidence. This made chef work feel rewarding and worthwhile.

We saw some crazy things at that place, especially amongst all the smackies we were dealing with. They'd sneak in behind our cars in the alley to get their fix. Now, buying stuff off them was okay, but if we caught them shooting up, we'd tell them to get the fuck outta there. One busy Saturday night, a group had slipped through our guard while we were under the pump cooking. Suddenly, one of the ladies in the group started screaming out to me from the back kitchen door, "Help! Help! Please boss!" She wouldn't stop wailing, so I ran out to see what was going on. Some cunt was passed out on the ground completely blue in the face and not breathing. I called out to Kirky who said, "Ahhh fuck 'em, if someone carks-it, maybe the coppers will come along and rid these junkies from the back alley for good." He had a point, but this dude was almost dead. I picked up the phone, called an ambulance and they arrived within five minutes. They managed to revive the dude with Narcan gas. The other junkies thanked me for saving his life, but Kirky was still pissed off, the incident had taken time away from his customers and I guess he had the right to feel that way. To my surprise on Monday the same misfits were shooting up in the back alley again. I told them to "fuck off" and they left. No point trying talk sense to a junkie, they're lost souls.

Kel would jump through hoops to ensure I got my training

in. If I missed days, he'd train me in parks or anywhere he could, but it was getting harder to coordinate with my work hours. So, I had to find another gym and I found the perfect place, which would end up changing my life forever!

The gym was called The Underworld and it was in the city, not far from the restaurant. I could walk there, plus it was open 24/7. I initially trained at the gym late at night after I'd finished shifts at the restaurant, then also on my lunch breaks. The facilities were great, it was decked out with weights, treadmills, exercise bikes, steam room, spa, boxing ring, bags and the music was always pumping! Sometimes I had the whole place to myself, but often I'd meet other boxers who were also training up for fights. With out a doubt I met many colourful characters at that gym. One of them was Luke who was just getting into boxing when we met and I showed him some moves. When he first started fighting amateur, he lost most of his fights but when he turned pro Luke did well, winning Victorian and Australian middleweight titles. He was also on the TV show *The Contender*. After retiring from boxing, Luke became a bikie and the national president of a very well-known club.

OLD SCHOOL, NEW TRICK

Rushing back to work one night after a sparring session I had an accident and wrote-off my Holden Astra, thankfully I wasn't injured, but I needed to find a new car. I'd been working hard and had some cream, so it was time to find something I really wanted. I bought a 318i BMW two-door coupe in red and over the next few weeks with the hot goods racket still in full swing I fully decked out the car's sound system with a Kicker subwoofer and amp in the boot, 2 x Pioneer 6 x 9 speakers, Sony 10 stacker and an Alpine CD deck. I also got sports suspension and lowered the vehicle, got a sports gear stick, alloy rims, tinted the windows, and added a performance enhancing exhaust. The car became iconic among my mates. I'd meet lots of girls and they would want to 'hit it' in the Beema after work. This took its toll on my driver's seat; during the last few months I owned the vehicle, the spring mechanism broke, and I was driving around with a milk crate wedged between the backseat and front seat to hold it up. This meant I was driving leaning right back with my head past my side window, with one hand on the wheel. Unfortunately, the jacks weren't too impressed and one day they eventually slapped a canary on my windscreen.

For a little while I dated a chick who lived in Brunswick, which was a lot closer to the Greek restaurant than my grandparents home. She was still in Year 12. I got to know her family and they would speak Greek to me. During this time in my life I got even better at speaking and understanding the language, coz customers in the restaurant were constantly speaking it with me. Plus, all day the restaurant would play Greek music.

At the first introduction to the family, I cooked something up and her mum loved me for it, returning the gesture by cooking for me when I visited, and she would even do my washing. They were cool with me crashing the night so I wouldn't have to make the hour drive all the way back to Mentone on the days I was working, but nobody wanted her father to know. He would say that if I was going to sleep the night, I'd have to propose to and marry his daughter. I was barely 21 during the time we dated, and there was no way I was ready to get married. She was the youngest in her family, and coz she was the baby, she could get away with whatever she wanted. Her mum and her sisters would help her sneak me in the house after her dad went to sleep. It felt a little disrespectful at first but most of the time we'd be hanging out late at night after work, so I'd be exhausted. After a while it basically felt like I was living half the time in Brunswick and half the time in Mentone.

I soon realised this family also had their fair share of drama. I was told that her mum had an affair with her dad's koumbaros. I actually didn't believe the rumour coz I always thought when people cheat and got busted, they just break up. It didn't make sense why they'd stay together. One morning I got up and went for a run before starting my split shift in the restaurant. I thought the mum was aware of my routine because she used to make me breakfast, coffee and have my chef uniform ready for me before I left. On this particular occasion I returned from my run and instinctively knew something was up. I was knocking on the door and she didn't answer.

I was still in my shorts and singlet and didn't have my car keys. I thought she'd gone shopping and forgotten I was out running. I went around to the back alley and jumped over the fence, and as I rebalanced my body from the jump, I saw her in the kitchen drinking coffee with someone. It was the koumbaros. The father had forbidden him from the house, so, what the hell was he doing there I thought. I had to get inside to get ready for work, so I let myself in the backdoor, and glared at both of them. It wasn't my house, but she'd treated me like her son, and I felt like she'd betrayed the family. I was offered coffee just before I left the house that morning, but I refused, I wanted her to know I was disappointed with what she had done.

Although that situation wasn't my business, I just couldn't help feeling that somehow I was gonna get thrown to the wolves in that relationship. I'd got caught up in another family's dramas and after what had happened with my mum and Wayno I was emotionally drained: I couldn't bear the thought of ending up in another entanglement. So, I called it off with the Brunswick chick and decided to see other girls. Just like the early days I was adamant; I would not take anything too seriously. How could I possibly get hurt by a chick when I had another one or two to fall back on? Hmmm, later in life I realised that it's better to focus on the prize than play the field: a winner knows that things can only hurt you if you let them.

Soon after that, I briefly dated a stripper who I'd met early one morning at a 24-hours Greek restaurant in the city. At this point our restaurant would turn into a bar at night and Kirky asked me if I'd like to work there as a busboy for some extra salad. I found the work a little degrading and didn't stick at it long, but I became friends with some of the bouncers and regulars and we we'd often go for a bite to eat after work. We were all about the same age. It was during one of these meals that I met the stripper, Davina Manic, who ended up being a complete pain in the ass, but she taught me something. If I was having trouble trusting regular girls, well to put it nicely, strippers were next level. They hustle dudes for a living!

Anyway, me and Davina arranged to head up to Sydney on a bus one long weekend because she had a well-paying gig up there and she thought that I should come along and party with her. This was towards the end of the year and I didn't have any more fights locked in, so I thought it sounded like a good idea. I'd never dated a stripper before this time, although when I grew older, I dated many and the thrill of the whole thing faded out pretty quick. I was pumped and told my mates about it. A few of my mates were partying hard on weekends and had started popping pills. Someone asked if I could try and hook them up some better produce up there, so he gave me a wad of notes and a stash of pills to party with the girls. This all sounded like a good idea at the time, but as we got on the bus Davina just kept asking me for more and more flippers. I didn't want act stingy or too straight, or anything like that, so I just kept popping those bickies with her until we'd finished what we had. By the time I arrived in Sydney after a 12 hour bus ride from Melbourne I was fucken flyin' and so was she.

We ended up at some crazy random friend of Davina's place, who told me she was Syrian. This chick was also a stripper, and she had a PhD in being dodgy as fuck. In the few hours I was there, she had a coupla different dudes rock up to her house. One of her Lebo mates rocked a big mono out the front with an R1 motorbike, no helmet and no shirt; just tearing around the back streets of Sydney. I was completely outta my mind thinking, where the fuck have I ended up? Next minute we were at some hard trance club on Oxford street, and they started flirting real bad with some dudes, what a fucken headache, I thought to myself. One of them said he was a bodybuilder and for some reason we ended up back at their apartment taking more gear with them, while one of their housemates DJ'd. Davina's friend was in the room all night banging this dude. Then for no reason she turned nasty on me and tried to hook up Davina with one of the dudes.

I was wired and just wanted to get the fuck out of there. I didn't trust any of them, so I kept the splash my mate had given me to myself. Except Davina knew about it, as she had seen the wad as I was getting pills out of my pocket on the bus. I guess it wasn't anything too full on but the next morning that dodgy stripper insisted we all go for exotic massages, and that it was her shout. She paired herself up with her bodybuilder fuck buddy and Davina with his mate and I got a solo massage with some Cambodian chick hitting me up for a 'happy ending'. I was like, fuck this I'm getting out of here, and got dressed.

Back at reception, the Duchess of Dodginess pulls out her credit card and it's declined. She looked at me for money, and Davina goes, "Yeh, he's got a stack with him." The massages were about $500, so I paid. Then both chicks started acting real nasty again. I told them what I thought of them and got on the first plane back to Melbourne. I was promised that they would pay me back, but they were scammers, and I'm just glad I caught on quick and got the fuck outta Dodge. There's no denying, it was a shit feeling knowing that the player I thought I was, got fucken played!

MORTAL KOMBAT ... BiTCHEZ!

arch 2000 I was advanced straight through into another Victorian middleweight state title fight against a fighter called Porky who was a couple years younger than me. The fight was confirmed last minute. Kel had called me that morning and said to meet him there, which threw me out of my usual routine of picking up Andy and driving to his place. In a daze I completely forgot to get off at the right freeway exit and got lost, which meant I weighed in late. By the time we were good to go, I didn't feel very switched on and was nonchalant about the fight. I'd seen Porky get knocked out in his last fight, so I felt I had him covered. But I broke rule number one: never underestimate your opponent.

Porky was hungry to redeem himself. He fought fearlessly and got the win on points. It was a massive crush to my ego, to be beaten by a younger fighter, and self-doubt started to creep in. I resorted to trash talking in the last round when I should have been throwing more punches. My head just wasn't there that day and getting it right is the most important thing in the fight game. Porky went on to become an IBF Pan Pacific and IBO Asia Pacific Super Middleweight Champ, winning the belts several times over the years. He had a massive following of supporters at the Reggio Calabria club that day, and they followed him throughout his pro career. I felt the fight between us was a turning point for both of our boxing careers. Porky was over the moon, he deserved to feel that way. He was a great fighter and I wasn't as great as I thought I was at the time!

The second fight I had that year wasn't until August. Kel had taken on a new middleweight fighter from Lithuania; it was good sparring with him. Kel was impressed with some of his tricks. We became good mates, and it was interesting adapting to his different style. Ironically Porky ended up beating him too when they fought later in the year. I felt that the spotlight had shifted away me as a fighter and my confidence sank down a little further. It was just like being back at Leo's again.

During that year another fight at the Calabria Club had fallen through and I was really pissed off about it this time. I was keen to avenge my state title loss, and get my mojo back. This had been the fifth time a fight had fallen through for me in two years. I was always keen to fight, I loved it, but with everything else going on in my life, I was feeling removed in general. In spite of the fact, I was convinced I was gonna become a world champ, but I was impatient. I wanted the opportunities there and then. I was now already older than Tyson was when he won his world title and that strangely frustrated me.

The Sunday night after the cancelled fight, Memo and me had planned a night out at Razers on Chapel Street. I was drinking away my sorrows and frustration; so we hit the Johnny Walker and coke and got plastered. As we were leaving to grab a taxi home, some drunk malakas were having an argument with the bouncers, who I respected because of the fight with the Turks a few years earlier. I just stopped and kinda stood beside one of the bouncers like I was backing him up and the malakas didn't like that too much. One of them yelled out at me, "What are you looking at, fuckhead?" I just flipped and started laying into both of them. Memo, who was grabbing his jacket from the cloak room at the time, ran out swinging punches too. They were fighting back, so it was a fair fight, but they didn't land any shots because I was all over them, unloading with 'fists of fury'. They both decided to run. It was a bad move for them because they ran into an alley. I finished the fight with a jab cross combination, splitting the main assholes eye open, splashing blood all over the night.

A massive crowd had formed around us, right in front of the KFC where everyone would hang out back in the day. I remember looking up after the final blow was landed and seeing Ike, my old school mate. So, I rubbed the blood off my hands and I went to say, '"Wassup," when once again 'We-oow', the Bulle were on the scene. I ran for my life down Chapel Street, the crowd in front of KFC cheering just like I was at the Calabria Club and actually getting a fucking fight for a change. I ran for about a kilometre with the smokey bacon continuing to chase me on foot about 20 metres behind me. I could have lost them, but I realised they'd already grabbed Memo and I didn't want him to take the rap for the fight, especially because I'd caused more damage. So, I stopped, put my hands-on top of my head, surrendered, and allowed the jacks to handcuff me.

We were once again chucked in the back of a divvy van and taken straight to the cells for the night on a drunk and disorderly charge, which was actually a great result considering all the violence. I thought I was gonna get charged with assault for sure. The fact I wasn't charged meant either the dudes I bashed just kept their mouths shut and didn't say anything or they were smart-ass to the jacks and got locked up too, coz I'm pretty sure I saw one of the dudes leaving in the morning, while we were waiting for a cab to get home.

Eventually, when my next fight came around in August, it was well worth the wait. I'd be representing Victoria in the middleweight category, against the champ from Adelaide in South Australia, travelling by bus with the rest of the state boxing team. The bus left about 7 pm from the front of the Northside Boxing gym in Preston. Walking onto the bus was intense. Just like I was in the change rooms at the fights, and then I saw Porky. I got a mad rush like, we were about to go another round, but he kept staunch and glared back. Andy, Kel and the Lithuanian fighter put their arm around me, gave me a high five and made me laugh, so I forgot about it.

All the other fighters on the bus had won state titles in their division either that year or the year before. The bus ride took about nine hours, which meant we arrived at the hotel around 4 am. The guy that filmed all the videos of fighters at the Calabria Club was driving and the Stucci brothers were sitting up the front with him. On the bus we were all joking around, a lot of us had fought each other in the ring and we started to form what I can best describe as a fighter's bond between each other. I ended up having a chat with Porky, who was injured at the time and wasn't fighting and just coming along for the trip. We were cool with each other and became mates. It felt more like a footy trip or a school camp rather than heading there to fight!

When all the fighters finally got up to the serviced apartment, we were exhausted. We looked for our beds. Okay, three bedrooms, a lounge, kitchenette, and a bathroom ... But wait a minute, how many fucken beds? Only five ... There's 10 of us ... WTF? Someone ran downstairs to tell the Stuccis. One of the Stuccis ran up to the room and said, "Ahhh they fucked up, you're gonna have to rotate them boys." I was like, for fuck sake! Some of the other fighters had been obviously worded up on how disorganised the whole process was and got their own transport and accommodation with their trainers rather than with all of us. We were the Victorian State Boxing Team getting Z-grade fucken treatment. It was bullshit but we had no choice. I wished they hadn't of let all the extra fighters come along. It was a waste of space, but I wouldn't change it for the world coz we had a mad time all of us there together.

I got first preference of a bed and I crashed out straight away. No more than four hours later someone was tapping on my shoulder, "Times up, it's four hours each," someone said, and we all rotated beds with the other five guys.

Next day, we were all pumped up to grab some breakfast and see the sites around Adelaide. We hit the streets till about midday, then woke the other five guys up and met up with our coaches and the fighters that had got their own way across. Some of the dudes were ripping bongs in one of the bedrooms when we arrived back at the room. I remember thinking that if they were fighting, they were gonna get fucken smashed!

We were meant to be at the venue for the weigh in at 4.30 pm, so the bus driver had planned to meet us at the hotel at 4 pm to take us there. He was late and arrived at the hotel 5 pm. Then he got lost on the way to the venue, meaning we arrived at 6.30 pm. It was fucken crazy. It must have been one of the biggest events in Adelaide that weekend because it seemed like there was about five thousand people cramped up in the stands of the basketball centre. Coz we were late, the crowd was already seated and when we entered the stadium still dressed in our tracksuits, the ring announcer goes, "And Finally the Victorian Boxing Team have arrived!" And the spotlight shined on us while the entire crowd let out a massive cheer and hysterical laughter, which was quickly drowned out with hurls of abuse and booing! I couldn't help laughing! This trip was messed up!

We had to jump on the scales straight away, got changed and pretty much had to head out for our fights with a limited warm up coz they wanted us all dressed, ready and presented to the crowd as a state-of-origin line up thing, and individually introduced to the crowd with our opponent before the fights began. I'd be fighting right before the intermission. My opponent was tall, about 6ft 4. The bell sounded and I moved, dodged, weaved well, and landed clean shots. But as the fight progressed, the guy would push my head down and hold onto me, when I got inside. This was a foul. The fight progressed but the guy kept applying the same tactic, which was really starting to piss me off, especially as the ref cautioned me for holding. I started cursing and then as I moved in, he did it again, but this time I head butted him and the ref deducted a point. I got more aggressive, and on the next exchange the guy locked up my arms and the ref jumped in and stopped the fight. I was officially disqualified for 'holding'. I was pissed off. The whole Victorian Team was behind me, heckling the ref and shouting out, "That's Bullshit!" I was fuming! But again, I shouldn't have let it get to me. The ref was favouring the local fighter, that's just how Boxing is sometimes!

It was time to let off some steam, so after the fights the boxing team got together and decided to get on the piss and hit as many clubs in Adelaide as we could find. It was a great night! We had all found our way back to the room in a rowdy state around 6.30 am. The bus was due to head back to Melbourne at 8 am. Some dudes had made it to the beds early and people were shouting, "Wake up ya Fuck heads!" The dudes woke up and were hostile as hell. Next minute a massive brawl erupted in the lounge room between everyone, but the violence was quickly defused with sniggering, so it was nothing too serious. In a playful but malicious way it kicked off again, furniture was flying around everywhere, the TV got all smashed up, a window cracked, people laid into each other with whatever they could get their hands on. Most people had their shirts off or were in their drawers. Then we heard a loud 'bang' on the front door. I thought it was security or something, but it was Andy. He was completely smashed out of his mind. He ran into the lounge room where everyone was fighting, pulled out his dick and started pissing everywhere. Man, it was really fucked up. But, he unquestionably put an end to the riot. So, I got dressed and just got the fuck out of there. Some dudes were passed out on the floor, coz they were drunk but not KO'd ... I think. I never bothered to find out if the Stucci brothers got left with the clean-up bill. Ten pissed boxers in a tiny hotel room... Seriously what were they thinking?

THE HOLY GHOST

n the bus ride home, I started feeling a bit down on myself because I'd lost my fight and I'd hardly slept all weekend. Kel could tell something was up and asked if I was alright. I said, "Kel what's all this is for?" I wanted Kel to tell me, you're doing this because you're going to be the next middleweight world champ, don't give up, things didn't go your way, you'll bounce back bigger and stronger, you're something special, destined to be one of the greatest boxers of all time. But Kel didn't tell me what I was expecting to hear. He just said, "You do this coz you love it!" That didn't make any sense to me back then. In fact, I took offence to his answer. I wanted to be the best fighter there was. I wanted to make millions of dollars from fighting. In my mind I thought it meant I wasn't good enough to make those millions. Being told I was doing it for the love of it just didn't resonate with me. In truth, Kel was 100 percent right. Many years later I understood why ...

I arrived back in Melbourne and intended on spending more time with my grandparents. I hadn't been home much since I'd moved in with them, and I wanted them to know I appreciated their love and support. When I arrived back home Oma and Opa we're excited to see me, they didn't ever ask me too much about my boxing fights. They were happy just as long as I didn't get hurt. Oma had made me a stack of one of my favourite dishes, Rouladen.

The following weekend a chick I'd just started seeing had told me she'd planned a romantic night for us in a luxury five-star suite at the casino. The weekend was a blur, but I decided to head into training with Kel and Andy early Monday morning. I planned to stop off and grab some flowers for Oma's birthday and then spend the day with her and Opa. I got close to the flower shop and my phone rang. It was my mum. I said, "Hi,

Mum, yeh yeh I know, I remembered it's Oma's birthday today." Mum said, "No, something's happened to Opa. Try and get back home as soon as you can, to see if everything's okay."

I got back home as quickly as I could, and in the lounge I found my cousin, my uncle and Oma all huddled up on the couch crying. Oma said, "Opa woke up in the middle of the night complaining that he had a sore stomach, I thought maybe it was because of the apple strudel, so I told him to go back to sleep, then the pains got worse and early in the morning he got out of bed and collapsed." Oma called the ambulance right away. When paramedics arrived, they told her he'd had a heart attack. They loaded Opa into the vehicle then drove him straight to hospital. Oma had wanted to wait for me, then we all drove to the hospital together. I was sure everything would be fine, Opa was very strong, so full of life and always joking around. He'd beat this...

I arrived at the hospital and a nurse met me in the foyer, "Are you here to see your grandfather?" she asked. I said," Yes." She told me, in a kind voice, "He didn't make it, but you can see him if you'd like." I was in shock, I repeated her calm words, "Didn't make it? But I can see him?" What is she talking about? ... No. Please God, No.... Not now. It's not his time.

The nurse led me to a ward and opened the curtain surrounding a bed ... Opa was laying there, not moving at all. His face had lost colour and the expression didn't look right ... This isn't him? It can't be? This person isn't real? It's just fake... Right Opa? opa... "Nooooooo!" I screamed and cried uncontrollably, and I threw myself on his body and hugged his torso. I said, "Come back Opa. Please, come back," as my tears streamed onto one of his favourite grey polo shirts. I felt his soul, but the body was cold. Other family members started to come into the hospital. We sat in a small room together for a while. Then everything turned into a haze, until we had the funeral.

On the way to my aunty's house in Mount Eliza for the wake, I was still rattled. I accidentally went the wrong way down a one-way street in Frankston. The fucken pigs pulled me over and gave me a fine, even after I'd told them it was an honest mistake and I simply got lost after my grandfather's funeral. My brothers were in the car and still pretty young. I didn't appreciate them being exposed to such disrespectful behaviour from the bacon burgers. Yep, just another reason not to trust the assholes. They totally fucked up my spiritual vibe and made the grieving process seem unimportant.

When I arrived at the wake, I was feeling agitated, more so than feeling sad. Opa was like a king to me and although he was humble, I found it frustrating we had to celebrate his life in such a humble way. The funeral service was in a small crematorium-type chapel, with only immediate family and a handful of friends in attendance. He was Catholic, it just didn't make sense ... I envisioned Opa being carried in a coffin in a Catholic Church which resembled the Vatican in Rome. I guess my family just didn't have the money. It hurt to realise, but that was the truth. Somebody mentioned he was cremated because he was claustrophobic, that was a lot easier for me to get my head around.

Later that day, I thought about a story Opa had told me a few months earlier. He said that in the middle of the night he woke up to a bright light that filled the room and Jesus was standing right in front of him. The way he described it was like the Divine Mercy. He said he shook Oma to wake her up, but she didn't wake up. Then oddly enough, on the same night that happened there was a death in our extended family. Opa believed the person passed at the exact time he had his vision. Neither of us were close with the person that died, but I have no doubt it happened for a reason. I've always had a strong feeling Opa's in a better place. I dream about him sometimes. I feel like he's always with me in spirit, or whenever I need him. One day, we'll share a beer again on a doorstep in Germany. He was 78 years old when he passed. On a lighter note, and in essence of his humour, which he'd appreciate, he'd be pleased to know I've never trusted eating an apple strudel ever again!

TURKISH FROM SNATCH

After Opa passed, I tried to get on with my life, throwing myself back into work and training but things just didn't feel right. Again I had to find a new place to live because Oma wanted to live in Mount Eliza, which was way too far to travel back to the city every day for work. I ended up moving out by myself into a flat right near old ill-famed Tooronga Station. A week later, I noticed our tags which Bronzer had written in wet cement at the end of the street many years before. It was meant to be. It had been a busy couple of years. Boxing, managing a kitchen, running a hot goods racket and attempting a social life. Then there was my mum and stepdad breaking up, moving homes, and now I'd been through the death of my Opa. Something had to give in my life.

I called my dad for a long chat over the phone. He suggested I retire from boxing, he said, "Ninety nine percent of the world's population wouldn't have the guts to enter a boxing ring in front of a crowd and face another man that wants to kill you. You've achieved that and you did well. Time to move on."

I'd never really thought about it that way. The fights weren't really that big a deal to me, each fight was supposed to be a steppingstone towards becoming a world champ. The loss in Adelaide and all the times I'd rock up and have the other fighter pull out of the contest or get stitched up in one way or the other still pissed me off. I was starting to think boxing was all bullshit, it's rigged, only the better-known fighters that bring in the crowd and sell the tickets got the wins or the easy fights. This may be true sometimes, but not always. I was thinking negatively because I was tired and emotionally drained from everything that had happened over the past few years. I wanted some much-deserved time out from my life, but there was no time to rest from my job because I wanted to make big bucks and not struggle like my family had all these years. I felt Dad was right. I needed to retire from boxing, and focus on getting that paper! I called Kel and told him how I was feeling. He suggested I take a break and see how I felt in a few months time. But this time my mind was made up!

One day back at the Greek restaurant, Kirky said, "Hey come sit down and meet a mate who's also a boxer, his name's Johnny." He was maybe late 30s at the time and we had a brief conversation about boxing. He told me he'd fought before. He was one of the blokes in charge of all the security guards working in the Greek bars. I asked him where he trained and he said, "The Underworld with Rock." I'd been training at that gym a while, but we must have been going there on different days and times coz I'd never seen him there, and at that stage I still hadn't met Rock properly, although I'd heard a lot about him. "What times and days you guys training?" I asked. "About 4 pm Monday's, Wednesdays and Thursdays," he said. "Sweet, I'll come down and train with you guys then and see if someone wants to spar."

Although I'd made up my mind about retiring from amateur boxing, the brief conversation with Johnny brought back an immediate and impulsive fire in my guts to get back into fighting. Rock trained some of Melbourne's best pro fighters, I felt this was my chance to get in with him and I could turn pro too. I could then make some cash from the sport, and I'd get to embrace all the fame and glory.

I went back to the kitchen and started packing up because it was towards the end of my shift. Kirky came back into the kitchen five minutes later and asked, "Hey have you got any sunglasses?" He knew I'd been operating the racket like a proper side business and was very organised with it all and when it came to impressing his mates it had its perks sometimes. "Yeh, I got some Ray Bans," I said. "Can I show Johnny?" Kirky asked. "Yeh, they're $100," I said. I might have paid say $20 from the junky but in the shops back then they would have been at least $250. Kirky came back into the kitchen and said, "Sold," and he gave me the cabbage.

I headed down to the Underworld Gym the next day on my lunch break from the restaurant, got changed in the locker room and started skipping, and then shadow boxing in the boxing area. An older man who must have been in his late 40s came walking through the back iron bar gate, which was right behind the boxing ring. He had a set of keys and a big training bag. It was Rock. I approached him and asked if he needed help with his bag, "Nah, I'm right mate," he replied.

I said, "My names Benny Sinclair, I'm an ex-state champ boxer, Johnny mentioned it would be cool to come train with you guys." "Johnny who? Ahhh ... Johnny the Greek?" he asked. "Yeh that's him," I said. "No worries, mate. I just have a few of my professional fighters to get through on the pads and then I might have time to give ya a couple rounds towards the end." I said, "Sounds great Rock, thank you."

I couldn't exactly expect him to put his pro fighters aside to train me, who had just decided to retire from the amateurs. I was just grateful Rock had given me some time and that he was approachable. Plus, I had to get back to the kitchen before dinner service. As training unfolded that day more and more fighters kept filing into the gym. One by one, round by round, they did either boxing or kickboxing pad-work with Rock. It was clear to see I was getting pushed to the back of the queue, but I was the new kid on the block training with them. I had to earn my pad-work, show him I was loyal and committed.

Rock was a well-known figure in Melbourne for several reasons. He owned the biggest nightclub security company in Melbourne. He was an ex-kickboxing champ himself. He'd been shot six times and he was good mates with Big Tony, a heavy hitting Italian with a lot of pull around the traps, if ya know what I mean. Rock had even starred in a Bollywood movie and other acting roles and no doubt, in his own way was a man about town!

Rock quickly started to show more interest in me as a fighter and I'd get some quality rounds on the pads with him. I liked his concept of angle work, which I hadn't focused on too much before we trained together. I started to spar with some of his fighters, like a fighter called The Horra, he was tuff as nails, with a big heart. He had a lot of fights, but lost more often than he won.

WHEN WE WERE KING STREET KINGS

One day I rocked up to Underworld to train and ran into Luke. During that time I noticed he was improving and I encouraged him to take his boxing more seriously. On this particular day I could tell he was hyped about something, coz he just ran up to me and said, "Guess what brother, you're not going to believe it. Rock hooked me up down at a club called The Hotel. It's money for jam Benny, get paid to stand around and chat up girls, you should get into it, bro."

Initially I was a little surprised that Luke, who was a little younger than me, was working as a bouncer. I assumed most bouncers were giants or ex pro fighters. I thought, damn, I could be really good at it with my fighting experience. This could be the way to get that paper, I'm gonna get it! Next time I trained with Rock after hitting the pads I asked, "Hey Rock, you need any more bouncers to work at the clubs?" Rock said, "I sure do buddy. You interested?" I said, "Yeh, why not.". He said, "Great. Here's my card, call the office on Monday and tell them you got the number from me. Alright?" I said, "Thank you Rock, I will." So, I called the office on Monday and was told to come in to sign some paperwork. They asked if I had a security licence and I said no. The office lady said it didn't matter, I could still work under a probationary licence, but eventually I'd need to attend a security training course to become qualified.

After the probationary license came through, I received a phone call from the co-ordination's manager, responsible for giving weekly rosters. He said, "Can you work on King Street, this Saturday night?" I said, "Yep, no worries." He said, "Good, you start at 10 pm. When you arrive at the front door ask for Jim, he'll show you what to do." So, I headed down that Saturday night after my shift in the kitchen.

King Street in Melbourne has a long-standing reputation as being a ruff and violent place. In the vicinity it hosts several nightclubs and strip clubs, a mixture of demographics in crowds due to its central location and the allure of temptation in all its many forms. There is also an entry to the casino at the end of the street and the Docklands sports stadium, which holds big events like footy, soccer and music gigs. King Street provides access to heavy alcohol and drug consumption for its patrons, and most nights of the week there's a lot of street violence. I knew about King Street's reputation, but I hadn't been involved in any fights or violent situations there until I started working as a bouncer. If Tony Montana ever came to Melbourne, he'd head straight for King Street.

When I rocked up at the club called Temptations for my first shift, I was 21 years old. It was months after my last amateur boxing fight in Adelaide, but I was still about 170 pounds at the time and same height I am now, which is a little over 5ft 10. I wore a long denim jacket, coz I thought it made me look bigger, with a white sheep wool turtleneck underneath. I approached the door and asked for Jim. The bouncers at the door seemed shocked I was there to work. I thought I looked a lot older than I did at the time, but I had a baby face, I just didn't realise it. Jim was a little frosty with me at first & looked me up and down. Almost straight away he asked if I trained and I said, "Yeh, I've been boxing with Rock. He hooked me up with the job. I used to fight." I met the rest of the crew, including a bouncer called Reza who was Persian, Ivan who was Croatian and a couple of others. I asked Jim if he trained and he said "Yeh, Ivan and me train with Colt Jones." Colt Jones was a big deal in the Melbourne bouncer and martial arts world for many years at that point in time.

The Temptations crew instantly had my respect. I was taken into a back-office room, given a black and white plastic security number on a lanyard to wear around my neck, and then told to sign the crowd controller's book. Lastly, I was issued a radio. Reza and me were working inside the venue together and he said I should go stand on the stage where everyone was dancing. I asked, "What should I do if there's a fight?" He said, "Call it through on the radio, jump in and break it up, then help kick them out."

It seemed pretty straight forward, and it is, except that's the easy part of security work, when things are straight forward. Most of the time it's not straight forward at all, there can be a lot of complications, a lot of politics, it takes time to get good at the job, and experience is everything. The job is more of a psychological game rather than physical. Just like boxing. When I was 21, I didn't understand that. There were no incidents that I can remember happening on that night except I felt people in the club didn't really like or respect me. They were drunk, having a good time with some baby-faced bouncer, trying to act all big and tuff up on the stage with his arms crossed. They didn't know I was a boxer and an ex-state champ. But why would they care? No one gives a shit about a boxer that wasn't a household name, they just thought you were dumb, punch drunk and washed up.

I wasn't told to do anything else like kicking out patrons that looked drunk or about the other liquor licensing laws we had in our city. The idea with the probationary licences was to learn on the job. Most of the guys I was working with weren't exactly the greatest influences. I just thought I was at that club working as a bouncer to jump in if there were fights and break them up or punch on with people that tried to punch on with me or the other bouncers. I honestly thought the rules were if people fuck up in the club or on the door and become abusive or aggressive towards the bouncers, we had the right to beat the shit out of them. Reza always remembers my first night and he says, "I was looking for you on the stage, but I couldn't see you at all, I thought you were lost, but you were actually standing right at the front and didn't move all night long."

He was right, I didn't move for four hours, and people were dancing all on top of me. I didn't move a single step until the other bouncers told me too, coz I thought that was exactly what I was supposed to do, and I didn't want to let the team down. Now that I wasn't fighting in the ring anymore, I could fight doing this job and get paid for it every night of the week.

I was fed up with working in kitchens and being confined to one space for such a long period of time each shift, and under stressful conditions most nights. One night I remember Kirky came running into the kitchen complaining that the baby octopus that we used to serve was undercooked. I didn't feel this was right coz I'd been cooking it the exact same way for almost two years, and we had a huge argument about it. I lost my temper and threw my tea towel in his direction and stormed off. This was uncharacteristic of me, coz I was usually very calm. I saw it as a sign. I was done with cooking! Not long after this I decided to give notice at the Greek restaurant and handed the reigns to Devious who took my spot as the head chef.

With the thrill of the security job, I'd quickly forgotten about my aspirations of becoming a professional boxer. But I still saw the bigger picture. I started to really understand my road-to Damascus moment and my true calling was to become an entertainer. Being around music and nightclubs might lead to better opportunities. Maybe I'd meet a DJ or a record label executive and show them how dope I could rhyme and record an album. I could work, get paid, network, and meet some ladies! Problem was, I wasn't getting as much work in the security industry as I'd hoped for, and some of the clubs would only give you the minimum three hours work and ask you to sign off. This would often be the case on weeknights, as the clubs weren't as busy, so I needed a back-up plan to get that moolah rollin' in.

WORKIN' ON THE STREETS OF CHAPEL I KNOCKED BACK THIS BLOKE WHO OFFERED ME A PINEAPPLE

Bouncer, *King Hits* **(2009)**

Fight Club3

decided to mix up my training and I started hitting the weights and I cut back on running completely. I would hit pads with Rock and train with other fighters when I could and I felt like I was in a new crew; Rock was the Boss. Sure, I'd still have my weeks when I dreamed of fighting pro. I would imagine myself relishing all the prestige that I felt had been missing in the amateur game, with bigger crowds, ring girls, TV exposure, longer rounds, and no fucken headgear. But, the reality was I had way too many distractions. I wanted to make cash and I wanted it fast, something lucrative. I was beginning to notice a lot of people around me were breaking into that hustling game, either that or they were already well established ...

I started to try out products like protein powder and creatine. It took some time for me to get beyond 180 pounds. I was living on my own and wouldn't cook for myself that often, kinda just eat the bare minimum to get by. I'd quickly fallen into the habit of popping bikkies like they were on prescription and racking up lines with the older bouncers, to keep ourselves awake and entertained. The drugs suppressed my appetite. I'd also stupidly started smoking cigarettes for the first in my life.

It started with just one or two a day, only if someone I was working with or one of my mates would offer, but within a year I got up to two packs a day. I could buy the packs of smokes through machines in the clubs, so that didn't help, especially if it was a quiet night, coz I'd smoke like a fucken chimney. I was getting fed up with people calling me the little guy and felt like I wasn't being taken too seriously when I was working. Often people would test me by being smart-ass, this would piss me off, I would snap and end up teaching them a lesson in respect by slapping them around and stuff like that.

The respect of my work mates came when they noticed how I worked. Initially, I thought the rules on 'ejection' were if you asked a patron to leave and they refused you had the right to take them out as hard as you like coz they were trespassing, at least this is what it looked like everyone else was doing. It was a fine line between going too hard or not hard enough. Nobody among the security crew said that my technique was wrong, just sometimes I wouldn't get any shifts back at a particular venue because the venue management would complain that I was too ruff. The co-ordinations manager wouldn't bother explaining anything to me, he'd just cut my hours or put me at another club the next week.

Most of the time I got sent to the venues with all the problems and violence. I didn't mind this at the time because it was more straight forward. The more frequent the dramas, the more the managers or owners of the clubs didn't mind me going hard when I needed to. This made my job simple, but very physically demanding some nights, and risky as hell. My life was literally on the line every night I worked, and so were the lives of my work mates. Apart from the ruff ejections and the occasional fight in the club, the first big all-in brawl I was involved in was on King Street on a Tuesday night.

BLACK HEART

I was working on the door of a strip club, which was only a few metres down the street from, Temptations. They used to serve cheap drinks in plastic buckets back then on Tuesday nights. As the nights unfolded each week, you'd see people getting kicked out and sometimes literally thrown out of the club onto the pavement, or people throwing up on the street. It was a chaotic night, but at the strip club I was working, it was usually pretty quiet on Tuesday's, so it was generally an easy night's work.

Just after midnight another bouncer, Kosta who was Greek, had joined me working on the door, while an Aussie bouncer, Dale, who was also a boxer, was working upstairs. I heard a ruckus down the street in front of the Temptations front door. Reza and some other bouncers I knew were working there that night. They were in a heated argument with five big Islander dudes and some big ladies too. The Temptations crew were behind the red velvet rope, standing on the front entry steps. Suddenly one of the Islander dudes undid the rope and threatened to smash them. Next minute 'boom!' a bouncer threw a big right hand from the top step and it landed right on the Islander's chin, putting him on his ass.

He got up right away, he was tuff, and a massive all-in brawl erupted between the bouncers and the Islanders, who believe me, all knew how to fight, even the ladies were throwing down, some better than the dudes!

The Temptations crew were outnumbered and in trouble. Kosta was a bit hesitant to get involved initially because it wasn't our club, but when that Islander dude got off his ass, I noticed someone had dragged Reza off the front doorsteps to the point where he was airborne. I left the strip club door and ran up to help out Reza, who, by the time I got there, was pressed up against a car on the street with the Islanders laying into him. I burst through the pack and grabbed the biggest dude in a headlock and started beating him. He had a hard head and my fist swelled up straight away. Then some others from his crew jumped on me and broke me off him. The big dude was bleeding, bruised up and out of gas, but he still threw a few punches back, which I blocked. The others jumped in and were fighting with the rest of the group until they all backed down and ran off down the street.

The bussie's came out of the club with buckets of water to wash away the blood from the street. The bouncers all embraced, checked for injuries and thanked each other, before we headed back down the street to the strip club. Our manager was at the door, he surprisingly wasn't too mad, we'd left his club unattended. It had been a massive brawl and if we were in the same situation, you'd have to think the Temptations crew would help us out too. Kosta had also hurt his hand and he grabbed us some ice, which I placed in my pocket with my hand to ease the swelling.

A couple of hours later a green 1980's Ford Falcon double parked in the taxi rank on the other side of the street. Two older Islander dudes got out of the car. One of them was holding a baseball bat. He looked about 500 pounds and at least 6ft 9. He slowly walked over to the front door of Temptations, the bouncers had already knocked off and locked the door. The guy started beating on the double doors with his bat. After about 5 minutes of beating the doors, the dude got fed up, after all they were fucken solid. He noticed that our club was just down the street and was still open, so he headed towards us. I was standing inside the doorway with Kosta, and Dale waited in the foyer behind us. We really couldn't afford to provoke another incident. My hand was sore, but still, I was prepared to do what I needed to do if this giant took a swing at me with his bat. He slowly walked past the door. He looked me in the eyes and said, "You fellas seen those bouncers who work up the road?" I said, "Nah, bro."

He stood there for about 30 seconds, rubbed his face and walked back across the road, dragging the baseball bat behind him, looking like an ogre. He then jumped back in his car and drove off with his mate. It was a relief he left. We were all a little bruised and tired from the first brawl, it was almost 3 am by this stage too and I was ready to head home and sleep. The brawl with the Islanders on King Street became legend. Legend became myth amongst bouncers across Melbourne. I'd earned a reputation of having balls and being a good street fighter. I wasn't the biggest in the crew by any standards, but I never backed down when fights erupted. I always jumped in for my mates no matter what. A few years later a coupla bouncer mates, who used to collect the security surveillance video tapes of all the 'King Street Fights' made a compilation video of their footage to music. They played it to us after work one night. I was proud to see the footage of our brawl made the compilation video. It ended with the big Islander dude tryna beat down the Temptations doors with his bat. We all laughed ... I would classify that video as a work of art ... Well done, fellas!

BLOW YA NOSE MATE

ife changed when I started working as a bouncer. I was sleeping during the day when most of my old mates were working, and I was working all night. Some clubs I used to work at would also run a day-club as well as nightclub on weekends, so they were literally open for business from Friday afternoon until early hours of Monday morning. Sometimes I'd work 15 hours straight at a club or finish at one club at say 4 am then start at another at 5 am, working right through to 1 pm at the next venue.

At this stage most of the people I was hanging out with were either other bouncers, dealers, weekend junkies, or chicks I was hooking up with. 'Recoveries' were the big thing in the early 2000s. It was ironic because initially the concept was that people in that scene had usually been out partying and smashing the gear the night before and needed somewhere to wind down during the day, then maybe blaze a spliff and eventually get some sleep before heading back to their regular lives and responsibilities. But this was just a concept. The facts were people would go to these venues and get more and more fucked up and sometimes continue partying for days on end.

I got caught up in this scene and it was common to start partying on a Thursday night and finish partying Monday morning without any sleep, or just a couple hours over the entire weekend. The music they played at the Recovery venues was EDM, but mostly the Hard genre like Progressive House and Trance; songs like *Cocaine* by Yakooza or Funkagenda, *What the Fuck* and *Zombie Nation* by Kernkraft 400 were massive, with smoke machines and lasers displays going off to the beat. There was a particular dance style that everyone got into, that I felt I had some influence on as the scene grew. I'd rip out a move and then I'd see someone copy the exact same move a coupla minutes later. I was just making that shit up, maybe those fools biting my style thought I was a professional dancer... Or maybe I was just trippin'? I was always high, outta my mind at those places.

Some of the moves were like Islander or Indigenous dancing, but more uptempo. We'd beat our chests, walk back and forth, rolling our arms and hands to the beat. People would howl, scream, whistle, clap hands, and yell stuff out. A lot of dudes would have their shirts off and girls not wearing much at all, with their glow sticks or whistles and sunglasses on. Sometimes it could get a little gross because people would be sweating all over the place. I thought I'd found my tribe, hanging out with a lot of different and random people. I'd finish work late and when I wasn't working at these recoveries I'd head out with my new mates or the new ladies I'd meet each week...

I used to go to venues like Viper Room, Cuba and other

random places around St Kilda or the city. There was also a venue I partied and worked at called The Dome, which was notorious for the high number of shootings that went down there. Generally, it was the places where I knew the bouncers at the front door I'd go to the most, coz they'd waive me straight through without having to pay the entry fee and often give me drink cards, or bottles of water or red bulls. Mega Bar on King Street was renowned for being one of the worst of the bunch. Its recovery session ran from 6 am Monday morning to 2 pm. If you ended up there too often on a Monday, you knew you had issues.

The crowd that went to Mega Bar was the biggest bunch of misfits you could imagine and most of them hadn't slept in days. You'd see corporate businesspeople walking down King Street heading to work all suited up with their briefcases and all these drug fucked raver-looking zombies hanging out the front of the club peeking off their heads. Thankfully, I only made it to Mega Bar once or twice. But one time I went right through to 2 pm Monday. Then we all headed to the casino where they had a video arcade called Barcode, which served alcohol and was open 24/7 back then. The session dragged on and I couldn't seem to get away from the misfits I was hanging with, so I wandered off to the nearby cinema and bought Gold Class tickets to watch the movie *Blow*, starring Johnny Depp. As I watched the movie, I imagined myself becoming a big player in the Melbourne drug scene; maybe I could get in with a large cartel and move some serious weight and make that serious paper I'd been yearning for. But as the movie went on things seemed to get progressively more tragic for Johnny

Depp's character, George, and I started to come down hard from all the gear I was on. I questioned would that kinda life be tragic for me also? When I got out of the movie it was dark, and thankfully everyone had left Barcode by then, so I went home and finally slept.

THE WEEKEND WARRIORS

ne morning after work I was hanging out with an old Italian gangster, who I'd briefly befriended. He used to frequent the Greek restaurant and hang around Lonsdale Street, when I was working as a chef. A bouncer called Eddie, who was Papa New Guinean, was also with us. There was also a Colombian dude I'd met a few times at random recovery places I was going to. He said he was from Sydney. That morning he was smoking something out of a glass pipe in the doorway of the bathrooms at the recovery club we were hanging out at, in plain sight of everyone. You could smoke cigarettes inside the venues back then, so he kind of blended in, unless you were close enough to see it was a pipe in his hand and not a cigarette. I was intrigued by what this guy was smoking and said, "Hey bro, what you smoking?" He said, "It's ice, u want some?" I said, "It's what?"

Ice was new to Melbourne at the time, I'd never come across it before and I was oblivious to it being highly addictive. He said, "This is the new thing up in Sydney, give it a hit if you like, just light it up like you're smoking weed and inhale."

I tried it and didn't think I felt anything. We moved onto the next venue further down Chapel Street, coz this place was shutting down. It was probably about 11 am Saturday and I hadn't slept since Thursday. Eddie came along with me. The next venue we went to had a kitchen area but it wasn't open. We hung out in the kitchen area with this dude and had more hits from his crack pipe. That shit got a hold of us, coz we kept going back for more. We must have been flying at 2000 mph, coz what seemed like 30 minutes had actually been hours of us getting high and all messed up.

We were hanging out until about 3 pm when we decided it was time to leave and try to get some sleep, coz we were working together that evening. As we attempted to walk to my car, I suddenly realised that I had no fucken idea where it was. I was high out of my mind. I crossed a side street and a car with four dudes around my age stopped to let us cross. I distinctively thought one of the dudes in the car yelled out "Hurry up ya fags," but Eddie and the girls we were walking with were adamant, I was trippin', coz they hadn't said anything at all. Regardless, I ran up to the car and hit the driver through his open window, right in the jaw, with a right cross. He said, "What the fuck did you do that for?" I then went to the rear passenger door and tried to get the guy in the back to get out of the car. He wouldn't get out, so I threw a front kick into the side panel denting the door. I then opened the car door and dragged the guy out of the car by the leg, who was by that stage screaming his ass off. I started beating him too, as he scrambled to get back in the car. The driver put his foot down on the accelerator and took off down Chapel Street, with the passenger door open and me running behind the car. By this stage Eddie had caught up to me, bear hugged me and pulled me away in the opposite direction. He said, "What the fuck are you doing?" I said, "They called us fags!" Eddie said, "Your fucken off ya head cuz ... They didn't say anything! Go home and get some sleep." I was in a state of drug fuelled psychosis. I didn't realise it at the time!

Somehow, I did get some sleep and rocked up to work on time. Eddie was a little shaken up when I saw him, he still couldn't believe what had happened. I think we were both coming down off the drugs in a big way, but thankfully it was a quiet night. It was a private function we were working at. We ended up poppin' some pills right at the end of the night and headed out to another club after work to party again!

Drugs had quickly developed into an issue for me. I just didn't want to accept it. I wouldn't say I've ever been physically addicted to any drug, but psychologically, yes definitely. I just couldn't say no to any drug people offered me, especially if I'd been drinking or had taken a little something already. I was self medicating. I convinced myself that it was making me a better person. More likeable to everyone. I was able to stay awake for crazy long hours, work, meet girls and still be able to party with my mates. I thought everyone was my best mate. I'd found a new crew, new contacts. I wanted to become like Bugsy Siegel, a player with the ladies, also a smart businessman, but hoped I'd have the brains of Myer Lansky. I felt drugs should be legal and that it wasn't doing any harm to anyone. Bouncers would open the ropes for me when I got near the door. I'd never have to wait in line like regular people.

THE CHEF OF GREEK STREET

I didn't fear anybody and I felt respected. I liked the feeling. I was making a bit of extra cash on the side, but I wanted to make big bucks. My hot goods racket had died off when I left the restaurant and although my shifts were long on weekends if I worked at the recoveries, the shifts would be short during the week, so my salary was less than when I was a chef. Getting sacked from particular venues for violent behaviour and other reasons didn't help the money situation either. Not long after I'd started bouncen', Devious called me up and asked me to meet him at his place, he wanted to make a proposal. I met with him on my day off and we talked. "Benny, I have an idea," Devious said. "What's is it Bro?" I asked. "We should all go into business together," he said. "What you got in mind?" I asked.

Devious's proposal was that we all chipped in and bought a large quantity of pills and distributed it to our contacts, then put our profits into a fund, which we could use to finance large investments on the stock market. He suggested we call ourselves The Alpha Crew. Alpha symbolising the first letter in the Greek Alphabet and to be superior. I liked his idea and was impressed with the details of the scheme my old childhood mate had devised. Devious kinda had me thinking, why the fuck didn't I think of that? He'd come a long way since we were kids with his white bandanna gang Columbo, and over the years he'd become more like a brother than a mate. The timing of his proposal seemed perfect, most people I was hanging out with were heavily into taking pills on weekends.

I asked Devious who else he had in mind to join the crew. He suggested a couple of aspiring dealers from the northern suburbs that he'd gotten to know through the restaurant. I trusted his new contacts would deliver as promised & it sounded like a good idea because we all had our own clientele. We sat down for a meeting and it was decided we would start our plan.

The pills were priced higher if they were imports, most of the time we were told they came from Europe. These pills were generally better quality than the local pills. Some of the imports were stamped with popular brand name logos. The local ekkies would imitate these stamps sometimes, but you could tell there was a difference in quality and were usually packed with speed and ketamine, not as much MDMA. There were so many different random stamps, and colours which made them more marketable as each week people thought they were trying something new. At first the average person couldn't tell the fucken difference after a couple drinks, just as long as they got a bit of a buzz from it, but after awhile people started becoming kinda like connoisseurs, or fucken food critics. There were even websites where you could rate pills and shit like that. Around about that time pill tester kits came out and you could test what was inside of them. Before that time, we would pretty much try whatever they gave to us, no questions asked. It was crazy when you think about it, so bad for our bodies and risky too, there was no way we could tell if we were feeding ourselves rat poison or something good. At the time I was convinced those fucken pills were like some kinda personality performance enhancing drug. The truth is I look back at these times and I'm not proud one bit ... But sometimes the universe, as Stephen Hawking says, just is.

Each shift I'd rock up to work with a couple hundred flippers stashed in my jocks. The other guards who knew what I was carrying would direct their friends or patrons in the club in my direction and the transaction was completed with a swift handshake. I'd hand out some flippers to the guards and we'd all party together whilst we worked. Just like back at the restaurant, everyone got fed!

We always tried to deliver the best product we could. At the peak of the racket, I was working at two venues where party drugs were high in demand. The strip club and the weekend recovery club. In addition to other bouncers moving our product, I'd also involve the strippers at the strip club, and I guess you'd call them 'trippers' at the recovery club. Their job would be to try to move the pills onto their friends or random patrons. As long as they weren't jacks, it was all good. Except I discovered pretty quick that off duty BLTs did frequent the clubs I worked at and surprisingly a lot of them would be taking way more drugs than me. If we got to know them and they were cool, well cool for fucken pigs meaning not red hot and about to do you in, then occasionally we sold to them. There were times at certain clubs we would be racking up with six off-duty motherfuckers in the bathrooms closed off to the public and it would be their shout, because they'd confiscated the gear from somewhere.

The owners of the clubs would fuel these dodgy copper fuckers up with drink cards too, so they had a real good time getting the VIP service. One of the bacon burgers that used to hang with us got kicked out of the force for an apparent sexual abuse charge, after he drugged a girl up and made moves. Dirty fucken Harry! It's no secret that coppers have never been friends of mine, during this time they were less than acquaintances to me, handy to know if you got in small time trouble, but still I couldn't trust them one bit. The type of shit they get up to in their spare time just proves how the system contradicts itself. Bad boys, bad boys, what you gonna do, what you gonna do, when they come for you ...

THE GODDESS FATHER

At 21 years of age working in a strip club, was the bomb! Damn I used to love that place. I was like a kid in a candy store, all the girls looked so beautiful, like sexy goddesses. I quickly learnt these girls were far from angels, they were more like porn stars both onstage and off. A lot of them had issues or baggage or had suffered sexual abuse and stuff like that, which did make me feel sorry for them initially. But I woke up pretty quick, especially having previously experienced the dodgy weekend in Sydney with Davina. It was like, wait a minute these girls are absolutely screwing these guys over and some of them are getting paid more than $10k per shift, all in cash from tips! It was crazy ... I just couldn't make sense of how these drunk, lonely, or desperate guys could feed these girls so much cash.

I hooked up with a lot of girls from the strip club. I was given the nickname 'The Quiet Achiever'. I got sacked a couple times for my sins, but they'd always ask me to come back and work again six months later. It was the same at the recovery club. The first times I was sacked was apparently because the word got out to the owners that I was hustling. I don't think that was the real reason, as the venues were full of drugs, and everybody seemed to like it that way. I'd even hook up stuff for the managers or owners occasionally too. It was more likely because I banged the wrong girl, or too many wrong girls! I convinced myself there really wasn't a great deal of difference between hooking up with strippers or the regular girls I was meeting in clubs, the strippers were usually getting paid more, but back then they all had drug and alcohol problems. Sometimes they were complete psychos, and it could be hard to tell at first.

There were a lot of rumours circulating around that I was working for someone. It was true. I was working for our crew, The Alpha Crew. Some people thought coz I trained with Rock that we were involved in this together. Rumours circulated about Rock's involvement in those kinda things. The truth is, I never asked him. That was his business. He was a good trainer and always good to me. He called me up one day to clarify, and without him going into too much detail he said that he knew what was going on and it needed to stop, especially inside his venues. He didn't like that people were linking the accusations made about me, to him. That's all that was said, and he moved me on to work at different venues, but with reduced hours.

In the meantime, with me in the limelight taking all the risks and getting my named tarnished as a dealer, the rest of The Alpha Crew decided to live the high life. They'd rock up to the clubs I was working at, with free entry, drink cards and I'd introduce them to girls, that they'd hook up with sometimes too. They'd also hire expensive hotel rooms with our profits and party all weekend until late Sunday night. I was usually either still working or out tryna get deals done at recoveries and would hardly visit the hotels. I was always busy working 24/7 one way or the other. I was obsessed with making as much cash as I could. We would meet mid-week to count the profits and every week I was way ahead of the rest of the crew in sales. I was getting irritated; they weren't sharing the hunger I had. This was no game, this was real life and if I got caught doing what I was doing I'd be doing time fosho. Before things got heavy, we held a meeting and Devious decided the crew should split ways.

After being involved in so many violent altercations and getting caught out hustling, my employer: Prospect, decided that it was necessary for me to get proper security training ASAP, so they enrolled me in a security course. The tip of the iceberg was a night I'd worked at Bobble. Two dudes I'd refused entry to, said something offensive and called the club 'a fucken dump'. I was working on the door alone, but my mate Luke was visiting at the time. I completely lost the plot, handed Luke my radio and left him standing on the door to stop people coming in and started giving those two cunts a fucken hiding down the street.

The manager ran out of the club, screaming, "Benny, get back inside, who the fuck is this on the door holding our radio?" I said, "Mate, they called the club a fucken dump." The manager said, "Who gives a shit, you should never leave the door abandoned". He was completely right, besides the place *was* a fucken dump! I was moved on from Bobble for a while, but for some fucken unfortunate reason, before too long they wanted me back!

I enjoyed the security training. I passed the first few parts of the course with ease and that was all I needed to become a fully licensed security guard, but I decided to stay on and do some more advanced courses. All through the training I still worked in the clubs during the night, so I was taking louee to help stay awake during the day. When the course finished, I'd have a short break, then head straight back to work again.

I THOUGHT I WAS SUPERMAN

No one could ever beat me in the street. I was too strong. Too sharp. Too quick. One of the security instructors got me good one night, when we were on training. He'd also trained with Colt Jones. All that crew knew how to fight. We were practicing simulated drills where we were wearing fake guns and utility belts and we had to patrol the building. The instructor would act drunk or do all types of crazy shit. The course was run late at night because he wanted us to feel what it was like in a real-life security setting, when you sit around all day then suddenly unexpected incidents go down. When it was my turn, he made out that he was drunk and asleep on the floor. He wouldn't move, when I asked him to. As I was Superman, I thought I should pick him up and carry him out of the place. Apart from the fact he was over 300 lbs, he was testing me and had other intentions. He grabbed onto my firearm right away, got it out of the holster and went 'Bam, bam, bam! You're all dead ...' It was an awful feeling ... It was only training, but I had fucked up big time. I should have simply used my radio to call for backup or called the cops as they have higher powers of arrest than security guards in Australia, a policy I was gonna have to learn to accept. It was the wrong decision, had it been real life, I would have got us all killed. I was disappointed in myself, but it was a valuable lesson ... And I have never forgotten it!

The last test I had to complete was to get my firearms licence, which would have meant more opportunities for highly paid work, such as being an armed bodyguard or armoured guard. This test involved a legal exam, which I passed easily and then a practical test, where you shoot targets at the shooting gallery. We got to practice with a Glock 9mm and .38 Smith and Wesson. I worked in a club the night before the test, so I went into the shooting gallery without sleep. My practice shoot groupings with the .38 the instructor gave me were not up to scratch. He said, "You shot two grannies ..." which meant I missed the target twice, and potentially could have shot two old ladies standing behind the target in a real-life situation. "You'll have to sit the final test out." I walked away disappointed, but I'd definitely learnt something from security training; I wasn't Superman. 'Be humble, violence is a last resort, use your brain and your words.' Oma's words of wisdom. Selah.

PULP FRICTION

There were some strange things that used to go down working as a bouncer and with all the heavy-duty shit going on around us it was good to be able to kick back and have a laugh with the crew on the odd occasion, if only to ease the tension. There was a serious war going on with rival crews which the media referred to as the 'Melbourne Gangland Killings', some of the gangsters involved were friends, associates or enemies of people I knocked about with. You always had to be on your guard when involved with those circles. Drug use was at an all-time high in Melbourne. Leading up to the new millennium there was also an underlining sentiment among my mates that the world was going to end due to the Y2K bug conspiracy theories that were going around at the time, I felt this really kicked things off. Then when September 11 went down things got worse, people were in fear that they could be attacked at any time. Everyone thought they were self-medicating. In reality we were just fuelling our paranoia, insomnia and declining mental health. Things got real weird and twisted.

I'd now been in the security game a little while and I got some work as a supposedly un-armed private bodyguard for a strangely named couple. An Israeli cosmetic surgeon Tolly, and his new wife, Dolly. These people were completely nuts. They were convinced that some low-level criminals and Tolly's ex-wife were trying to kill them and stand over them for money and drugs. Tolly's family owned a big law firm, so he regarded himself as a potential target for extortionists or standovers.

When I arrived at their Toorak mansion, I was immediately greeted by Dolly. "Oh, Benny we're glad it's you," she said. I had no idea I'd be body-guarding these guys. They were regulars at a club I worked at and were strange but nice people, coz they'd often bring food and drinks for the security crew. Dolly led me straight into the front room where the video surveillance camera system was set up. She said, "What would you like? The SLR, shotgun or the crossbow?" I was thinking, wait a minute, what's going on here? Then Dolly said, "Let's take you on a tour of the house. Come on Tolly." It was like an episode of Playschool on the ABC channel except the hosts were fucken crazy and packing some serious heat!

Tolly looked scared but he was head over heels in love with Dolly. Apparently, she'd been one of his patients and he had left his ex-wife for her. I noticed skulls with love hearts painted on the walls with craft paint all around the house. We got up to Tolly's daughter's room. Thankfully, she wasn't there coz that's where they stashed the crossbow. Dolly explained it was strategically placed there coz it was the room closest to the staircase and I could shoot a hitman if he was running up the stairs to get them. Hmmmm. Next, we went to their bedroom, where there was a loaded double barrel shotgun under their bed. I decided to hold onto this while I continued my tour with them, coz they were starting to freak me out.

We entered their walk-in robe and Tolly reached into a box up on a shelf. It was the SLR Light Machine gun. This thing was a beauty, but I advised them to leave it in a good hiding place coz semi-automatic weapons in Australia are highly illegal. Dolly then said, "There's just one more thing I want to show you." They led me down to the basement garage and Dolly said, "Now, here's a roll of carpet we've conveniently placed here, so we can roll up the body and place it in the back of the SUV before we find a place to bury them." By this time I'd lost all the entertainment value I was getting out of the conversation. "Dolly," I said, "If anyone suspicious even gets close to your house, I'm calling the Five-O. These weapons here are a last resort." The reality is, in Australian law, even if an intruder breaks into your home, you can't shoot them coz you'll get done for murder, you're suppose to just apprehend them or call the bacon in blue.

I sat in the front room and played around with the shotgun whilst I watched the video surveillance footage with Dolly. She kept playing back a scene from the previous weekend, over and over again. "Wow did you see that?" She asked, "It was a trace from a bullet, someone shot at us I felt the wind brush past my ear." Realistically, it could have been anything, but I agreed that it certainly looked that way. After all, their paranoia is what had gotten me the job in the first place, at a better pay rate than normal too. Ironically, they took me out to eat with them at the first restaurant I had worked at and some of the staff recognised me. I kept things low key and told them I was just there to have dinner with my friends.

When we got home, we watched telly together, but they insisted it was strictly the Crime and Investigation Network only. I remember watching a show on John Gotti's hitman 'The Iceman', Richard Kuklinski. I slept in a spare room with the crossbow and shotgun close by and headed home the next morning. I called the office and said, "Don't send me back to that place, they are outta their fucken minds!"

A little while later I got asked to do a private bodyguard gig as a one off in Launceston, Tasmania. The guy I worked for, Ron, a Canadian dude, who was involved in the adult entertainment industry and a small-time porn star. He also organised swingers parties with catering. He was dating a stripper. Come to think about it, Ron probably deserved a reality TV show, what do ya reckon? Anyway, Ron had only recently branched out into the swinger party scene in Tassie. He told me he had run many successful swinger events in Melbourne. Only thing was, there was another dude that already had the lion's share of the market in Tasmania, in particular, Launceston where Ron would be holding the next event. The dude got a hold of his phone number and he began harassing him over the phone and via email. He made some serious death threats. So Ron hired me as his bodyguard.

It was my first time in Tassie and as soon as I arrived at the "Lonny" airport from Melbourne, I knew something wasn't right. The locals called us "Mainlanders", meaning that we were from the Australian mainland as opposed to the island of Tasmania. This job was gonna be different alright. I headed straight to the hotel room where the party was planned to take place coz Ron wanted to set things up. I took this opportunity to walk around and do a perimeter check and conduct a risk assessment. I was basically trying to look like I was doing some kind of work coz I seriously didn't think that somebody was going to do over a swinger's party.

Next, we headed to our room at the hotel, which was next to a bar called the Cougar Saloon. Ron bought us dinner and a whole lot of drinks and this got me rocking on the dance floor with a strange crowd that looked either too young or too old to be there. Ron told me that most people in their 20s got the hell outta Lonny and headed to the mainland to find work. One lady started coming onto me pretty strong and before I knew it somehow, I ended up back at her place. Before I left, I said, "Ron, call me if anything goes down." In essence, I abandoned my client in a pub, picked up a local lady, who took me back to her house to hit it in her room, while her son smoked billies in the lounge room with 15 of his mates.

I got back to our room in the morning and was happy to find that Ron had survived the night completely unscathed and without a sign of 'The Lonny Swinger Party Death Threat Bloke'. After a late breakfast Ron needed to get groceries coz he had to cook up a storm of hors d'oeuvres for his crowd of swinger enthusiasts. He was adamant he needed me by his side in the supermarket, just in case something went down and basically give him a hand carrying the groceries. It was at this point I saw what can only be described as a pure-bred Tassie stoner bagging up some broccoli in the veg section of the supermarket and realised I'd need some choof to get through the long night ahead. So, I walked straight up to him and said, "How ya going mate? Can you get choof?" "Fucken oath cunt, yeh no fucken worries," he said. It was $80 for a quarter ounce and I had only a day to smoke it all before I flew back to the mainland, aka civilisation.

Later that night, as the swinger party began, I took up a post in the hire car parked near the front entry of the hotel where the event was set to occur. I immediately kicked back and started blazing up joint after joint thinking how cruisy this gig was. Suddenly, a suspicious vehicle pulled up out the front of the hotel. Ron had given me a list of his guests, how they would be arriving, and the license plate numbers of their cars. This vehicle was not on the list and didn't look right at all. I switched on the high beams of the car and the suspicious vehicle quickly drove off. I put my foot down on the accelerator in pursuit of the vehicle, they were onto me and they quickly turned down some backstreets and shook me off their tail. But it had been a diversion. While I chased the suspicious vehicle "The Lonny Swinger Party Death Threat Bloke" had struck. The cheeky fucker had placed advertising flyers for his next organised swingers party on the windscreens of Ron's guests' cars.

I removed the flyers and tore them up. Ron was very pleased and brought out several rounds of me good ole mate' Johnnie Walker and coke to the car. After midnight he came out again and said, "Benny, not enough blokes have turned up, so I'm gonna have to ask you to take care of some of these lonely ladies in there." I looked at my reflection in the rear vision mirror and said, "Duty calls." Upstairs in the hotel suite, I sat on the couch for five minutes and watched a porn movie on the box with a lady who told me she could do a better job than the actress. The rest of the night is best described as an obscure borderline traumatising experience, which I survived and as far as anyone knows without a trace of PTSD or for that matter the other similar acronym with less letters. All I know is that it was an interesting and memorable weekend's work, but at the end of the day swingers parties ain't really my thing and Kevin Costner ain't got nothing on me!

GANGS OF BURN CITY

I used to run into a lot of childhood friends, working at clubs. Old friends from school, gyms and the neighbourhoods I'd lived in. Some of these people treated you differently. I tried my best to be the same person I always was, but you had to know when to draw the line, coz they would try and use the fact they knew you to their advantage sometimes. It was fucken draining if you didn't know them too well, their intentions were always obvious, they showed their cards. It made me think, when was the last time that person called you up to hang out when you weren't standing on the door of a club? Then those people had friends too and they'd try and take advantage of the fact you went to school with a friend of a friend and stuff like that it. With the genuine people and my genuine friends, we were always just happy to see each other and naturally I'd look after them with things like free entry, or getting in at times when we were close to capacity, or if they were half cut. People would recognise me wherever I went. It was cool when you wanted to head out to other clubs, coz not only was I getting looked after by the other bouncers, owners or managers, but regular people would be buying you drinks and giving you all kinds of stuff and rack all the time. I never had to reach into my pockets on a night out.

There were some nights I'd go to a club completely broke and leave flying with a pocket full of cash, bags galore and maybe even a nice lady or two. People would ask me to hook them up, and I'd just point them in the right direction and make a cut. I'd get free meals at restaurants. Anything I wanted from Footlocker and other stores like that, free of charge. I even had a dude give me a brand-new monkey bike in the box, delivered by courier express to my home, just so we would let him in the club without any hassles. While we were working people would bring us pizza and burgers, even protein bars and fresh juices.

Most of the time being recognised got on my nerves. Like being in the supermarket and people coming up to you saying, "Excuse me do you work at that club?" Me being caught off guard saying, "Yeh." Then they might say, "Is it ok if I come down on the weekend with my friends?" I'd be like, "Stop breaking my balls, I'm doing my fucken groceries man, go on the website and register on the guest list." Sometimes it was best to walk off and not say anything at all.

There was a club I worked at where the DJs would mix in hip hop, funk, techno and house music. They had live acts, mostly electro or hip hop music in the front room on certain nights. Black Eye Peas once graced the stage while I was on shift there, it was surreal; I got the privilege of meeting and chillin' with Will.I.Am. We spoke about hip hop and I told him I also rapped. He was very supportive and suggested I come along to the festival they were playing at the next day called The Big Day Out. He mentioned he'd hook me up a backstage pass if I could make it. They were still more or less underground in Australia back then, but blew up to the mainstream after Fergie joined them. It sounded like a great idea, but I'd been hooked up to do security work at the same festival the next day. When I signed on early that morning, I thought it would be easy to get across and catch up with Will.I.Am but I got stuck working at a different stage, with a couple local hip hop DJs, which was alright I suppose; but chillin' with Will again just wasn't meant to be.

Locally the hip hop scene was growing and I'd often hang out at Obese Records which was a big part of the movement. The owner Shaz was a childhood mate from the crew EMB. During those days he was kicking it with a heavy from the Westside who was like Melbourne's biggest gangster in more ways than one, a big fan of fried chicken, and was in the news almost every day! Shaz also had some up and coming Aussie rappers working at that store like Brad Strut, Pegz and a producer named Jase Beathedz. I grew tight with them all and it was great to see positive things happening for local hip hop. But at that stage I guess I was more occupied on 'tryna get that paper', so our conversations would revolve around 'the next big hustle', rather than how things were going with my rapping.

As Scarface called it, 'yayo' started to be the preferred drug of choice. Far more prestigious and way more expensive than other substances, which also meant way more profit. Most of my clientele were loaded, so I wasn't dealing with street junkies so to speak, but cashed up junkies more or less and other hustlers too. I'd get it by the ounce and wouldn't cut it. For a while I stuck with the 'Tony Montana' motto 'You fuck with me! You Fucken with the Best!' I had fewer customers, fewer transactions, less risk and most importantly more dinero. But let's not falsely discriminate here 'Cocaine is a Helluva Drug', and addiction does not discriminate.

THE GERMAN SCOTTISH IRISH AFRICAN MAN

Pieces were often carried and traded amongst my associates, with all the murders going on in the background, there was good reason to be extra cautious. Between the bouncer crew we use to share around a small gat, when we were working at the recoveries and some other clubs. It was a .22 and coz I was the head bouncer during my shift and always on the door, it would be handed to me, and I'd stash it under my belt. I tested it out a few times by firing it in the back alley. I'd sometimes show it off to certain chicks I'd mess around with that would think its gangsta and get turned on by it and want to hook up in the club. We had our spots, like the green room. This spot was tight as they had acts on regularly and it was decked out with couches and mirrors. It was like a pimp's office to me back then. Flashen' that roscoe to the nightclub groupie chicks was the most work that gat ever got, I was doing all the shooting from the hips!

One time I headed to the casino after work with the crew. We had been taking all kinds of shit, weed, racking up, flipping pills plus drinking before we got there. We had a good racket going at the time where all the known dealers in the clubs would need to pay us 'rent money' to sell their shit in the club. We'd accept cash or drugs; basically the rule of 10%, as it was known.

We got some more drinks at the bowling alley and bumped into some strippers from the club. We then ran into our mates the infamous Tongan Twins, and a Serbian dude that would frequently go to the recovery joints named Zoran. He was involved in something, but I never did business with him or asked any questions. He was good mates with Joey who I hung out with a couple times briefly. I remembered Joey clearly coz he had asked me to hook him up with some goey in the past, that was not long after he'd gotten out from jail for murder. Goey for Joey, it wasn't hard to remember! From what I could tell he was always high and was shot dead not long after this period in time, two men were charged with the murder. On that night Zoran had also just gotten out of jail after a brief stint. What I didn't realise was that he was being watched. We decided we were all gonna head back to a mate's pad not far from Southbank to party and try and get some action from the ladies we were with. The Tongan Twin, wish I could tell you which Twin it was, but I had no fucken idea – those cunts were identical – was carrying a nice 9mm Glock, which he'd shown me in the bowling alley. I was carrying that little piss weak .22.

Before we left the cas and got in Zoran's car to drive to my mate's place, I gave the .22 to my mate coz he asked for it. He must have caught up on a vibe that Zoran was being watched and decided to walk. When we sat in the car the Tongan Twin pulled out his 9mm and stashed it under the seat. I remember this clearly coz he was sitting in the front and I was sitting in the back seat behind him. For a brief moment when I saw him draw out his piece and being high out of my mind, I was like, WTF is this cunt playing at? Is this some kinda fucken standover? But that wasn't the case at all, what he did was smart, he just stashed it real good. Just as Zoran started the engine, there was a tap on his window and an undercover BLT flashed his badge and made sure he showed us he was carrying a .38 Smith and Wesson on his belt. He asked us to get out of the vehicle while his partner came around to our side and directed us out of the car.

He then ID'd and patted us down for drugs and weapons. Luckily none of us had anything on us. We'd given everything to my mate, but we were sweating though, coz the 9mm was stashed under the seat. The coppers searched the interior and the boot of the car for five minutes. They must have been tired or something coz by this point it was 7 am on a Monday morning, when the rest of the city's inhabitants were getting ready for their normal jobs. They didn't find the piece or anything else, and we were free to go. Zoran and the Tongan Twin were fucken rattled and decided to leave. The rest of us went back to my mate's place to party, with the girls.

ALL I DO IS JUST DRINK, AND I'M CUTTIN'
THROUGH THE LINES LIKE A VIP

B.O.P, *The Impeccable Word* (2017)

2001: A Melbourne Odyssey

eptember 11 2001, about 11 pm, I was waiting in my car in the middle of a drug deal with a fucken idiot named Slovenian Casper the Friendly Fuckwit and one of his mates. A news flash suddenly came up on the radio, that at approximately 8.46 am a plane had hit the world trade centre in New York. It was like I was listening to *War of the Worlds*. The idiots in my car cheered, "Yes, World War 3 is about to start ... Fuck America!" I just looked at them and glared thinking just hurry up and get this deal done and get the fuck outta my car. I didn't know what to think about what had just happened in New York; I just knew that something definitely wasn't right.

Something wasn't right with the deal either, Casper was stalling. He'd promised to get me an ounce at a good price but each location we got to his contact wasn't where he was supposed to be. I had a meat cleaver in my car, which I showed him, and said to Casper, "Your mate waits in the car while you get the fucken bouba," and I gave him the money. But once again the contact wasn't there, and Casper told me his friend was waiting in the casino. I was starting to think this fuckwit was planning to do a runner with the cash, but I kept his mate close by and my meat cleaver closer.

We got to the cas and Casper wandered around the gaming floor, while I waited at a table playing blackjack. When he eventually showed his face again, I took my money back and basically told him to fuck off coz I was busy, and he'd wasted my time. I ended up blowing away the most money I'd ever lost at the Casino that night. I'd played 18 hours straight and at one point was winning big and thinking crazy shit like buying myself a yacht, but I was popping pills and the greed kicked in. I'd evaporated away all my winnings and all my hustle money into a cesspool of misery and no return. I felt shit for weeks and officially retired from gambling after that day and never looked back. Slovenian Casper the Friendly Fuckwit, had indirectly done me a favour, he'd cured my gambling addiction.

About eight months later I was working on the door at a pub in Dandenong, when who should come walking down the street but Casper. The first time I'd met this goose he was hanging around the stripper Davina who I'd gone up to Sydney with. She'd proven to be un-trustworthy bitch and this dude was just about to show me what a snake he really was. He said, "Hey Benny, do you still know anyone who wants Charlie?" Initially I said "Nah, fuck that," after all the bullshit at the casino, but my mate Slim had been asking me for an ounce nonstop all week, and I couldn't get it from any of my regular peeps ... "Can ya hook me up this time for real?" I asked "Yep, it's pure," he said. I didn't believe it was pure, it never is on the streets of Melbourne coz it comes from so far away it's way more expensive than other countries and everyone jumps on it to make better profits. I said, "My mate will contact you. If he likes it, he might buy it." I put them in contact with each other coz I couldn't be fucked dealing with the idiot again and I figured Slim would be able to suss out if Casper was talking shit or could deliver the goods.

The weekend kicked in and on Saturday night I was working on King Street when my phone started to ring. I couldn't get to the call right away coz I was working, so I looked at my phone again and noticed a text on the screen, *Can I trust ya mate?* I figured he meant Casper and responded with, *No.* But my phone kept ringing and ringing and ringing until eventually I found a quiet spot to chat with Slim. He said, "I gave ya mate the paperwork 30 minutes ago to grab that thing and he hasn't returned to the car." Right away I said, "That fucken cocksucker."

Slim and I met up after work to devise a plan. Casper had blatantly taken Slim's stacks by pretending he was collecting from the Collingwood flats, but played ghost and ran off with the bones. Slim didn't need my help finding him. He'd done a twelve-month stint inside for aggravated assault and had made some solid contacts, plus his family were connected.

A coupla nights later he called me up and said, "We've got him. I'll meet you at your place in 20 minutes." This issue wasn't really mine to deal with, but I'd introduce the two of them and I was pissed off at what Casper had done to my mate, and apart from being a snake he had been extremely disrespectful.

We drove to a Macca's carpark where we met with another car full of mates. Apparently, Casper had tried to ghost them too. They must have gotten their money back coz they were happy to hand him over to us. They popped open their boot and there he was. "Get up ya fucken cunt," Slim said as he punched him a couple times in the guts. Casper's hands had been tied. Slim slapped him across the face as he stood up and pushed him into the boot of his car and we drove off, thanking the others for their delivery.

With Casper in the boot, we quietly discussed our plan. Killing him and dumping the body couldn't happen, coz Slim would never get his money back and it was just not worth taking a life over. So we organised to take him to the house of a Greek associate who happened to also owe some rhino, kind of as a sign that if he didn't pay up this is what was/ gonna happen to him. The plan was to torture and interrogate Casper, and above all else ensure he paid what he fucken owed. Problem was when we arrived at the Greek dude's house he unexpectedly said, "My mum's home."

Slim just said, "Too bad, we need to use your backyard." It was a cold July night in Melbourne. Slim told Casper to take his clothes off. When Casper refused, he elbowed him in the face splitting his eye open and blood gushed out fast. He started to moan and groan. We told him to, "Shut the fuck up, if you wake up his mum or the neighbours, you're dead, cunt". Casper complied and got naked. Slim told the Greek malaka to grab the hose and water down the maggot. He got hit a couple more times and now had two black eyes. Slim then 'lost the plot' and decided to sadistically beat him with a broomstick; all the Greek bloke kept saying was, "Shhhhh ... Shhhh ... My mum will hear ... Shhhh."

The more Slovenian Casper groaned the more he copped it and after 45 minutes of humiliating torture, he was given a towel from the garage and told to get dressed. He was then allowed to sit in the back of the car and explain how he was going to get the money back. He started rambling some nonsense, so we dropped him off in a park and told him to get his shit together. I never saw Casper again after that, and I'm not sure if Slim ever saw his money. Which lead me to draw to the conclusion that if you believe in ghosts, never give them cash, the cunts will haunt you for the rest of your life!

For a while, Prospect moved me around to different clubs and only gave me hours on weekends. It wasn't enough money to get by without hustling and everyone was onto what I was doing. I think I worked at almost every club that they had the security contract with, after being moved on several times for being too violent. One of the clubs I was back working at was Bobble.

MOGUL OF THE WOGS

I got a phone call from Kosta one Saturday night. "Hey, where you workin'?" he asked. "Bobble," I said. At that point I hadn't seen Kosta since I'd been sacked from the strip club. At one stage we'd been working together almost every night. We had formed a close bond like a brotherhood, after all the "punch ons" with pissed assholes who groped the girls inappropriately and stuff like that. But now I was now back working at that dump of a club, Bobble. It felt like punishment, with all the trouble I'd gotten myself into. I was heavily into hustling during that time, and I was looking to extend my network further, with the right people. The higher up the food chain you got, the better the prices, and the more respect you got too. It's just the way it was back then.

"Cool, can you meet me, Pavlo and some of his crew, down at the door in 30 minutes?" I said, "Yeh no worries, text me when you arrive. I'll get you guys in." And 30 minutes later they arrived.

I couldn't remember meeting Pavlo before that night, but I'd met so many different people during that period of my life, it's hard to say. He greeted me with a kiss on each cheek. Pavlo and his crew were Romanian, and this was a common greeting amongst gangsters, particularly those who were European or Middle Eastern in Melbourne. I would get greeted this way a lot when I was working as a bouncer. It wasn't my thing, but I didn't complain, it was a sign of respect, but a handshake, fist pump or even a hug would have suited me fine. A lot of my mates were involved in crime back then and it was all over the media that there was a gangland war going on, and people were getting whacked, left right and centre. I had to keep on my toes, I couldn't risk upsetting the wrong people.

I led Pavlo and his crew through reception, so they didn't have to pay an entry fee. Then I went back to my post. On this night, I had some White Dove's on me. I'd taken two before they arrived. I was fucken flying, but I'd gotten use to the feeling by then. I was taking them so often it just felt normal. So, I told myself, why the fuck not and just like that I popped another flipper after I let them in.

I had a vibe that Kosta had brought Pavlo to the club to discuss bizzo with me and as expected, about 30 minutes later, he came down to my post on level 2 looking for me. I initially thought sweet, they're ready to have that meeting now. But something was up. I could feel it in the air, my heart started to race, and the adrenalin started to pump. "Hey Benny, Pavlo's about to smash some fucken idiot, you better do something," Kosta said. "What happened?" I asked. "The dickhead asked if he could get him some pills and Pavlo's paranoid as fuck. He thinks the guy's a Jack and wants to Bash him." "Okay, where is he? I'll kick the cunt out," I said.

After circling the club with the crew looking for this guy a few times, Pavlo eventually stopped and pointed towards a booth on Level 3, which had about eight people sitting in it, chatting amongst themselves. I walked over to the booth with him and the crew. Pavlo said, "That's the cunt." And everyone stepped back to let me do my job. "Hey buddy, you gotta go," I said. The guy stood up. He looked smashed. "I haven't done anything," he said. I said, "You've been going around askin' people for pills and you're off ya face."

The guy started to make a scene and shouted out, "That's bullshit!" I grabbed him, locked his arms behind his back and manoeuvred him towards the nearest exit, which lead down three flights of stairs to the back door. Apparently I was supposed to take this guy with eight raver-looking mates standing around him to the front entry door coz there weren't security cameras covering the back door. How the fuck was I supposed to know that the rules had changed on my first night back at that shit hole of a club? In my mind the nearest exit was the best exit coz I could imagine what Pavlo and his crew would do to those raver dudes. Plus, Pavlo was strapped.

As I led him down the staircase to the street, the guy was resisting my hold on him. He wasn't a massive dude, but he was wriggling around and wouldn't walk like I told him to, so I had to restrain him a bit more. In my mind I was thinking, "I gotta get this guy out quick." Pavlo and his crew were gonna eat him alive. If he'd just walked out and not resisted, things would have gone smoothly, but everyone including Kosta, Pavlo, his crew, a tall skinny Indian and a 400-pound Fijian bouncer named Junior followed behind me like some kinda fucken entourage. Pavlo was like a wild dog and sensed fear in the guy's face. When I took my arms off the guy to open a glass foyer door leading to the back street exit door, Pavlo got excited and went for the kill.

Boom! He hit the guy with full force, knocking him off his feet. He literally flew down about six steps and into a basement area where the manager's office was. I ran down and got the guy back on his feet and asked him if he was okay. I felt bad for the dude, but I was pissed off he hadn't just walked out like I told him, too. Pavlo and his crew were still hovering around, so I quickly opened the back door and let him out.

The other guards worked for a different security company as contractors, and they were asking me a lot of questions about what had just happened. I didn't want to rat out Pavlo and his crew, so I just said, "They're mates with the boss." It was a fucken naive thing for me to say, but at the time I thought it would keep them off my back.

Pavlo wasn't mates with my boss, but he was definitely known to him. He was one of the biggest drug dealers in Melbourne, leader of a staunch crew from the Western suburbs.

He was a heavy, a standover man and a professional debt collector. Definitely not to be fucked with, and I didn't want that kind of heat on me. Months later he would be murdered by a notorious gangland hitman in his bathroom. The body lay there for days until his mum found him half seated on the floor next to the toilet, with three bullet wounds in his head.

The tall skinny Indian guard ran straight to his security boss, who ran straight to the Bobble manager. They called me to the office and bombarded me with like a 100 questions all at once about the incident, "Why didn't you use the radio?" "Why didn't you use the front entry?" "Why didn't you get back up?" "Why this, why that ...?" I just flipped out and told them all to "Shut the fuck up!" The manager said "Right...! Sign off Benny... Security, make sure he leaves!" That was the start of a lot of trouble in my life; all the heat I was trying to avoid.

I felt like I'd been accused of committing a crime and all I was tryna to do was kick out some dude who was wasted and tryna score some fucken flippers. This shit was crazy! I signed off and headed straight to the front door, to get the fuck outta the club. I turned around and realised that one of those scumbag contractor bouncers was following me. I stopped, gave him a shove and told him to fuck off. He fell into a crowd of patrons and backed right off. I left and didn't give it much more thought, until about two weeks later when I received a call from the fucken Hungry Jacks, the lowest of the low Senior CUNT-stable Bacon Sandwich.

In the most polite and un-accusing tone he called me on my personal number and asked me to attend his station in the city, to answer some questions regarding 'An incident at Bobble'. I realised what he meant, but at the time had no idea they suspected me of committing a crime. In my mind I'd saved that dudes life that night, I'd done everything right, I had nothing to hide, apart from the fact I was hustlen' and popping pills. But this was different. I'd been to the cop shop two or three times in the past to give statements on fights involving pissed or drug fucked cunts while working security, and I guess that kinda gave me the false impression that they understood our job was tuff too. Usually, once I got my story right regarding those incidents, things went away. This time it wasn't the case.

Bacon Sandwich was a dog and a stupid one too. The bitch had a hard on for me that's for sure. After I hung up the phone, I got distracted and completely forgot about meeting up with the copper. I thought it was just a routine thing and I wasn't concerned at all, couldn't give a flying fuck TBH. I went about my normal routine of hustling, working, training and partying. Two weeks later on a Monday morning after a big night out at Viper Room I heard a loud knock on the door. I'd been fooling around with a coupla chicks and thought it might be some kinda booty call; I heard, "Open up it's the police." I thought, oh man it's a fucken raid, but luckily it was the end of the weekend and I was out of stock, so they could have searched all they wanted if they had a warrant.

I opened the door to hear, "Benjamin you're under the arrest for the assault of Blah, Blah, Blah...." They were in plain clothes, wearing shirt and suit pants coz they were detective pigs. They handcuffed me and took me for a ride to HQ. I never saw that lady again.

Apparently, the wasted dude at Bobble had suffered a broken jaw after the incident and spent a week in hospital and missed a month of work coz of his injuries. He was just after compensation, so he'd pushed to get charges laid. And coz I had a number around my neck, I was an easy target.

Out of ignorance, and to a certain degree arrogance I suppose, I answered all the jacks' fucken questions. They recorded on an almost antique looking device from the early 80s. By that stage of my life, I'd been through the interview process many times, but my underlining attitude was that this whole thing is bloody ridiculous. I was just doing my job and when they asked me about the identity of the bloke that threw the punch, I stated I had no idea who he was. In reality that wasn't too far from the truth. Pavlo was by no accounts a close mate of mine. I knew he was heavy but not any more details than that unless I went and fished more information out of Kosta. But why the fuck would I do that? I wasn't a dog. Later I learnt it was always better to answer the jack's interviews with 'No comment' and let your lawyer handle things! I just said a whole lot of jibba jabba on the tape and it all fucken backfired. I should have learnt from my bullshit juvenile 'hottie' trial years back; pretending to be a dumb cunt plays right into the jacks setting an easy victim trap!

The jacks caught on pretty quick I was hiding something and about a month later they found out where I was working on a Saturday night and hand delivered a summons to appear in court. The assholes hit me with six serious assault charges. I looked Bacon Sandwich in the eye and said, "But I never hit the bloke?" he coldly said, "Well tell us who did, and you might get off." Fuck that I thought, I didn't trust this prick one bit, he was a different breed a Senior CUNT-stable alright!

I met up with Kosta and told him what had happened. He said, "I'll speak to Pavlo about it." The message that came back to me was, "Pavlo said he's proud of you and to show his gratitude for not lagging on him, he'll pay for the court costs." That all sounded well and good, but how was that supposed to happen? Plus, I'd be forever indebted to this guy and he'd shown his true colours. He'd hit a guy for no good reason and left me in deep shit. I didn't trust it for a minute. If he came forward and gave me paper for my legal fees, then great, so be it, but I was wise enough to know not to expect it. I was also pissed off with Kosta for bringing him to the club in the first place. My life was spiralling out of control. I felt like I was red hot. I was gonna have to be a helluva lot smarter and get my shit together!

YOU GOTTA STIR THE SAUCE

Could I possibly put all the violence and hustling behind me and just move on? The Obese crew seemed to be going well, their rappers were breaking through on Australian radio, but it felt like I'd gotten real heavy and couldn't escape the violence. Shaz and me were on the same page, problem was he'd recently been raided by the pigs and was facing the pen. I felt my lyrics which reflected my life, were a little too 'gangster' in comparison to what was breaking through at the time, but I wasn't about to give up. I

2001: A Melbourne Odyssey

needed to kick my bad habits and get fucken serious about it!

After a crazy couple of years, it was time to pull my head in. I decided to cut down on all the drugs I was taking, and I started to get some rest. It was like my body was catching up on all the sleep I'd missed over the past few years. Sometimes I'd crash out for up to 15 hours straight, it was insane. An Italian American chick, Mother Teresa, I'd been seeing, gave me a book called 'The easy way to stop smoking' and it worked a charm. I quit cigarettes completely after reading just three chapters. She moved into my apartment with me for about 6 months and she seemed to take great pleasure in taking goofy photos, playing board games, Sony playstation and watching DVDs, which made me feel like I was a kid on school holidays hanging out with my cousins. It definitely took away my gangster edge, but just behind closed doors.

Teresa was working as a stripper and it used to do my head in, so I guess I retaliated against my feelings and I wasn't committed to our relationship. Think about it. Anyone, and I mean anyone, could just walk in off the street give my girl $50 and she would get completely naked for them, and who really knows what else she would do. It's tuff, no matter how serious or not you are about your girl. You gotta be the kinda bloke who simply doesn't give a fuck and remember that you're the one who gets to take her home each night, but that wasn't me. I was still young and realistically not mature enough for anything too serious.

At the same time I was working on being smarter and less ambitious with my aspirations to become a big-time gangster. I'd had some close calls, lost out on some deals and I also had the court case looming, with six serious assault charges against me. I was pretty sure I was being watched by the jacks. I'd regularly see the same taxi with the same number plates parked in front of my apartment and following me around when I left home. Either I was under surveillance, or I was extremely paranoid from all the drugs I'd taken over those years. I felt like Henry from *Goodfellas* when he thinks the helicopters are following him around. Well, it didn't end too well for Henry, so I decided it was best to keep tryna work regular jobs and less bouncing work.

Teresa was persistent with me cleaning up my act and suggested that I should look in the back pages of the newspaper for different kinds of jobs. She'd say, "Here you go, look at that security job, give them a call." And I did. It ended up doing a door-to-door sales job, selling home security alarm systems. I was initially thinking no way do I want to do that, but the boss seemed to like me due to my security guard experience and promised within weeks I'd be making $1500 a week, which was real good money back then.

A couple of weeks before this job there was a similar gig selling mobile phones door-to-door but I got kicked out of the training course for falling asleep. Again, they promised over $1000 per week but it just didn't ring true, no pun intended. So, I rubbed my sleepy eyes and told the instructor to stick his job up his ass that time: "Why don't ya try sticking this fucken phone up your ass and see if it fits." Scarface's voice ran through my head. Back then they were small enough to fit too, unlike a modern smart phone. Daaamnnn!

Anyway, the Alarm business gave me a uniform and for the

first few days I was in training, which entailed walking the streets of Ashwood, where I'd lived with Mum as a kid, and knocking on doors with an older Queenslander who was good at his job and made some sales. I was given a trainees cut by the boss. Parts of Ashwood used to be housing commission zones, but over time people had bought and sold their houses meaning that some of the houses were now known as ex-housing commission. So, I guess the boss figured it was the right neighbourhood to sell home alarm systems.

After a few days on the job the boss said, "On Saturday I'm driving everyone up to Shepparton, it's easy to sell alarms there, you'll make good money. I reckon you're ready to try and sell some on your own. So, can you come up on the drive with us?" I said, "Yeh okay...I was born in Shepparton, I've never been back there, coz my mum moved to Melbourne not long after I was born. I don't really know much about the place. Have they got a lot of crime there?" The boss said, "There's a bit of a ruff element to it, but it's not too bad, they just don't have alarms." I said, "Ok cool".

Three of us hit the road with the boss. I was the youngest by at least 20 years, but I did manage to sell an alarm system to a family. I really didn't like the job at all. Unexpectedly invading people's homes and trying to convince them they needed something they probably didn't want or need. That day, I made my mind up the job wasn't for me, but the boss was happy and, on the drive, back to Melbourne he bought a slab of XXXX beer coz of the Queenslanders we had working with us. He let one of the other guys drive who wasn't drinking and we kicked back and had a couple of beers each on the drive home.

The drive back to Melbourne went faster than the journey out of Melbourne. Before I knew it, we were driving through the outskirts of the city through an industrial suburb. It must have been about 6 pm coz it had only just turned dark. Then out of nowhere, the boss yelled out, "OH FUCK!" I looked up and saw what I initially thought was a kangaroo's body flipping through the air tumbling down the road towards our car. Our driver slammed on the brakes and stopped the vehicle quickly before we hit the carcass. I immediately thought, fuck me, lucky the driver wasn't drinking.

We all got out of the car. It wasn't a kangaroo. It was a person. A man to be exact. And it was a horrific scene. Fragments of his brain, skull, hair and blood, were scattered all over the road. His body was twitching. Someone grabbed a blanket from the boot, and I threw it over the body. The 4WD drive in front of us had clipped him with its mirror at a speed of about 80 kph. The occupants of the 4WD were a couple in their mid-40s. Just as the blanket landed on the man, the couple came running out of their car screaming, obviously deeply traumatised. There was a caravan park right across the road from the scene of the accident, and we assumed he'd walked across from there to go to the shops across the road. Maybe he was drunk, but either way he misjudged the distance between him and the vehicle and the rest, including him, was history.

We were all interviewed by the jacks as witnesses. His death briefly made the TV news. At the time, I remember feeling like I'd just seen an animal killed and not a human, but the truth is after so many years I've never been able to forget the graphic details. I never went back to selling security alarms again and just stuck with being a bouncer. The boss called me to see if I was okay and totally understood my decision. He said he was more shaken up than me and thought I handled the situation very well at the time. I still find it spooky that the first time in my life that I'd gone back to my birthplace, I'd witnessed a life taken right before my eyes. I've never been back to Shepparton since and I don't plan to any time soon.

GYM WARS

haz ended up coping two year's in the nick, it was a fair whack. He'd been dogged and there was no doubt the pigs pocketed whatever they could and paid themselves bonuses. We had minor issue with some bad bizzo; but he did everything he could to make sure we were square before he went inside, and I had a lot of respect for him for doing so. Unfortunately, he needed to sell the record store at a fire sale price, to finance his legal cost, so he turned to his staff. Pegz stepped up, embraced his purchase and turned Obese Records into a multi-million-dollar business. It became the first label to sign one of the most successful Australian hip hop acts to date, Hilltop Hoods.

I was getting stronger and had put on a lot of solid muscle, by lifting heavy weights and eating well. There were times in clubs where fights would break out and I'd drag two blokes out at once. I'd still hit pads with Rock when he was at the gym, but boxing wasn't a priority to me anymore. However, at the Underworld they'd built a new section specifically designed for MMA and I decided to give that a crack for awhile. It was a dope challenge mixing things up and I was getting a kick outta sparring some quality fighters, which was very handy for all the violent altercations I was getting into at work!

I was still on King Street on weekends, and would work at the pub in Dandenong during the week. Meanwhile, Teresa was making ridiculously good money stripping; she was one of the best-looking birds in the joint. Still, it made me wonder, what she was doing to get paid so much? She would say stuff like, "I'm just playing them," or "You got to know how to work it!"

Even though she was killing it on the dance pole, there were days when Teresa just wasn't herself and she'd be completely down in the dumps. It was like her moods were extremely high or extremely low. This wasn't so noticeable when we were both partying hard, but when we had slowed down on all that shit, I started to think that her behaviour was manic. She actually reminded me of Saving Grace sometimes, coz they both had deep emotional trauma inside of them that I just couldn't fully understand. They were looking for a saviour, not by fighting for them, by loving them....I just didn't see it. I always thought I was the one who needed the saving and the loving, due to my feelings of non-acceptance and my violent behaviour....I was caught up in my own struggles and not ready to give them my heart. But, I felt for what ever it was that Teresa was going through and wanted to support her the best I could. She came along to some of my family functions, and got to know my close mates. Things were still changing for the better and I felt an edge of normality slide into my life, but I still had the court case looming and I had no idea what lay ahead.

THE JAW BREAK REDEMPTION

One Wednesday arvo, I bumped into Kosta who was hanging out with one of the Tongan Twins, again I had no fucken idea which one it was, at the gym one day. I didn't have any time for people who would try and prove they were heavy, especially in the gyms, coz you only had to watch me workout to find out I could handle myself. I had nothing to prove. When I saw Kosta and the Twin hanging out my gut instinct told me it could only lead to trouble. I was still pissed off with Kosta for bringing Pavlo to the club that night and I hadn't spoken to him for a few months. Kosta thought that coz he was with the Twin, I should show him more respect, but I just looked straight through him and kept walking. I could tell they were off their fucken heads. They were smoking crack together regularly and although I wasn't officially in the fight game anymore, when I worked out in the gym I was there to train hard, not to play gangster and fuck around. Kosta came running after me saying, "What's your fucken problem?" The Twin, which ever fucken one it was, no doubt had his 9mm Glock on him, was standing behind him. I gave Kosta a cold stare and said, "What the fuck you want me to say after all this shit I've been going through?"

Surprisingly, Kosta immediately changed his demeanour and became humble. He said he understood; he apologised, and he kept it between us, leaving The Twin out of it. Kosta promised he would come to court with me as a witness, to explain what had happened that night and we were all good, or so I thought.

Shortly after that day, Kosta rang and gave me the 411. Pavlo was dead. I decided to adjourn the court case to work out my new legal strategy. Just like a set of steak knives on an infomercial – 'But wait there's more' – right when I finally thought I had this fucked-up situation all worked out, I was thrown by another bizarre turn of events. Kosta and a coked-up Tongan Twin and his girlfriend were 'on the pipe' one night, while watching a TV show about a woman who sleeps with her boyfriend's best friend. The Twin completely lost it and in a state of drug fuelled rage and psychosis pulled out his 9mm and shot Kosta three times and his girlfriend once. Both Kosta and the girlfriend were lucky to survive. The shooting happened on a Friday night, three days before my new hearing was scheduled. My main witness, Kosta, was now in ICU and we needed to adjourn the court case again. I was living my own private *Groundhog Day* in hell.

So I put my head down and continued working. The crew on King Street grew close, including the venue staff and the manager of the club, who'd give me access to an open bar after work. This led to many loose Sunday morning drinking sessions, with the crew. It was a good opportunity to bust my rhymes. I would rap about the shit we had gone through the night before, or freestyle if it was someone's birthday, and stuff like that. It was good bonding time and a great distraction for me.

I was growing more anxious with my court case coming up and I'd run out of reasons to keep adjourning. Kosta had now recovered from his gunshot wounds and, as he promised, was committed to coming along to court. He was lucky to be alive coz one bullet had narrowly missed his heart and another narrowly missed his spine. With Pavlo gone, and Kosta on my side committed as my witness, I was convinced the court would understand that this has all been a massive mistake. I didn't assault the victim and justice will no doubt prevail!

Someone introduced me to a young lawyer at the pub in Dandenong who met with me several times while I was on shift, and we ran through our strategy for the court hearing. He said he'd do my case pro-bono, so I called off my previous lawyer coz I thought the new lawyer had it under control. My thoughts were that the trial would just be a trivial matter, it'd be over quick, and I'd go back and work my security shift at 6 pm when it was all done. But of course, things didn't go as planned ...

On the Friday night before the court case the young lawyer called me and said, "Benny, I have some bad news, I'm unable to represent you on Monday. I just realised I'm not licensed to practice law in the state of Victoria!" I'm not sure if what he told me was true. I never saw or heard from the guy again. I'm guessing he was full of shit from the day I first met him. Surely, he would have known if he could represent me and at least told me before it was too late for me to hire someone else. He also mentioned to just show up at court on Monday and let them know you are Indigenous, as they have lawyers at the court that can represent you for free. I said, "I'm part black but I'm not entirely sure if I'm Indigenous or not" The lawyer said,

"It doesn't matter, just tell them you're story, they won't know the difference." Seriously, I thought, what a fucken wanker! He totally screwed me over.

That same night, Tanya a female duty manager who was ironically Indigenous Australian, decided to hold a big housewarming party at her house in Narre Warren. She'd recently divorced from her husband, who originally came from a remote island in the Philippines. Inside her house she'd kept a totem pole her husband had purchased from his hometown where it was common to practice the ancient Filipino traditions and the belief that everything contains an essence or spirit including objects. The totem pole was said to contain the spirit of a Mumu (a ghost or evil spirit).

My Punjabi workmate and me organised to finish work early and got some other guards to work the later shift at the pub. Tanya was a big weed smoker, so there was plenty of skunk floating around the party. After a few bongs, my workmate decided to practice his kung fu moves on me like he'd seen in the *Matrix* movies which were popular at the time. He was starting to piss me off a little bit, so I let go with a quick front kick. It connected well and he literally became airborne and flew about three meters across the room, headfirst into the Mumu totem pole. Crack! The Mumu spilt in two. Tanya came running into the room freaking out, "Noooooo. What have you done! Oh my God, what have you done?" She then grabbed the biggest part of the broken totem pole and swung it like a bat into the back of my workmate's head, dropping him to the ground. I jumped in and apologised but she was still mad at my mate for starting the fight in the first place. I helped him back to his feet and into his car to sleep it off. My mate wasn't in a good way and I think he was a little concussed. I decided to leave the party too. As I was leaving, Tanya shouted out, "Wait! Wait! You don't understand! The reason I wigged out was not coz you broke the statue. I bought an identical replica just in case it ever got broken and my ex won't know the difference. The reason I reacted that way is coz you've now released a curse. There was the spirit of an evil Mumu inside the statue." I was like, "Ahhhhh okay" and got the hell outta there.

The next night I was back working the door at the club on King Street. Before the night got busy a fight broke out right in front of me. I grabbed the two guys fighting in headlocks, one on each side, and started to drag them out of the club, when 'BOOM' what the fuck? I tripped over a small drinks table, which I swear wasn't there a second ago. I still had a hold of the dudes, but I strained my calf muscle, so I was kind of hopping and dragging these guys out at the same time until I got to the exit door. I finished my shift taking it real easy, just in one spot but limping around the whole night. Mumu 1, Benny 0.

I arrived at court on Monday morning limping. The first thing I did was ask to speak to an Indigenous lawyer. I was sent to an office and I spoke with some man in a suit. He asked, "Are you Aboriginal?" I said, "Yes, my Great Grandmother was black." He said, "I see, but she's not Aboriginal?" I said, "I'm not exactly sure where she's from, my family mentioned she was Islander so maybe she was a Torres Strait Islander or South Sea Islander?" The man said, "If you're Aboriginal, why didn't you mention it when the police asked you if you were an Aboriginal or Torres Strait Islander?" I said "Coz I didn't know what to say. I'm part black, but not sure if we are also indigenous." He said, "Well if you're not sure, I can't appoint a lawyer to you." I was just trying to be honest. I can't lie about who I am, but I told him what I knew at the time. The reality is that I probably should have just said I was Indigenous, and everything would have taken care of itself, but morally I was opposed to such a contradictory system, I just couldn't bring myself to give into it. I just wanted to be accepted for who I am. I was simply in need of a lawyer and the system took no pity on me, I felt it discriminated against me. I'm sure all black people in white man nations have felt discrimination on countless levels. I knew for a fact my ancestors had felt that pain, literally to the point where they were beaten up for asking too many questions. If that didn't happen to my Nana Mary, maybe I'd have a little more information to share with Mr. Man in the fucken suit!

The man in the suit advised me to contact legal aid instead and try to find a lawyer that could represent me, but said that coz it was last minute the chances were slim. The Judge, the Police Prosecutor and all the witnesses were ready and waiting for me. I had no choice but to run with the case. I found a barrister that said he would take my case on board, but he was shocked I'd left it so late to contact him. We delayed the case two hours while I worded him up, and we read through the police brief of evidence. When I told him the full story about Pavlo, he was convinced that as I hadn't assaulted the person, and if I was comfortable explaining the full story to the judge, all should be fine. Our assumptions were wrong!

When we finally got into the court room, I quickly realised that Detective Senior CUNT-stable Bacon Sandwich had gone to great lengths to ensure all the witnesses were prepared to say everything they could to make sure I looked guilty as hell. To make things worse, I could tell the time delay really pissed the judge off. First outta the blocks was the manager: "Benny was signed a radio and should have called me to tell me there was an ejection." "Benny was told to use the front door for ejections, coz the CCTV cameras are better quality there." "I asked Benny to sign off, he got aggressive!" Blah, blah, blah.

Then the tall skinny Indian contractor bouncer spoke: "Benny didn't call me for back up." "Benny had the guy in a headlock!" "Benny was acting strange."

Junior, the 400 lbs Fijian bouncer, was next. He was a lot vaguer but didn't do me any favours: "Benny just told me they are friends with the boss, so I thought it's all good."

The wannabe head of security contractor made things worse: "Benny didn't follow procedure."

"Benny didn't call for back up." "Benny got aggressive with me."

And finally the victim spoke: "Security lead me down a dark back entry corridor for no reason and bashed me. I suffered a broken jaw and was in hospital for a week and needed to take a month off work. I've been extremely traumatised since."

I got totally set up. I was really pissed off with the dogs that got up on the stand to save their own asses. I'd actually bumped into the victim, ironically near Bacon HQ, a few months before the trial and apologised to him in person and explained who Pavlo was and why he bashed him. He seemed like he got it then. Perhaps he was scared. I treaded very lightly, when I saw him, it was a fine line between standing over him and getting in more trouble with the cops or peacefully getting him to retract his statement. There are only two possible explanations for why I was targeted in this way. Firstly, the victim wanted financial compensation. Secondly, Bacon Sandwich saw me as an easy target, didn't like me from the moment he laid eyes on me and wanted the case closed to further progress his career. He would have advised the victim that this was the process in order to get compensation. I could smell bacon all over this one, and it was greasier than an extra bacon double cheeseburger deluxe meal on a tweaking truck drivers lap during a heat wave...Or something like that!

As promised, Kosta got up on the stand for me and gave our side of the story, which were the actual facts of what happened. Kosta also told the court Pavlo had been murdered and was a big time standover man and known to always carry hardware. Kosta then explained how he had been capped multiple times by a mate out of jealousy and he was feeling extreme discomfort while sitting in the stand. He was breathing heavy.

I was then asked to take the stand and I told my story. The truth. The barrister I hired that day didn't say too much. The judge heard me out and she wasn't impressed with me one bit. She bluntly said, "Security Guards are hired by venues to provide safety and to protect the patrons that attend the premises via the laws set by the governing body, the Victorian Private Agents Registry. They must not allow their friends to beat innocent people up while they stand aside and watch. I hereby sentence you to eight months inside a correctional facility."

My barrister requested bail but it was rejected. I was like "Huh? What she just say?"

Teresa had come along for support, so I handed her my mobile phone and said, "Call my boss and tell him I'm not coming into work tonight." I was then handcuffed by two officers and lead to the holding cells, underneath the Magistrate Courts, known as the Melbourne Custody Centre. The nickname for these cells among crims is the Yellow Submarine or the Dungeon. I was then strip searched, yeh bend over and spread em' and all that bullshit. Some of my clothes and jewellery were placed in a plastic bag, including my shoes. I'd been convicted of a crime I didn't commit. I was pissed off! But at least I now knew how The A-Team had felt. Mumu 2, Benny 0.

DUST STORM CARTER

The screws showed me a little compassion coz they realised I was a bouncer. They actually said, "Damn she was harsh on you brother, we'll get you a cell to yourself for a couple nights coz we can tell you're limping, you classify as medical." After the screws processed me, I was walked to my cell, and I crashed out almost straight away. I was woken up about 7 am the next morning with bright lights. There was no natural light coz the cells were underground, just a small window on the door and a trap door big enough to fit a tray of food through. Two screws came to the window and asked if I wanted either tea or coffee and a cigarette. I got coffee and although I hadn't smoked in months, I took the rollie. The screw struck a match and I smoked it.

About an hour later the guards came back with breakfast and my TV, which was bolted up high to the ceiling switched on automatically and played the morning news. Breakfast was another tea or coffee, Weetbix drenched in milk and sugar, two pieces of stale white bread, an apple, a plastic disposable cup for water and another rollie. Near the basin was a metal toilet without a seat and it was positioned right near the window where guards or other prisoners could watch you take a dump. My bed was a thin foam mattress, without a pillow, with a white sheet and blanket, on top of a concrete slab. I'd been too tired and drained the night before to even pay attention. I surprisingly slept well and was feeling okay.

After breakfast, the screws came back to collect the tray and asked me to make my bed and sweep out my cell. I felt like the compassion they'd shown me the night before was quickly forgotten. I was just another crim in their eyes. The others were now walking around the concrete yard and peering through into my cell with curious eyes, as if to say, why does this cunt get a cell to himself. I could read those looks like a book and I knew I couldn't take any shit from anyone. If I had to bash the first cunt that got cocky, I was prepared to. I quickly stood up tall and proud, and strutted around my cell, to show them I'm fit and not to be messed with. I then ripped into some push ups and other exercises to keep myself occupied.

After a few hours it was my time to stretch my legs and mingle. The cells on the westside had an hour in the yard, then the cells on my side, the east-side got an hour. Later in the afternoon we showered in a separate section. While we waited for our turn we all mingled, apart from the crims waiting to attend court for their appeals or committing crimes while incarcerated. The first questions I got asked by the other crims were, "How ya goin'? What ya in here for?" It wasn't that different from the prison movies I'd seen. "Assault," I said. It was so cliche my mind was telling me don't say you're 'innocent' coz they are gonna say 'we're all innocent in here mate' and start laughing like in *The Shawshank Redemption*. To change the subject I just said, "And you?"

"Road Rage" said one guy who was a meth-head looking truck driver. I didn't really need to hear his war story about smashing a carjack into someone's windscreen. Like he was working on a production line, the meth-head truck driver was asking everyone, "How about you mate?" Next guy was like "Smack," he was Filo and about my age. Next guy, "Too many speeding fines." One Islander dude a bit younger than me was there for murder. The meth head didn't ask him, everybody knew why he was there. I'd already overhead people talking about him from my cell. And the last guy just kept quiet for a bit and then said, "I was a drug mule." He was also about my age but pale and skinny, and with a distinguishing feature; he had an American accent.

The week before while working in the pub in Dandenong I'd read a small article in the newspaper that got my attention, 'American man caught attempting to smuggle 6kg of cocaine into Australia'. He was that guy. He kinda flinched when I looked at him. I said, "I read about you in the newspaper." He looked scared, but noticed my Australian accent and he seemed to become more comfortable. He said, "I got myself a drug debt with a cartel. They said they'd clear my debt if I smuggled the blanca across to Australia. They taped it to my body real tight and I couldn't breathe. I went to the bathrooms on the plane and tried to cut it loose, but I fucked up and I cut into one of the bags and it was leaking. The air hostesses grew suspicious and told the authorities." He said he thought I might have been Latino, that's why he was worried at first. He explained that he was pretty sure they'd try and set him up to be shivved, so he didn't rat on them. I just said, "First thing you should do is try and lose the American accent, coz you stand out like dogs balls in here, I knew who you were right away just from reading the paper."

The next day the routine continued, except I woke up to two full-blown junkies, pacing the yard and making a ruckus. They were from Port Phillip, aka Guantanamo Bay, which is a maximum-security prison on the outskirts of Melbourne. They must have committed another crime in there coz they were awaiting trial and thought they'd get a kick out of terrorising all the 'newbies' in the joint. I thought, okay this is it; these will be the cunts I'm gonna have to bash. But instead, it was like they were trying to harass every other prisoner and trying to befriend me. "Hey Bruz, where do we know you from?" One of them asked as they both stood at my window and looked into my cell.

I looked at them straight in the eye and said, "I don't know, maybe Russell Street?" They looked shocked, maybe they thought I could score them some smack. As the screw came into the yard to hand us our brew, rollies and apples they pleaded with him to let me into the yard to hang out with them. The screw said "No," and gave me a look like you don't want anything to do with these scumbags, and he was right, I didn't need the drama. I'm sure I would have lost my patience. When the screw left, they came back to my window, "Hey Bruz, gimme a squiz, aww sweet shit yeh, ya gonna smoke that dart?" I was starting to feel sick from smoking so many cigarettes, after being off them for so long. I said "Nah," and passed my rollie to the junkie through the meals flap in the door. He traded me back an apple, so I guess they figured I deserved their respect, not that I needed it.

They ended up turning on the Filo smacky dude. They could tell this dude was going through cold turkey. They called him over and in dodgy Asian accents, kinda like Mr Chang from the *Hangover*, they yelled, "Hey you! You want heroin? Okay you want heroin? You want heroin? You want heroin you give me sucky sucky I give you heroin, okay? Sucky heroin, okay?" This went on for three hours. It was fucked up and everyone else was locked in their cells with these junkies running amuck. What made it worse was the Filo dude was just standing by the window not saying anything. It seemed like he was contemplating doing what they said; just for the chance to bang some H. It was disturbing. Those junkies deserved to get bashed, but the screws came and took them up for their court hearing and we didn't see them again.

Another younger dude became my celly the next day and a few people came and went. The most common thing I'd hear people say to me is, "It's your first time in here, yeh? Don't worry it gets easier than this. Wait till you get to the MAP, conditions are heaps better." In Melbourne, after you're sentenced by the judge, the usual process is that firstly you go to the Dungeon then to the Melbourne Assessment Prison. Sometimes it's just straight to the Map, depending on the crime. That's where they work out which prison they'll send you to, to complete your sentence.

After three days, which seemed more like three weeks, I finally got a visit from the barrister who ran my trial. He said, "I have good news, I should be able to get you bail." I said, "Great, when can I get out of here?" He said, "We'll have to sit another trial and if bail is officially granted, you need to get someone to organise the money for you, pay the amount, sign some papers and you'll be released until your next court hearing."

I made a call to Mother Teresa who organised the resources and coordinated getting it to the barrister. The judge accepted my application, and I was released on the Thursday night. As I left the cells, everyone stood at their cell door windows and waived and nodded goodbye. I knew then and there I was never going back. Dr. Evils version of *Hard Knock Life* ran through my head, but all jokes aside ... Freedom is everything!

Teresa picked me up from jail. She'd been wigging out with her mates doing rack and shit like that. I felt like I'd been inside a long time, but it had only been four days. I was stressing out thinking about how much it was gonna cost me to get a good lawyer to appeal my sentence at the County Court. I decided I'd go back and work at the pub in Dandenong the next night.

It wasn't a good move coz my mind wasn't right. My workmate was asking a lot of questions about my court case and what I'd been through that week. It was good to get it off my chest and talk about it, but it made me more pissed off that

I had to go through all this shit for a crime I didn't commit. Just before closing time, six Albanian dudes were drinking in the bistro near the pokie machines. The duty manager was getting pissed off with them coz they must have said something sleazy to her or they were getting too smashed.

She came over to us and said, "Can you tell them it's last drinks." I went over to them and said, "Fellas it's time to wrap it up, last drinks." One guy stood up and in his thick Albanian accent said, "Who the fuck are you?" I said, "Who the fuck am I? Who the fuck am I?" And then WHACK! I slapped him. It was 3 am and I was tired and overstretched. It rocked him but it didn't connect that good coz usually I'd put them on their ass with a slap like that. Another guy, who I think was his brother, came over and WHACK! I slapped him too. Again, he got rocked but not as clean as I'd liked coz he came back throwing punches. Then WHACK! A third guy came, and I just punched him and from there it was complete chaos. "Yep, That's Me!" ... Punching on with a pack of pissed Albanians while my Punjabi workmate was hanging a shit in the fucken dunny!

It got real messy, real quick. The duty manager called the jacks. I was out of control, swinging wild punches and doing okay until someone jumped on my back and we tumbled over a table together in the bistro. Tables, glasses, plates, chairs and cutlery were flying around all over the place. Someone smashed a bottle across the back of my head, and I was greatly outnumbered but I just kept fighting. The brawl progressed into a scrappy wrestle; I survived the best I could and gave back as good as I got. It continued for almost two minutes before my workmate came running out of the toilet and we managed to get them out of the venue.

When the jacks rocked up, the Albanian's started shouting, "He threw the first punch! He started it arrest him!" I just thought, oh fuck, here we go again. But apart from a few scratches and bruises no one was seriously hurt. As usual the bacon double cheeseburger deluxes were not on my side, but they let it go. In a strange way I guess I kinda took it as a compliment that I did pretty good. Six on one and the Albanians wanted to press charges against me. Mumu 3, Benny 0.

I woke up the next day to a few missed calls from Tanya. I called her back and she said, "Oh my fucken god, I'm so sorry. The fucken Mumu. You've been cursed. I'm going to burn the remains of the statue tonight. I hope that makes things better." While I worked on King Street that Saturday night my mate went back to Tanya's to ensure they burnt the curse out of that fucken statue, whilst they blazed up. Apparently, they threw the Mumu into a bonfire in her backyard. My mate called me the next day and said, "Dude, you shoulda seen how that fucken thing was burning man, it was un-fucken-believable. Blue flames coming out and shit, I've never seen anything like it, dude. I'm sure that whatever the hell was in that thing we killed the fuck outta it ... And you ain't gonna get any more problems from it." I said, "Thanks man, I appreciate it!" With the Mumu sent to hell, I could see clearly at last.

TRY TO LOCK ME DOWN & I SAY NO WAY

Lockdown, *Don't Take It Personal* (2018)

Scarface the O.G.

Supernatural curses aside, I was going through a ruff patch, but I'd learned a valuable lesson. Never put your faith in the system. It's not designed that way. If the system is the answer, it must have been a stupid fucken question! There must be millions of people around the world that have been jailed coz they couldn't afford decent legal representation, or their legal team just got it completely wrong and made them look guilty. Perhaps no one is completely innocent in this world, and I'm definitely no exception, but with regards to the crime I was convicted of, I was not guilty. I had been charged with six variations of assault. I did not assault the dude or have any intentions of letting anyone assault him. I was simply trying to kick him out of the club and do my job. So, was I guilty of being reckless? Well, the pigs insisted I was. I didn't think so. The facts were, I believed the person was intoxicated. He made a bad choice and asked the wrong person for pills, which he admitted in court and shouldn't have been doing. I had the right to eject him from the club, but unfortunately things went fucken pear shaped.

Life was twisted working as a bouncer and incidents were rarely straight forward. Just coz Bacon Sandwich thought

I could have done a better job, it didn't seem right to press such heavy charges. I think he wanted me to feel not only the emotion of guilt but the financial penalty of appearing in court, which would ultimately lead to my incarceration. However, there was the whole covering for Pavlo aspect that I couldn't just brush aside. In reality, Pavlo was never a mate of mine, still I'll never be a dog. The law of the street prevailed, things caught up with him and inevitably he was murdered. I don't know if this helped the victim at all, with seeking some kinda retribution, but I'm sure there was an underlining sense that karma had caught up with the cunt that bashed him. As for me; well let's not beat around the bush; with all the wannabe gangster bullshit I'd been getting into, a stint in the boob was a forewarning.

Bacon Sandwich was looking for his Underbelly scalp and coz Pavlo was now six feet under, I was guilty by association. Bacon Sandwich had lost out on his moment of glory, so he was taking his frustrations out on me. He'd convinced the victim that it was me who hit him and with everything happening so fast, it would have been easy to do. But one thing was for sure, there was no way I was going back to the clink.

Most peeps that I've ever known that've been inside haven't come out reformed at all; they've come out worse, with better criminal connections and more driven to defy the law, intent on making smarter choices in how they go about it, and inevitably learning the skills required to make more cheddar. Sometimes they develop drug addictions or a mental illness such as depression. Some have even taken their own lives. I could see through the agendas of the police prosecutors and it smelt like rotten bacon. My appeal was set for the higher level County Court the following year.

I needed to be a helluva lot smarter. Get a better lawyer to properly explain my side of the story to the judge at the retrial. I hated the fucken system, but I was in quicksand now, I had to think like MacGyver and somehow get the fuck outta that shit! I contacted the same lawyers who'd represented me for my juvenile auto theft charges back in the day, to take over the case. With the auto theft charges I pleaded guilty. I was just given a small fine without a conviction, which meant under Australian law there would be nothing on my criminal record that would affect future employment, hence why I was allowed to hold a security license and travel to most countries. My lawyer did say at the time that there was one negative in my guilty plea. Some countries, such as the USA, may not allow you entry coz it may be seen as a crime involving moral turpitude. I was still a teenager at the time of that court case and didn't quite understand what the lawyer meant or take the time to do my research. Still, those lawyers had gotten me out of doing time back then, I trusted they would get me outta the shit once more. Under the bail conditions for the new offence, I was granted my passport and was allowed to continue working as a bouncer in order to make a living.

I felt like I needed to get away from Melbourne and avoid trouble. Teresa needed to renew her tourist visa so she could stay in Australia longer, so she booked a trip to New Zealand. I decided to just stay in Melbourne and work while she was away. But she fucked up and was detained at the New Zealand airport and completely banned from re-entering Australia for a long time. She had left behind all her possessions. She ended up extending her stay in New Zealand before returning to the USA. She stayed in contact and was upset about what went down but seemed to be enjoying being back at home. I planned to visit her in USA, so I bought myself a return ticket to Las Vegas, where she'd decided to work as a showgirl. I was thinking of looking for work as a bouncer in Vegas and try and launch my rap career in the States. Teresa was encouraging and agreed there were better opportunities for rappers in the USA compared to Australia.

I took myself down to a travel agent in the city and took the plunge. Just after I paid for my tickets the travel agent said, "Oh there is something I forgot to mention ... Ummm ... You haven't been in trouble with the police before, have you?" I embarrassingly said, "Ahhh yes I kinda have." She said, "Don't worry you'll just have to call the US consulate here in Melbourne and make an appointment. They'll probably just ask you to apply for a different type of Visa coz the US government is now very strict with who they let into the country since September 11." I disappointingly said okay, and she gave me the phone number to call. She actually shouldn't have sold me the ticket. No doubt, like Bacon Sandwich, she was working for her commission. I called the consulate and I was told I needed to apply for what is known as a B1 Visa, and that the process was a little complicated. I needed to wait to be given an official appointment time, provide full identification, my passport, a separate passport photo, a copy of my police record history and a few other things.

While getting everything ready to head to the States, I

moved in with my mum in East Malvern and continued to work security for Prospect. I'd lost my other security job at the pub in Dandenong coz the venue manager was concerned I'd now started an outright war with the Albanian community, who at the time made up 80% of the customers. I was happy to get out of the place. Rock had shown a little bit of compassion during the court case, and he spoke to me over the phone and in the gym after I'd been released. I was hesitant about getting him involved in the first hearing coz I honestly believed I had it all under control. He was there for support but there wasn't any offer of financial assistance or anything like that, but again if you accept too many favours from people you are forever indebted to them, so I preferred to handle it myself. Rock spoke to the operations manager, and they got me work at more venues again. I was now back at the strip club during the week, and a brand-new R'n'B club called The Kremlin out in the eastern suburbs.

The club was run by two Russian brothers. We became mates and they were happy to top me up with a cash envelope once a week and provide free meals from the restaurant whenever I was hungry. The brothers had rivalries with the other owners of the bars in the area, particularly an Irish pub directly next door to the venue. Coz of these rivalries, combined with a ruff suburban crowd of mixed ethnicities that clashed with each other, they wanted to run their club with a staunch security presence.

From my experience though, whenever paranoid nightclub owners wanted a heavy security presence there was usually something shady going on, or the security company would basically milk the owners for as much 'cha-ching' as they could. Each time the security company sent a new guard to a venue the more profit the company is making per hour. There were also bouncers known as 'sleepers', in reference to the secret agent term often used by the KGB, a highly dangerous asset when activated, aka a drunken brawl breaks out in the club, these guys had permission to unleash. They were usually a little older without official security licences, usually due to criminal records and getting paid straight cash from the venue at a higher rate than regular guards. Most of the time the sleepers would be packing heat, or it wasn't too far away if needed.

EASTERN MELBOURNE PROMISES

When I first arrived at The Kremlin the venue had organised a couple dudes to do the sleeper work. Problem was, while these dudes were at the club they were getting on the gear and fucking up! For some reason they smashed a shopping trolley into a shop window nearby and were caught on CCTV. Then they got into a dust-up over it; and the club got hot. The Russian brothers complained about all the questions from the cops, so Prospect decided to move them on and that's when the venue decided to top me up instead. They also organised a Samoan fighter known as Crusher to work at the venue with me; we became mates and got in many scuffles together. I was the official head of security and Crusher was the sleeper. We came to blows often at that club, there was no choice. The older brother wasn't scared to let his hands go. We stood by and watched him smash a few blokes and didn't have to do much at all; just jump in if things got out of hand.

Once someone threw and beer glass at us from next door at the Irish pub. The older brother ran into the Irish pub and hit the guy that threw the glass. I ran in with him like his bodyguard and hit some other guy that tried to jump in. It was a ballsy move by us to just run into the neighbour's venue and start hitting people, but the security from the venue were our mates, so they stayed out of it. We basically had a silent pact with all the security guards that worked in the area, no matter what security company you were with, that we'd jump in for each other when required.

I finally got my interview at the US Consulate. Disappointingly, my visa was rejected due to the pending County Court trial. I was told to re-apply after the hearing, if I was found not guilty. But it still meant I couldn't go to the USA and I'd already bought the ticket. Teresa was crying when I told her the news. I spoke with Mum and she said that I should go to Germany and stay with the family over there for awhile to get away from it all. I was getting in more and more fights at work, especially with the added responsibilities of being the head of security at The Kremlin, although I was careful to ensure that any time things got physical it wasn't excessive and within my legal rights. Or in the security game, the law that we came to know as section '462A':

Use of force to prevent the commission of an indictable offence: "A person may use such force not disproportionate to the objective as he believes on reasonable grounds to be necessary to prevent the commission, continuance or completion of an indictable offence or to effect or assist in effecting the lawful arrest of a person committing or suspected of committing any offence".

This law was meant to be known word-for-word by every licensed security guard. I heard a guard once tattooed '462A' on his forearm. Still the violence at work was so frequent, I thought it was just a matter of time before someone pressed charges against me. And coz I was still out on bail, I'd be thrown straight back into jail. Plus, it was a dangerous time with all the *Underbelly* killings going on in the background. I could never tell exactly what was gonna go down from night to night, so it was definitely time to leave Oz for a while. But it's funny how used to these things we get. Looking back, I wonder what the fuck I was doing!

BOOMERANG BOOM

When I arrived in Munich, I stayed in an apartment with Oma's childhood best mate Ula. Technically we were not related, but she started to feel like a second oma to me, straight outta Breslau, I knew my real oma back in Melbourne appreciated that I'd re-united with her peeps. After I'd settled in, I again met up with Klaus. Nothing had changed between us, he was still like a long-lost cousin. We hit the Hofbrauhaus in Munich but this time our adventures were all pretty low key. I didn't want to risk getting in any volatile situations and Klaus had just broken up with his latest girlfriend, still half a dozen steins of weiss beer didn't go to waste and its was great to catch up with him. No doubt, Ula was a charismatic old lady with a great sense of humour, and we did some sightseeing around Munich. I enjoyed making her laugh. Again, I felt like the little kid that my grandparents called Benji-lein, a long, long, way away from King Street and the gangland wars.

Getting away from Oz was a circuit breaker. It gave me time to breathe and to focus on what was important to me. And it reconnected me with my past. I also decided to head to Bad Endorf. Mum had been pen-pals since childhood with one of her cousins who lived on the farm in Bergham, they never got into the family feud which inevitably had driven my opa to migrate to Australia. Between them they made arrangements for me to stay on the farm for a couple weeks. I was a little nervous initially, when reflecting on how my opa might have felt. But when I finally got to meet the family who lived there, they welcomed me with open arms. It gave me comfort to believe that I had somehow settled the bad blood my opa had felt towards his family after loosing the farm. Whilst I relaxed and unwinded I looked towards the Austrian Alps from the timber balcony of one of my cousins cottages. I felt like Opa was sitting next to me slicing up blood sausage and sipping on beer. It's a beautiful part of the world and the spirit of the land my ancestors lived on will always be with me, just like my opa. My European trip couldn't last, though – I had to go back home and face the music.

My court hearing was about a week after I arrived back in Melbourne, so I had a little while to sleep off the jet lag, settle back in and prepare for my battle with Bacon Sandwich and the law. My trip had been an educational experience and I managed to catch up on sleep and enjoy some additional daylight hours that I'd been deprived of working night shift. I had grown my hair and I'd lost weight. I showed up at the King Street club to meet the crew and they nicknamed me Jose Romero after a Chilean, North Melbourne footy player, who they thought I resembled.

The morning after I got back, randomly out of the blue my dad rang me and said, "It's good to have you back son! I nearly fell off my chair. He continued, "You're not going to believe what's happened since you left Melbourne." I said "What?" He said, "An ex-cricketer was hit by a bouncer and died, it's been all over the media here. I'm worried this is going to make you look bad at your trial." "He was hit by a cricket ball?" I asked, surprised as to how that would make me look bad. "No son," said Dad, "He was punched by a nightclub bouncer". I paused in shock for a moment, then replied, "I didn't hit the bloke I'm up against Dad, the jacks just hate my guts!"

I didn't know the bouncer in question but I found out he was a boxer and that he'd fought against fighters like Porky. Dad then said, "Wait a sec it bloody gets worse, coincidentally a couple days later another bouncer hit some other bloke and killed him too". Surprisingly, I didn't really know that bouncer either, but I later heard he also worked at clubs I had and it was something personal with a punter while he was out at a bar.

Mum had contacted Dad when I was away and filled him in

with what had been going on and although the circumstances were grim, it was nice to share that moment with me old man. It felt like he showed some compassion towards my situation, something I'd never experienced from him before. Facts were though, it was some bad news. We both thought that, maybe the Judge's opinion of bouncers will be tainted. There wasn't anything I could do but rock up to court on the day and find out what the consequences would be.

KING OF CLUBS

On the day of the hearing, I put on a suit, made sure I was clean shaven, and I purposely combed my hair down and parted it, so I looked like a nerd. My mum, dad and Oma all came along to court with me, so it looked like I had a loving family who cared about me. And you know what, they actually did, I just didn't realise it for many years. Well, I never doubted my oma's love for me, but my parents I wasn't so sure about. I think a lot of kids from broken homes must feel that way, it's something I know I never wanted to admit, or feel sorry for myself about, but deep down that's how I felt.

The County Court hearing was the first time I could recall seeing my parents in the same room together. My lawyers had organised a better barrister to represent me this time. His last name was Germanic in origin, so Mum and Oma liked that and had faith that he was definitely the right man to clear my name.

The hearing went on a lot longer than the original Magistrates Court hearing. I was in court for three days. Most of the witnesses completely backflipped on their stories this time, except for the victim and Bacon Sandwich, of course ... Some of the witnesses didn't even show up. At one point I told the judge that I'd be happy never to work as a security guard again after everything I'd been through. Over the course of the three days, I could see Bacon Sandwiches greasy face get more and more disgruntled, until he looked like a man who'd just discovered that his balls had run off to join the fucken Chinese circus.

The judge reached a verdict on the third day of the hearing; 'Not Guilty of all Charges'. I was also granted court costs, which meant responsibility for covering the majority of the costs of the hearing fell onto the prosecutors. It was an expensive trial, the costs grant didn't exactly cover all my legal expenses as I thought it would, so I was still out of pocket big time and my life had been majorly disrupted. It didn't feel like justice had prevailed entirely, but I didn't have to serve jail time and now that was my prerogative! Perhaps all the hustling I'd been doing over the past few years had come back to bite me with a hard dose of karma. I did feel this victory in court once and for all signified the final death of the dreaded Mumu, who I'd come to think of as Chucky from the movie, *Child's Play*. But, most importantly all that stress was behind me, I could finally move on.

As soon as I was cleared of the charges, Rock called me up and asked if I wanted to pick up some more shifts. Most of those venues were topping me up with extra cash on top of my hourly rate, plus the tips, bribes and rent money I used to get working the doors. So, it was too hard to knock back the work.

Plus, I had to make a living somehow and I couldn't see myself working in a kitchen as a chef. Bouncer work and court had brought out a lack of empathy for humanity and I completely lost the passion for feeding people who I now viewed as obnoxious and non-appreciative strangers. I preferred to make a semi legit living and was hoping to not fall back on my old ambitions of becoming a big-time gangster.

There was just one more little hurdle I needed to get over. A Private Agents Tribunal hearing. There was still a chance I could have my security licence revoked if the registry decided I was not a fit and proper person to work as a security guard. This division was also run by the jacks, so I was expecting the worst.

I couldn't believe Bacon Sandwich rocked up to my tribunal hearing to try and prevent me from making a living. He wasn't legally required to be there; it was his choice. He was obviously bitter and twisted that I was found not guilty by the County Court, coz this made him look incompetent and he'd wasted taxpayer's money; the majority of the court costs fell on his department. Funny thing was, he looked even more pathetic when his own kind, who were running the tribunal, dismissed all allegations he made against me. Bacon Sandwich even said, "But in court he said he really couldn't care less if he worked another day as a security guard after everything he'd been through." At that point, my lawyer almost started laughing out loud. But the fact he took the time to write down what I'd said in court was disturbing. I highly doubt he's still working as a cop, at least I certainly hope not. I was fucken pissed off Bacon Sandwich had stooped that low, back in a land Down Under, I will not run, I will not take cover, from the messed-up system that tries to plunder...No, there would be no celebration from me, only relief and a little satisfaction...

After two successful hearings and returning to my job as a bouncer, there was one more thing I wanted to sort out. My US visa. I was not ready to give up on the dream of making it as a rapper in the USA. I was confident I'd get it this time, having been cleared of all the charges. I went through the same process again and attended my appointment at the US consulate, with all the required information. I waited in a waiting room while the admin staff processed my paperwork. They called out my name and I excitedly walked up to the service officer behind the glass window.

The officer said, "Mr Sinclair, unfortunately your application has been denied due to a breach in relation to a charge of automotive theft on your police record dating back to 1997. Grand Theft Auto is a serious felony under US law and as the offence occurred less than 10 years prior to your application we cannot permit your entry into the United States of America. You can however apply again in 10 years from now, thank you for your co-operation ... NEXT!"

I was shattered. I released then and there Mother Teresa and me were never meant to be. It felt like my dreams of making it as a rapper in the states were slipping away. However, I was determined never to give up, so I worked hard for many years and I prayed that my dreams would become reality...

8 KILOMETRES

ome crazy shit went down at the Underworld gym during the time I was overseas, and they were forced to close the doors for good, which meant I needed to find a new gym to train at. I was also back living with Mum since I'd arrived back from Germany. Driving to work one day, I noticed a sign above the door of an old run-down weights gym in Prahran. The sign read, 'Kickboxing'. I recognised the logo and realised my former kickboxing trainer Nick was taking classes at that gym. I hadn't seen him since 96'. I started to think about giving kickboxing another shot, so I signed up at the gym and joined in one of Nick's classes. I was happy to see him and that my old training buddy Mick had been fighting professionally over the past few years. Nick was a great trainer, but it just didn't feel right for me anymore. Things were never going to be the same as when I was training with him when I was younger. I'd changed a lot since then.

Coincidentally, a few days later, the owner of the gym who I found to be a little sketchy, coz when I signed up my membership, I could see a crate of empty beer bottles on the floor of the office and he told me he lived there, learned of my boxing experience and asked if I could run some boxing classes at his gym. My reputation as an ex-state champ had grown around the neighbourhood, especially after four years working as a bouncer. I was fed up with my job in the security industry, but I kept getting more shifts and the additional work hours kept me busy. Plus, I felt that all the nightshifts and exposure to violence had numbed my mind like I was some kinda fucken nightclub zombie. Love it or hate, all the stress and almost doing eight months jail time aside, I continued to get a lot better at the job. I worked smarter and became a good communicator, with the ability to distinguish which patrons you needed to shutdown quick and when you should grant some leniency. Fighting became a last resort. Although sometimes unavoidably that last resort was exercised more often than planned. As one of my managers at the recovery club would say, "That's why you're on the Big Bucks Benny!" when my hourly rate went up went up a couple dollars to the permanent supervisor rate and he would pass me my top-up cash envelope at the end of the shift.

I decided I'd take up the offer at the gym as a side gig and I had some ideas on how I wanted to run the boxing classes. I was hoping eventually this would be my way out of the security game. I asked the sketchy gym owner if I could invest in his gym and develop a fighters stable. He was more interested in starting with a few classes and seeing how things went. Before I knew it, I was running four boxing classes during the week, starting out with training other bouncers. I was starting to feel like like Obi-Wan Benny Kenobi!

Nick, the kickboxing trainer, would take two classes per week, just after mine but of a longer duration. Initially things were a little awkward between us given he was always eager on me going further with my kickboxing and I had now become a trainer where he worked. The truth, which he grew to accept, was that boxing was and always will be my true passion when it comes to martial arts. My classes were one hour in duration. I figured people would prefer to train the way fighters train, hit and go, get the skills and fitness work in fast and efficiently, then get your track work in between sessions or early mornings. I paid the gym rent and Nick chipped in; we made a great team. And Nick was an inspirational mentor to me!

One day, after taking classes for a couple months, a kid who was about 14 came into the gym with his parents. The father told me they'd like their son to learn boxing coz he was being bullied at school. I let them know about the classes, but his father asked if I could train him privately coz he felt his boy was a bit uncomfortable around other people. He said he was happy to pay me extra coz he appreciated the individual time I was giving his son. It sounded like a good idea to me, and coupla days later we started training.

I had my first official client and he ended up being one of my favourites. After training with me twice a week for a few months, the bully at his school finally got what he deserved: a broken nose. And my client walked away without getting in trouble from his teachers coz it was done in self-defence. He never became a fighter, but no one ever messed with him again! This was the most rewarding job I'd ever had.

Sadly though, time has no mercy and life is not measured. Nana Mary developed dementia during this stage and eventually she passed away. I attended the funeral in Corowa. The last time I saw her before she got sick, I did ask her, "Nana, where is our heritage from?" She was drinking beer at the time and just shrugged her shoulders and with a sad look in her eyes she said, "I dunno, black of some kind." This felt like the end of the trail ...

HUSTLE AND FLOW BRO

One day down at the gym I bumped into a fellow bouncer who was known as Perv. A few weeks earlier he'd realised I was into hip hop and he burnt me some CDs, it was a cool deed. I hadn't seen him since then and he said, "Hey man you been listening to those discography's I burnt for ya? What did you think, dope huh?" I said, "Hell yeh, it's inspired me to get back into writing lyrics." He said, "Really, you rap?" I said, "Yeh, I've been rapping since I was a kid. I've just never really had the opportunity to officially record a track or anything. There's nothing more that I wanna do with my life." He said, "I can help you record, man." I said, "You know someone with a studio?" Perv said, "Nah man, we can lay something down over my computer, it'll sound just as good. Trust me. Just bring all your lyrics over to my apartment and I'll go through them with ya."

I was a bit hesitant sharing all my written lyrics with someone I didn't really know all that well. I thought, what did Perv want out of it? But at that point no one else had ever really shown a great amount of interest in me as a rapper. I felt like my mates treated me like a novelty act with a party trick up my sleeve. I just didn't know how to make it happen and I'd been given limited opportunities to show my talent. Rap had always been there for me. I met Perv at his place a few days later and I busted out some of my best written raps from my notebooks.

My flow was raw as hell, but he liked my lyrics, so he suggested we type them up into his computer, then he downloaded a video game called *Ejay Hip Hop*, so I could lay something down over the beats. At that point in time, I didn't own a computer or need to use one at work, so I wasn't at all tech savvy or even familiar with the type of jargon he was using.

I left my notebooks with him for a few weeks whilst he read over them. My gut instinct was right. What he wanted was to learn how to rap. As he typed up my lyrics, he studied them, but rapping is not that simple, it comes from the heart. It's your own life experiences, fact or fiction combined with passion and delivery. After a couple weeks I asked him, "Hey have you finished typing up my lyrics?" I was keen to get them back and still feeling a bit uneasy with the sitch. He said, "Almost. Why don't you come around to my place Friday, I've got something cool to show you.

When I arrived at Perv's he'd typed up about half of the lyrics I'd given him, and he told me that he'd read through everything and just typed up the songs that he felt were the best. He'd cut up some loops from old '70s funk songs and uploaded them to his computer. We just needed a mic, so we went down to JB and bought a couple. We weren't sure about what to buy, so we just bought something cheap and simple. I was pumped!

When we got back to his place to start laying down vocals he said, "Wait before you start, what do you think of this?" Perv, started reading a couple raps he'd written. That shit was crude as hell, real simple and basically an attempt at comedy coz he couldn't help chuckling, while reading them out. I initially thought, oh man God help me, and tried to refrain from dissing his raps. I felt like he'd done a lot to try and help me record my first official demo, so I took a look at his lyrics and fixed them up the best I could without taking away from the style he wanted. He called himself Merv da Perv and I was Bugzie. And at that moment, the original hip hop outfit, Bouncer, was born.

We had a feeling no one would take us seriously and they didn't at first, it was definitely something we were a little self-conscious about. I'd tell people Perv was the lighthearted comical edge to our crew, kind of like Easy-E or Flavour Flav and I was a little more serious like Ice Cube or Chuck D. Most people laughed when they heard our tracks but overall, there was more love than hate. It was definitely entertaining and different to the other Aussie hip hop that was popular at the time. I would take a notebook and a pen along with me to every shift at the various places I was working and when things got quiet on the door, I would start writing. My lyrics were based on my experiences, so they were 100 percent authentic to my lifestyle.

The first track we recorded and gave out to our mates and DJs at the club was self-titled *Bouncer.*

ALL EYES ON US

Our raw demo version of that track went off, in a good way! It was humorous, realistic and relevant to everyone that frequented the clubs we worked at. The hook was simple and catchy. Perv had done a great job of looping a very cool old school funk beat. We must have burnt about 200 CDs with that track on it, and he gave it to everyone. We'd be standing at the door of a club and people would drive past with the track blaring through their speakers. It was a great feeling! Hip hop purists would say, "Oh that needs a lot of work," or "You need to work on your flow." But the positives far outweighed the negatives and people wanted to hear more tracks, so we got back to Perv's on weekdays and recorded more songs. Before we knew it, we had 10 tracks done. We recorded the tracks live with our two mics, similar to if we were recording a gig, coz we weren't familiar with proper recording techniques.

We'd started a buzz, then to top it off outta nowhere one Saturday morning something else came to fruition. I was on the door at the recovery club, chatting with a Jamaican mate of mine, discussing tryna get a singer on board. When he randomly goes, "How about Leigh from Past 2 Present?" and just like that Leigh appears walking down the street. The spiritual connection was again with us that morning!

Leigh reminded me of the guy from the old 1970s series *Kung-Fu,* played by David Carradine, but a Maori version. We organised to meet again a couple days later, and I officially played him the demo CD through the speaker of my BMW. Leigh was feeling it and he instantly dropped some dope harmonies and added in his own hooks, which sounded great, while I rapped along to the CD in the car. Perv couldn't believe who I'd got on board to join our crew. Lee's old R'n'B crew, were very well know across Australia and had top 40 hits in the past. But as the buzz grew louder, I made it clear to Leigh that 'Bouncer is now the Present'!

We had a couple of jam sessions back at Perv's apartment. Leigh spoke of his experiences with his old group, and we learnt a lot from him. Next, we had to find the right producer to properly record our LP. The idea was for me to be the warrior of the crew, Perv the comedian and Leigh the smooth R'n'B cat, so we nicknamed him Kool Kat.

We began recording with a local DJ who we nicknamed Shotgun. We'd met him at the recovery club. He had a good name for himself in the local scene but was predominantly into progressive house and trance music at the time. The first time I jumped up in the vocal booth to lay down a verse I can remember getting in a heated argument with everyone in the room, after being told that my timing was out. "What the fuck do you cunts know? I've been rapping since I was a fucken kid," I shouted. Leigh tried his best to calm me down and assure me that everyone feels that way the first time, it's just the adrenalin. My passion "Was great," he said, "but you need to know how to accept constructive criticism in the music game if you're going to make it." I felt a little embarrassed after that; I'd acted like a real novice. Leigh was completely right, and I tried not to make the same mistake again. Shotgun was big on quantisation, going through our music with a fine tooth comb and this took up most of our time during our weekly catch ups, leaving not much time to work on our vocals. But he was a good dude, so we persisted with this routine for a couple of months until I decided it really wasn't working and we had to find a more suitable producer.

One night I was working security at the boxing. I knew some of the fighters on that night. During the main event I switched with another security guard so I could watch the bout. That's when I noticed Olinda, she was one of the ring girls. I'd be lying if I said she didn't catch my eye straight away. She looked beautiful that night. The fight ended and after about 30 minutes I was in the process of asking the remainder of the crowd to finish their last drinks and leave the venue. Olinda was now dressed and was kicking back drinking champagne on a table with one of her friends. I noticed she kept looking over at me and smiling. So, I went over, and we started a conversation. I brought up I'd seen her at the RZA gig at The Palace a little while back. I was there only briefly that night due to work commitments, but I walked in just in time to see that she'd been called up on stage by RZA and another one of the Killa Beez. The crowd were chanting, "Show us your tits!" like they did back then. She just showed them her bra very quickly, which I thought was kinda classy. Olinda said, "Really? You remember that?" I said, "Yes, of course I do, I was really impressed with how you handled the situation." She laughed, I got her number and she kissed me before she left.

Out of the blue, on the Queen's Birthday public holiday, Olinda called me up and asked what I was doing. She said, "Come over and see me. I'm at a house party, not far from where you live." I was exhausted after a long shift, but I could hear the music pumping in the background and her girlfriends were in the background shouting, "Come hang out with us Benny!" I got dressed and headed down.

There were some sexy girls at the party including an Argentinian chick who was a soapie star. There was also a DJ playing house music and I started talking to him. Olinda came over, officially introduced us and mentioned to him that

I was a rapper. The DJ took an interest and said, "Have you got anything I can listen too?" I said, "Nothing official just yet, but I got a ruff demo CD in the car. You wanna hear that?" He said, "Yeh Brah, go grab it!" So I did, and I mentioned we were looking for a new producer. He told me he was gonna have a listen and then show one of his mates who might be a good fit for the project. I gave him my number and continued to party with Olinda until later that night.

A couple days later I got a phone call. It was the DJ, "Hey Brah I'm here with my mate CJ, we're loving your demo man, it's a pissa and the beats are catchy AF, let me put him on the phone." CJ jumped on the phone, and we organised to catch up for a meeting a couple days later. He was a well-known producer and had a massive dance hit in the '90s called, *Dreams* by Quench. To this day it's one of my favourite EDM tracks, and the irony of living out the 'dreams' I had envisioned, which for so long had seemed like an infinite black hole was finally turning into reality.

The meeting went well, and CJ was genuinely thrilled about our project. He hadn't produced hip hop music in years. He'd previously won the Australian DMC championship before progressing into EDM. For many years house music dominated the clubs in Melbourne so that's where he got most of his work, but hip hop was what had inspired him to become a producer. CJ became the fourth official member of Bouncer and we started officially recording our LP, *King Hits*, in 2006. I focused on bulking up as big as I could for the 'warrior' look: I was still in the gym at least five days per week. Things were definitely getting better.

GƎT RiCH, OR GƎT RiCH

t was dope having a creative break after all the violence and chaos of my working life and the recording of our album was going better than I could have imagined. CJ had a sick studio setup and I started to get more comfortable with my vocals each time we recorded. He was patient with us wanting to change stuff, when we thought it didn't sound right. A lot of the time we would get into his studio on not much sleep and in between shifts, but still I felt that I was learning and improving throughout the project.

During this time, I started to connect on another level with some other local rappers. Some of those connections came via my involvement in boxing and they went on to feature on our album. There was Billy Bunks, who trained with me. Eloquor who was from Leo's gym. Also Blades, who worked at the recovery club. Even Rock got involved and our mate Flash who once had 15 pro fights in seven months. Then there was Pegz, the new owner of Obese. I was digging his music at the time, as were my younger brothers, who now attended High School.

But at that point in time something was missing from the musical journey that had started off so positively, with aspirations of greatness, fame, glory and wealth. It was Leigh. His energy was second to none whilst we were recording the first nine tracks, then completely disappeared from the face of the earth. When I tried to call him to see what was going on with him, his phone had been disconnected. It was disheartening, and the seeds of doubt started to creep in. I thought, maybe he thinks we're no good and doesn't want to be part of Bouncer. I later found out that this personality trait was just how he is, and it was pretty well-known within the local scene, "It's just Leigh being Leigh, bro". Unfortunately also during that time, Perv would sporadically lose motivation. He was opinionated and negative a lot of the time and wanted to do things his way. He didn't want to do gigs unless they were massive. He'd say things like, "The world will love it, it's never been done before, we're gonna be the next NWA trust me, then we will fill stadiums," to reassure me. It was an interesting project, that's fosho, and I just wanted to see it through no matter what. But the truth was, I wanted to make music from my heart and soul.

I felt like I'd been carrying the project on my own two shoulders, writing most of the lyrics and doing the hundreds of other little things you need to do in order to establish yourself in the music game. But we did split all the costs. Perv was convinced he'd get us signed through MySpace. Like a man on a mission, he would spend a crazy amount of time adding anyone and everyone. We had millions of friends. He also uploaded some of our first ruff music videos to YouTube, it was basically candid footage of us in the studio or at the door of the club, which he'd taken on his personal camera. Somehow he got millions of views on those first videos but then YouTube took them down, claiming it was spam. Perv definitely had his positive contributions and we were similar in our borderline obsessive compulsive personalities at times. Let's face it, there would have been no Bouncer without Merv

Da Perv and he was the first person to really get behind my lyrics and support my dreams of making it as a rapper. He also had improved a lot over the journey, and I wanted the heads of Australian hip hop to take him seriously.

I had a good feeling that Pegz was going to sign us to Obese coz he'd showed a lot of genuine interest in us. He'd featured on the track *The Heavies* and in the video too. Plus given us a stack of Obese merchandise like tees and hoodies. He'd even taken the time to give me CDs of most of his artists that he wanted me to study and sound like, saying, "This is what sells, check em' out!" But we didn't want a bar of trying to sound like other rappers, although I did respect what they had accomplished. I preferred our tracks, the way they were.

We hang out a coupla times, music biz aside. The Russian brothers had re-opened a new club in the city. They had Mobb Deep and Alchemist performing a Live Gig there one night and invited me down to hang out. We kicked back with Havoc, Prodigy and Alchemist up on stage, and backstage we blazed up and got lit. It was a dope night! I drew more inspiration because I could confidently connect with the rappers I'd respected the most for so long, and deep down I knew I could rap just as good as them when given the opportunity!

When it was basically time to make a decision on signing us, and after Pegz had a good listen to the finished LP, he simply said, "Perv can't rap," and laughed. He didn't sign us, but he offered digital distribution through his label, which just meant uploading the tracks to iTunes for us and he let me put some CDs in his store on consignment. Pegz also put me on to the publicist he used, who told me, "It's too ruff around the edges.

I can't help you." She was extremely blunt and rude. Saying I felt let down was an understatement, I was devastated. From that moment all I wanted to do was prove them wrong!

UP iΠ SΠOKΣ

No record deal aside, Pegz was alright and I genuinely respected what he had done with Obese, but when his business was flying he did manage to piss off some of my mates. I remember when Shaz got outta the nick, Pegz had given him a job back at his old store to get him back on his feet. It would have been hard for Shaz to see his old business turned into a multimillion-dollar record label. But that wasn't what bothered him the most. He felt he was getting treated like a shop assistant. He mentioned one time Hilltop rocked up to the store and Pegz told him to unpack boxes. He'd had enough and he left the business to go back and do what he did best. Hustle. I guess sometimes, as a mate of both Pegz and Shaz I just wish that business was run better, it could have been anything and most importantly, still around today. There was nothing better for Australian hip hop than Obese Records (it was)– 'Fatter than ya Mamma'.

Our first Gig was at a club called The Prince of Wales, in St Kilda. It was a massive event called 'Roosistence', held as a fund raiser for the North Melbourne Football Club organised by Tim Rogers, who's a legend in the Aussie Rock scene and hooked us up our spot on the bill. Leigh was still M.I.A, so my big Samoan mates, Freddie, took his place. We rehearsed three times a week for about a month leading up to the gig at the rehearsal studios, which were located right behind the recovery club. We were determined to nail this gig and most rehearsal sessions we did. Until the big night.

When the day of the gig arrived, I remember feeling exactly the same way I use to feel before fights; elevated, but always tryna hide the fact that I was nervous AF. It's like a kinda cold sweat clammy feeling. Anything else I tried to do that day wouldn't take my mind off the gig. Before I knew it, we were up for the scheduled sound check, we didn't really know what to expect so we just kinda rocked up and winged it, busting our verses into the mics like we expected the sound crew to stop and give us a roaring applause. As we stood on a stage in front of an empty room we paused for a moment and looked at each other. "Yeh great guys! Who's up next?" one of the sound engineers yelled out, as the rest of his crew murmured, something which to me sounded like, "Who the fuck are they?"

It was time for us to go home get some rest, grab a shower, and get ready for the big night. I actually felt like I had to remind myself that while on stage I wasn't going to have punches thrown in my direction, at least I hoped not. When we arrived, the club was packed out and well over capacity with at least 2,000 people. I was sharing the backstage green room with football stars, rock musicians and comedians who were all frequently on mainstream TV and radio back then. We were the only hip hop act on that night. Given the demographic of the audience, I got the sense that this gig could be challenging. But I told myself, honestly who gives a fuck, just get out there and smash it!

Everyone in the green room treated us fine. No one was overly talkative, including us, it was the nerves, exactly the same as being in the change rooms before a fight. Glenn Archer, the North Melbourne legend, was on stage giving a speech right before we came out, so our plan was to dedicate a song to him. As he finished his speech the crowd erupted into a cheer which resembled the roar at a stadium after a goal is scored. So we decided we would run onto stage like we were breaking through a banner, which all seemed like a great idea... Apart from one small technical issue. Perv had forgotten to ensure his chord was attached to the mic and it fall out as we ran onto the stage. As we had A TV version of the hook on the beat CD we were rapping to, nobody noticed at first "Bouncer! Bouncer! Bouncer! Bouncer! Bouncer! Bouncer! Bouncer! Fucken Bouncer!" Yep, awesome sound, I thought, smash out that verse of yours Perv! Perv! Perv! I could literally hear the crickets chirping. There was no fucken sound on Perv's mic!

I looked at Freddie, and Freddie the Big Samoan looked straight to the ground in sheer embarrassment, or to avoid cracking up. I had to think quick, timing, timing ... Boom! "Number 323 and I'm hanging with my set," as I began rapping out Perv's verse. I saved us, but I'd probably missed one bar, about three seconds worth of rap, and I knew the crowd could tell. I could hear the murmurs, "Did they say Bouncer, Fucken Bouncer?" Ahhh yep, we did! The Perv fixed his mic and we finished our set solidly and received a rowdy applause at the end. But did we really win them over? Who knows?

Regardless, I got the vibe that we warmed up to the hearts and minds of that hostile Aussie Rock crowd. Especially from the ladies, coz quite a few were coming up wanting to introduce themselves, but I was high on adrenalin and not interested. Besides Freddie and Perv were both 100 miles and running. There was no way they were sticking around after the whole mic chord drop thing. I didn't hang around too much longer myself.

I TELL IT HOW IT IS ON THE MELBOURNE STREETS USE TO WHEEL & DEAL NOW I'M BUSTIN' OVER BEATS

Hustler, *King Hits* (2009)

No Jacks City

he boxing gods were smiling again when a couple of hotshot videographers, Sony and Heata, joined my classes one fortuitous sunny and hot afternoon. A brief conversation about our mutual passions for hip hop led to locking their crew in for the shoot of our first music video a couple months later for our track *Crime Doesn't Pay*. The track title and lyrics made a statement. Perhaps a statement that wasn't entirely true from my perspective, but a statement that signified my longing for change. It was time to put the hustling game behind me and it was the fucken real deal this time.

Perv was big on me changing my ways and was undeniably a positive influence on my life. Drug abuse cut deep through his heart, he had lost family to that shit over the years . Saying 'No to Drugs' was his stance on the topic. The location for our shoot was a place of significance for both of us. The Prahran Flats. The same block I had lived as a kid until Oma threw a brick threw the drunken wife-beating neighbour's window. And we would be back at the basketball court we had both played street ball on as kids, with one degree of separation between mine and Perv's childhood crews. We organised a posse made up of our old mates to come through on the day, including Memo and Devious, as well as some local peeps we knew from the flats and around Prahran who were feeling what we were doing and were eager to get involved. The buzz was dope and, on that day, I knew that we'd cemented our place as one of the first successful underground rap groups of Melbourne. We'd created Bouncer rap, to be specific, we were rapping about our lives un cut, lining the clouds with silver, no bullshit and a bad ass gold chain. We went on to film more videos with Sonny and Heata, and a dude named Johann, who we got to know through the clubs.

As soon as the LP was released Leigh showed up like Kwai Chang Caine and appeared in our next few videos. We had professional photos taken, which signified we were again a winning team heading in the right direction. Shortly after that we performed the *King Hits* album launch gig at the recovery club, and we packed out the venue. We promoted it well in a newspaper called MX (which people read on public transport), a music guide magazine called Beat, on student radio, via posters around Melbourne and through SMSs or phone calls to friends, coz social media wasn't as big back then. We used some of the footage of the show for our *Back in The Day* video, with snippets of our mate: Break, from the graff crew MSA (Melbourne Street Art), cutting loose painting trains. There was no mic chord drop incidents during this set, it was fresh, and the crowd were all there to see us fucken bouncers rap, including the owner of the recovery club who had proven to be a loyal fan and who offered his venue for video shoots whenever we needed it!

We were feeling the love from a variety of industry peeps

who were into our style. Typically, we attracted the type of fans who liked our raw underground edge, along with bouncers or punters that frequented the clubs we worked at. *Rage* on ABC played the majority of our videos over a couple years on various weekends in the early hours of the morning. The rush of seeing me and the crew rapping on national TV, even if it was around 4am most of the time, was second to none. We had a positive, full one-hour album review on 3RRR and got regular air play on other community radio stations. We were also getting asked to perform at boxing events, clubs and an outdoor all-ages festival. I always made sure we got paid at the gigs, or if not, made sure it was worthwhile in terms of our exposure. Oh, yeh and both my brothers sold a stack of CDs outta of there school bags in the yard or at train stations, so we now had a young teenage, testosterone-fuelled fanbase that knew my lyrics better than I did!

But as I'd always kinda known, the project meant more to me than just an experience to tell the grandkids about. I was in it for the long haul, but life is never planned and always uncertain, and that simple fact applied to all of us in Bouncer...Firstly CJ could no longer commit to our schedule, so we found a new producer called DJ Rellik, who was also a former Australian DMC champion. Rellik technically wasn't officially in Bouncer, but we went on to record a couple singles with him. Then I noticed, I just wasn't getting the same sense of drive from Perv or Leigh. Perv's lack of motivation was understandable; he had found himself a nice lady and ended up getting married to her. Well at least I got to be in the bridal party, paired up with her fit bridesmaid cousin. As for Leigh, well once again without a word of explanation he pulled a Keyser Soze and disappeared, or did he really? Nothing is truly watertight until you hit the iceberg ... But, as they said on the Titanic, the band played on... Unfortunately I was lost at sea...

Then suddenly... Like a lightning bolt from the hands of Zeus, a voice entered my head and said, "You need to settle down, Benny Boy." I listened to the voice, things happen for a reason. ...

HISTORY OF STONE

Ahhhh where do I begin... Well, to cut a long story short, pardon the pun, life moved on and the road got real twisted and fucken bumpy. I got involved in a serious relationship and I thought it would be the start of something great, but it all came crashing down again. After years of hard work tryna get ahead, I had ended up exactly where I'd started back all those years ago in the creepy house in Malvern, dead broke and fucken miserable.. Sure, I was a changed man but marriage simply wasn't my thing and I learnt the only thing that can heal me is me. The quest for salvation was in fact a search for self-value and acceptance.

Bouncer had split and I was feeling flat. I was thrown to the wolves and ended up in court. Yep, you guessed it I got completely cleaned the fuck out man and needed to sell the home I was living in to pay out the settlement, leaving me in search for a new place to live, plus child support and all that jazz, will always love my kids might I add! How could I possibly get shit back on track now, I asked myself. Well, I figured boxing had done so much for my life, why the fuck wouldn't I need it now? I decided I was gonna try and make a living as a full-time boxing trainer, that would keep me fighting through yet another challenging period & again take control of my life, fulfil my destiny. However, things don't always go as planned and ya know what sometimes that's not necessarily a bad thing.

My boxing classes just weren't growing the way I'd hoped and I barely had enough bread coming in to survive. It was tuff tryna motivate people to get fit and keep healthy, when I was feeling so stressed and burnout on the inside, but I just kept on pushing through. I needed to make some changes but the more I thought about it the harder things seemed. What was I gonna do? Hustle? I'd moved on from that, and I wanted to be a better role model. Bouncer or chef work? No fucken way! I felt like with any of those options I could flip my lid and possibly end up serving time in some fucked up twisted kinda way. I needed some balance and to find that balance I needed focus. Alotta focus ...

I guess there was some kinda focal point, but it's fair to say it strayed towards life's vices. I started drinking more than I ever had. I had a couple brief relationships and a lot of meaningless one-night stands. Good ol' sexual healing to make myself feel better. I was going on benders with so-called mates, hittin' the clubs and downing bags like a fucken hoover, gettin' myself in more debt, if it was my turn to shout. Around about that time one of my cousins told me about a dating app he was on called Tinder. At first I kinda gave him a look like, "Cuz are you fucken kiddin' me? Isn't that for desperate computer geeks who can't pick up in clubs?" But he caught on to my vibe and quickly responded with, "Give it a crack, cuz!" So, I did ... This was the age of smart phones and anything was now possible. I downloaded the app, logged in, uploaded some pics and boom, it was on like Donkey Kong. It felt like I'd clocked that game, the first time I played. Match, match, match, every time I swiped.

I'd dropped a lot of weight living on my own and was in the gym most days with the extra time I had to myself, so I guess my photos must have come up alright! Where had this shit been all my life? I was hooked like a mofo! I was momentarily distracted by the thought of banging away the pain, but it cut deeper than that. Things seemed bleak and my life felt broken again. The real question was, had my life ever really been broken? Or was it just different? Everyone's life has it good and bad moments, and when they're bad it really isn't the end of the world, life goes on and happiness is everything. I grew to accept that fact and embrace it. It took time though!

THE PURSUIT OF HAPPY DAYS

There was something rubbing salt in my emotional wounds. Oma had developed Alzheimer's disease and was rapidly deteriorating. I'd been so preoccupied with everything I was going through to really notice how fast I was losing her. My mum had volunteered to be her full-time carer and it was a battle from start to finish. I found a new level of respect for Mum after seeing how she handled Oma, who had basically transformed into the teenage refugee marching her way from Breslau to Bad Endorf, stashing things around the house as if she was hiding food rations and valuables from her enemies. Oma was relentless with her missions 24 hours a day, seven days a week. She would be lucky to sleep three hours a night for the last two years of her life. Mum would bring Oma to visit and stay the night over weekends. Oma once jumped in my bed in the middle of the night and scared the absolute shit out of me and I'd find the weirdest objects stashed in my sock drawer; basically the kinda stuff you could turn into makeshift weapons. It was breaking my heart seeing her this way.

Mum slugged it out as long as she could but the war on Alzheimer's was drawing to an end. Oma was moved into an aged care facility in Mornington where things seemed to go downhill a lot faster than expected. I did get to visit Oma a few times and had a laugh with my aunty and Mum hearing the nurses tell us a story of how another old lady had gotten in Oma's way during one of her marches through the hallway of the building. It didn't go to well for the other old lady, my oma punched her to the ground and bit her on the face. That was my oma alright, a fighter to the end! Mum said that when they wheeled Oma's body down that same hallway the nursing staff formed rows on either side and saluted her as a show of respect, an occurrence that didn't normally happen, she was told. Oma had taught me a lot throughout my life, most importantly to be kind and to stand up for myself no matter what. These words never came from her mouth, but she led by example. I miss her, just like I miss Opa, but I know she is always with me in spirit and my faith in that is reinstated when she visits sometimes in my dreams.

I was fed up with working at the gym in Prahran, it was a dead-end road. The final straw was the time I showed up at the gym one Friday early in the morning to train a corporate client. To our surprise there was a poker game going on in full swing and these blokes weren't playing around, there was some serious chips being thrown across the table. It reminded me of back in the day down at John's Pinnies, with 10 Greek dudes sitting around playing cards. These dudes were smoking and drinking, with souvlaki wrappers and beer bottles all over the floor. "Come on man this is a fucken gym, how the fuck am I gonna train my client with all this shit goin' on?" I said as I walked towards the table. The owner laughed it off with a "Benny the Boxer...Benny the Boxer, fellas meet Benny the Boxer, haha!"

He was off his fucken head, as we say in Melbourne, a pissed cunt. There was no point in tryna talk sense to him, or to his buddies. I packed up my training gear, told my client we needed to postpone and left the gym. It sucked, I needed the cash, but I wasn't one for playing poker and couldn't tolerate another hit to the pocket. So, right then and there I decided I needed to know where the hits are coming from, just like Rocky said, "Nobody is gonna hit as hard as life. But it ain't about how hard ya hit. It's about how hard you can get hit and keep moving forward. How much you can take and keep moving forward. That's how winning is done!"

That afternoon I searched online and I came across a solution to two of my problems – I found a place to work and a place to rest my head! It was a small shop to rent not too far away. It had a small kitchen and a bathroom, plus just enough space to train people. That shop became my gym and my home!

Partying with my so-called mates and random chicks all seemed fun and carefree to begin with, but it was only masking my depression. Sometimes I found myself back at work training clients early the next morning after big nights out. I wouldn't sleep and I would still be smashed from the night before. At that point I was mostly training tradies. These guys would wanna spar all the time. It was an easier option for me, I wouldn't have to talk too much, just defend their punches and land a couple shots of my own every now and then. Some mornings I'd get 15 rounds in a session, split between clients. Sure, it hurt mentally pushing myself through without sleep but I wanted to punish myself, for my lack of discipline and letting myself get so wasted on a school night.

Physically I was getting fitter and more conditioned, but I had accidentally hurt a few of my clients in the process by breaking ribs or accidentally knocking them down. I had to be careful, these guys were cashed up blue-collar workers which meant they were a lot more cashed up than me, and could potentially sue my ass if they lost work due to their injuries. Even though I was enjoying it, the sparring with my clients needed to stop, it was too risky. I thought about getting back into fighting, or at least join a fight gym where I could get some quality sparring in again with pro fighters.

I walked into the local PCYC one Saturday afternoon. Given this gym was run by jacks it wasn't exactly my gym of choice, but I noticed on Facebook that some pro fighters I'd befriended were training down there, and the facilities were world class. I trained at that gym casually a couple times a week for a while and hit the boxing bags along with the other fighters. Sparring wasn't allowed at the times I was at the gym, but it felt like the good old fighting days again and I started to feel a lot happier. Some of the fighters I was training along with noticed I was getting sharper, and they asked if I was still fighting. I told them it had been many years since my last amateur fight, but it suddenly struck me: so I said it out loud, "I'm gonna fight again, I'm finally gonna turn pro!" Those fighters supported me right away and the Australian cruiserweight champ, Kane, said, "If ya need some sparring, meet us down at Don's gym Friday nights!" Don's gym was primarily for professional muay thai fighters, but they liked boxers working with their fighters to help them improve their boxing skills. So, I rocked on down.

I had started running again four days a week and I felt I was on top of my weight. I was a little nervous before I arrived at the gym. Kane was the Australian champ and I'd seen him in action, the man could hit! There was also a tall muay thai fighter originally from Belgium called Kim who was there to spar with us. He was a legend in the scene. We sparred each other one round in, one round out. I got some quality rounds in with these guys, and I held my own. The routine continued on for the next few months and other fighters would join in and spar with us every now and then. Things were going good, but if I was gonna fight again I needed an official trainer to look out for me and be in my corner.

There was no point sparring at that level without a fight lined up. I'd get marked up a little from time to time, but I was as tuff as ever and I never got hurt. Kim and Kane were both active fighters. Kane suggested I chat to the old fella that looked after him. I headed down to The Melbourne Pavilion one night to watch Kane fight, and when the show was over I met with the old fella, Ray. His reputation stood as the wisest boxing trainer in Australia and had trained many world champions along the journey of his decorated career. We had originally met back in my amateur fighting days, but it had been a long time between drinks. Still, he liked my story. "No worries, son, here's my phone number, training days are Tuesday 12 pm, Thursday 12 pm and Sunday 9 am," he said, and just like that, I was welcomed into one of the best fight teams in Australia!

It took me a little while to break outta the sex, drugs and gangster rap lifestyle I had been living. It wasn't happening as often as before I'd lifted my training game, but it was happening often enough. I'd have my very good days and I'd have my very bad days. There still wasn't a fight date locked in for me and the old flashbacks of feeling neglected down at Leo's gym played on my mind. Was a fight really gonna happen and did Ray believe in me? Either way I needed to believe in myself. And I needed to make it happen. During all the random partying I'd befriended some Salvadorians who were supportive of me getting back into the fight game, but who understood I was doing it tuff in my personal life.

I've always had a spiritual side, but it had taken a back seat in my life and I'd been more focussed on the physical stuff; making paper, partying, getting fit. I knew there was something missing. This changed one day while I was hanging out with the family of my Salvadorian mates.

RAFiKi

They introduced me to a shaman who said he had a message to share with me. There was an eerie but cool vibe about the whole experience, and at first I didn't know what to make of it. Whatever you want to call it, a vision or a dream, or just making sense of things through symbolism, I had this revelation and found my missing piece. This was important as I had never felt complete. During this revelation I saw myself as a primate with a blue and red face, like Rafiki from *The Lion King*. I had never given any thought to these animals in my life, truth be told I found them fierce and kinda intimidating, but their colours were unique and beautiful. In my vision I felt anxious, there was a lot of disruption and turmoil, the other primates were attacking me and I was forced out of their tribe. I needed to fight my way back in. Mentally I tried, but I was weak, it felt like I was suffocating, my hits were missing the target. Each time I tried I got beaten, but nothing hurt more than my pride. It felt like my lifelong battle with acceptance. I decided to retreat into the rainforest. I rested and relaxed my mind. I became patient, fed myself on the fruits and insects I found, I drank and swam in the fresh water from the natural springs, ran through the jungle, climbed the trees, and swung on the branches alone. I roared as loud as I could. I became strong and confident in my ability.

When the time was right, I approached the tribe. Again, the primates became hostile, but they were intimidated this time, they shied away like I was 10 feet tall. Some of the cocky ones came charging in, swinging their arms in my direction but I fended them off and they hit the ground, then got the hell outta my way. I felt satisfied, I'd accomplished what I wanted to on my terms and showed them whose boss! I climbed a large baobab tree, all the way to the top. When I looked down at the scenery below, I felt like I was in paradise. I could see mountains, a beautiful waterfall in the distance, amazing tropical birds, and other exotic animals. As well as baby primates wrestling playfully around the base of the tree. I gave out an almighty roar and all of the nature around me seemed to stop for a moment to acknowledge my voice had been heard. It was like everything around me understood who I was, embraced my story and my message. I felt fulfilled; I had been accepted; I was a mandrill …

After this experience I felt like I now knew more about myself than ever before. I googled more information on mandrills. I found out that they are the largest of all monkeys. They're often described as shy and reclusive, yet intelligent. Sometimes their energy and appearance is viewed as intimidating, but when entering groups or attracting mates they display their prowess through vocalisation, colour and size, rather than aggression. But still, they will not shy away from a fight when there is a need to defend, and they know their own strength. They live in an apparent democracy without a clear leader. As a totem, the mandrill signifies being able to see things for what they really are and not just what we are told to believe, as well as strength, self-control, integrity, empathy, spirituality, and the ability to embrace a unique approach to life.

A few months later I took a DNA test and I was amazed with the findings. The test confirmed that my black ancestry came from Nigeria. Coincidentally mandrills live in the rainforests of equatorial Africa, which includes West Africa. The DNA test also confirmed all the other ethnicities that I believed to make up my heritage, exactly as I was told over the years. The only exception was there was no obvious trace of Islander heritage, but it's possible it skipped a generation or two, given it has shown up in other family members on Dad's side who also took the test. The fact that I had to go to such great lengths to finally get closure on my true heritage after so many years frustrated the hell outta me. But all that didn't matter anymore; my new-found totem made perfect sense to me and I was proud of who I was.

I decided to celebrate the fact I'd finally got the answers I was searching for by going to the casino. It was the night of the birthday of my old mate and ex state champ, Dragon. He'd hired a luxury suite at the casino hotel with his girl. We'd been talking about the topic of heritage over the past few months, and he thought my findings were great so recommended a big night out to celebrate, his birthday being just the excuse we needed. I'd been pretty good up to that point since the mandrill revelation, focusing on training and being the best person I could be.

We started the night on high spirits with a couple bottles of Moet Chandon and I racked up some rails of Bolivian, but when Dragon's girl passed out from drinking too quickly he suggested we hit the clubs downstairs, so she could sleep it off. It was a massive night! I was fucken flyin', just like Choppers ol' mate Neville Bartos, to the point when we arrived at the club it felt like I was fucken gliding. So what was the best solution, to level things out? Yep that's right, we hit the bar for more drinks. Ahhh bad move Benny!

The margaritas and espresso martinis were floating across the bar like we were in the movie *Cocktail*. Then I got stuck into the tequila shots. We were getting fucked up and having a blast. I was getting haggled by a group of 20 ladies on a hen's night, wanting me to sign their tits with a red marker, which I did without hesitation, tagging them with my infamous 'Bugzie, RSH' tags. Then there was all these other messed up hen's night games and shit that they wanted me to do with them. I was too smashed to remember the details and I faded into a state of semi unconsciousness. I turned around to try and find Dragon, hoping he'd fly me out of the bachelorette quicksand. He was nowhere to be seen. He'd turned Jet Li on my ass and got the fuck outta there. The ladies decided they were leaving, and I decided it was best I leave too. I got to the main street out the front of the casino and out of nowhere I felt a push in the back ... WTF, was that?

I thought one of the drunk hen's night ladies was playing one of their stupid games. But it wasn't them. It was four blokes and they'd surrounded me. "You fucken right?" I said. These cunts were looking for trouble, I noticed they were all African. "Fuck you, cunt!" one of them said. I was fucken wasted and completely taken by surprise, I had no idea who they were, or what I'd done, but my mind flashed back to my mandrill vision. I thought it's best to try and defuse the situation. "Where you guys from?" I asked nervously. "We're fucken Somali, what's it to you, ya dog?" the same cunt said. At this point it was clear to me these fuckers weren't fucken around, but I gave it one last try to prevent a fucken riot. "I'm part African," I explained. "You're full of shit, cunt!" someone replied.

These cunts wanted a fight! From that point I had no choice. I let loose with a big right hand hitting one of the smart-asses in the mouth, simultaneously I felt a roundhouse kick land across my back. The guy in front of me hadn't been dropped by my big right hand, I guess in reality I was just too wasted. He threw a punch back which I narrowly ducked, but a sharp object scraped me across the top of my shaved head drawing blood. I turned around to hit the cunt that had thrown the kick but before I could, I was kicked again from behind, this time to the back of my knees, causing one of my knees to buckle and hit the pavement.

I was under attack. I felt like I was drowning. I couldn't breathe, for what must have been only seconds, as I knelt on the road on one knee, with kicks and punches coming at me from all directions. I prayed God give me the strength to get back on two feet and let me fuck these mother fuckers up. I told myself I've never been knocked out or seriously hurt in a fight, like hell these cocksuckers were gonna get the better of me. I rose to two feet and started swinging punches. My punches started landing, although not as cleanly as I would have liked, and the Somalis backed off, heading down the street.

I was fucken fired up at that point. I felt like I'd sobered up real quick and was now ready to finish them off, but the jacks had rolled up by then and pulled me off to the side of the road to question me. I had fought for survival, it was a tuff fight, but the bacon burgers weren't interested in my side of the story, they just wanted me off the street. Fuck 'em I was no dog. I jumped in an Uber and headed home … No one was arrested. On the ride home I flashed back to my childhood and my mum's words ran through my head … There's good and bad in every race …

COCONUT CRUSHER

As much as I was in denial about the effects drugs and alcohol were having on me, I realised after the brawl with the Somalis that I had to put the binge drinking and partying behind me once and for all. A long absence from the fighting arena aside, it was definitely affecting my training. Sometimes I'd have mediocre sparring days, getting hit more than I should have been getting hit, which played on my mind, allowing the seeds of doubt to creep in. "Things will only get to you if you let them get to you, son," Ray would say. He was right.

One day after training I got a random text on messenger from my big Samoan mate, Freddie. It read: *Bro, Crusher was hit in a drive by last night!* I replied: *WTF? Is he ok? Where's he at?* He replied: *Not good Bro, he's at the Alfred Hospital, we are all heading down, meet us there 2pm?*

I was shook. Crusher and me went way back. He was fucken tuff and a stand-up guy, who the fuck would do this to him? I got my shit together and drove down to the hospital expecting the worst. When I arrived to my surprise Crusher was smashing down a bucket of KFC, surrounded by friends and family. He was having the time of his life; the meds must have been fucken good. "Hey bro, wassup!" he said cheerfully. "Damn bro, did the doctors say you can eat that shit?" I said. He replied, "Fuck em, cuz!" as the whole room erupted in laughter. Then I asked, "WTF happened?" He said, "I was walking to my car and a black SUV pulled up and boom, boom, boom, the mother fuckers popped me six times, lucky I managed to turn around just in time. A coupla shots hit me in the back of the legs, better than my fucken balls, ay cuz?" The room erupted in laughter again. I said, "Who the fuck did this to you?" He said, "Don't worry about all that, bro, we got this shit covered... But ya know what, why don't you write a song about it?!" I said, "I will, Uso!".

Word on the street was, Coconut Crusher had been stalked then gunned down by bikies after an altercation at a nightclub he was working at. I didn't pay too much attention to the details or involve myself in any acts of retribution. I just went back home and began writing the track and recorded it a few weeks later.

After about a year of hard work in the gym, Ray finally agreed I was ready to fight; I was given an opportunity on one of Big Tony's Boxing shows at the Melbourne Pavilion. My professional boxing debut was locked in almost 15 years to the day since my last amateur fight, the DQ in Adelaide. This time I wasn't chasing a title of any kind. I was doing it for the love of it. My story was different to most fighters, almost unheard of, well at least I'd never heard of anyone doing what I was doing. I was starting to get nervous, and I hated admitting that to myself or anyone else. I was putting myself out there to be judged. Leading up to the fight I started over thinking stuff, fearing losing, failure, embarrassment, or worse still, humiliation. I told myself I wanted to just get in the ring, pretend it was no big deal. I was back to show them how it was done and get the 'W' to make my kids proud. The opponent I had been matched with didn't have a great record, but he didn't have 15 years of ring rust like I did, so my team believed the match was fair. I was fighting in the cruiserweight division; I had a much more muscular physic than I had all those years ago in the amateurs and weighed about 185 lb. The heaviest I'd been in a fight.

Pro fighting is a different game to the amateurs. Ray would say, "It's the difference between a sword fight and a gun fight. I know which fight I'd rather be in." He hated amateur boxing. He was strictly a pro boxing trainer. From my perspective it meant I would finally get paid to fight in the ring and relish all the prestige I'd dreamed of all those years. When you're starting out in the professional game you get paid by the round, but the majority of your purse comes from getting a cut on the ticket sales, or from sponsorship deals. Given I'd been involved in boxing for so long I managed to sell more tickets than most fighters on debut. I also got some sponsorship on merchandise through a local boxing brand, who supplied my robe and shorts.

Nerves do funny thing to people. My problem was acknowledging that was a fact. I was feeling uncomfortable, the mandrill revelation played on my mind, and I questioned whether I had really been accepted by my boxing team or if I was simply there to sell tickets and spar with the other fighters. It was all in my fucken head, but I let it mess with my focus and on the night of the weigh in I rocked up 45 minutes late. By the time I arrived Ray and all the other fighters, including the main event guys, had left the building. I was left to weigh in alone with my opponent, his trainer and one official. We didn't even square off and take photos. Although I had let myself down by being late, I felt abandoned.

I woke up the next day feeling like I had a hangover, with a nasty headache, which was probably from all the tension and nervous energy. I tried my best to sleep it off before leaving home for the fight, but I just had too much bullshit running through my head to sleep. Instead of learning from my mistakes, I again arrived late to the change rooms. Ray wasn't at all impressed, so I copped a spray; "Mate, are ya fucken switched on tonight or not?" I said, "Yeh, sorry Ray just got held up in traffic." He said, "I can't do ya corner tonight, as you know I've got these other two fighting 10 rounds for a WBA ranking, you're only fighting a four rounder, those two other blokes over there will look after ya!"

I started feeling sick with anxiety, my mandrill vision was becoming a reality; my pride was hurt and I hadn't been accepted. I was given two ex pro fighters to coach me in the corner, but they'd never had much to do with my training. I just prayed my punches would hit the target. I'd decided I was going for a knockout win. Ray passed on the game plan to my corner man. I was to slip, bob and weave my way inside and keep up on his chest, closing up his range given he was much taller than me, and throw my punches from the inside. That was the plan I stuck with … It almost worked.

The fight started and I was clearly beating my opponent in the first round, but something just wasn't right. The whole experience felt surreal, I couldn't actually believe I was finally back in the ring. I didn't see a boxer in front of me. I saw Frankenstein's monster. His head was kinda green and purple, and he seemed to be moving in slow motion. I kept hitting him with shots like I was playing *Zombie Apocalypse*. Yep, those nerves were getting to me like a bad acid trip!

In round two I came out with the same game plan, then suddenly boom, I hit him with a big left hook which sent him crashing into the ropes. As I stepped inside to finish him off, I got my timing and distancing wrong. We ended up clinching and wrestling, which made me look scrappy. From that point on there was something critical I failed to do. Adjust! A good fighter always adjusts when they realise things aren't going as planned.

For the rest of the round and the third, every time I got inside my opponent held onto me, causing me to wrestle more often than punch. By the last round, my arms felt so heavy from all the wrestling it felt like I had cement in my gloves.

And not in a good way; my arms felt way too hefty to let my hands go. At the final bell I wasn't hurt, just ashamed of my performance. The judges scored against me, and my opponent got the decision. But I guess it didn't matter too much, I was now officially a professional fighter. Win, lose or draw, at least I'd earned a quid this time.

A coupla days later I put 10% of my prize money aside in an envelope and visited Ray at the Gym during the week. No one seemed to care that I'd lost my fight, just me. Everything was as normal. I'd thought that maybe I'd get kicked off the team, or I'd loose work coz my clients would wanna stop training with me. Again, it was all in my head and all I'd done was given myself excuses as to why I didn't deserve to win that fight. My biggest opponent was myself; I'd lost that fight by thinking about everything but the objective, hit the dude and don't get hit, and control each round. I was fit enough to go 10 rounds that night. I'd been holding my own sparring with some of the best fighters in Australia. I had to get my head right. Just get in there again and do what I do best, fight! Ray didn't accept the 10% I offered him. He told me to have a week off and come back to training when I was ready.

BENNY EL TORO

I realised there was something very simple missing from my training routine; a bit of R&R. I decided that would help moving forward. I was keen to keep sparring, continue working on new drills, and also to help out in the corners of the fighters in our team and continue to learn. But most importantly I was hungry to fight again!

I also needed to drop more weight and work on agility. I started swimming once a week, which made me feel revitalised and helped my body recover from the intense training and pad holding at my gym. I had a routine including laps of freestyle, backstroke, and breaststroke. I focused on my breathing and technique during the laps. Then, when I finished swimming, I would bob down under water to the bottom of the pool, hold my breath and throw punches as fast as I could, until I couldn't hold my breath anymore, just like I'd seen Muhammad Ali do in some vintage training photos. Although apparently the photos were a hoax created by Ali and his trainer, I felt it actually helped with my breathing by strengthening my lungs under the additional water pressure, and it also helped psychologically.

I'd then finish the session by praying and meditating while in the steam room or spa, which was good for my mind. I was running twice a week and two additional days would be sprint work. I'd train with Ray and the team on Tuesdays and Thursdays. Then I'd either workout on my own, or sometimes train with old mates of mine the rest of the time. All the pad holding and drills I was doing with my clients was constantly sharpening my reflexes, and I'd noticed that since turning pro my boxing business was getting a lot busier.

I cut down on using Tinder, it was just too much of a distraction and TBH I felt like I was breaking hearts. It's all fun and games until someone get hurt, right? I was now a lot more careful about who I let into my life. I decided to concentrate on recording new music and before I knew it, I had almost completed my first solo album. I also kept busy in my spare time watching a range of fighters on YouTube. Some of my favourites were Floyd Mayweather Jr., Manny Pacquiao, Canelo Alvarez, and old school Latin fighters like Edwin Valero, Julio Casar Chavez, and Oscar De La Hoya.

I started to appreciate the Mexican boxing style, and I began to reach out to random Mexican fighters and trainers on FB. Social media became a great way to chat to other boxers, give each other advise and share boxing videos. One day I posted that I was looking for sponsors and immediately one of my old Syndal mates who ran an air-conditioning company, jumped on board. A merchandise company run by a Mexican American family posted me out custom-made head gear, a groin guard, shorts, a robe, 10oz fighting gloves, 16oz sparring gloves, hand wraps, t-shirts, the fucken works! All customised in my favourite American football team, The Raiders, with calligraphy stating my boxing alias, Benny the Bull. I was really starting to feel like a professional and in turn took on a professional mindset towards my training. My confidence grew!

The name, Benny the Bull, was briefly given to me in the gym during my amateur boxing days, coz I had a reputation of charging in like a bull. This was to get in close range with the mostly taller opponents I fought, with gloves up high protecting my head. Although we never officially used this name in fights back then, the name stuck. When I turned pro, the bull boxing-style analogy resonated with my new team, and with a new Mexican American sponsor on board it was appropriate to adopt a Spanish interpretation. So, *Benny El Toro* became my nickname!

IMPECCABLE, WORD UP

hrough the hip hop scene in Melbourne I had befriended Beanz, a rapper who was originally from Brazil. He took an interest in the direction I was heading with my music. We recorded a track together and discussed running some future events as a side hustle and to help promote our music. I still had solid contacts in the night club scene, so finding a venue that could run our events was the easy part. Finding a loyal crowd of supporters for our nights was a little more challenging.

We planned to shoot some music videos and started a small entertainment business called Dime and Ruff. The first video was for my track, *Vices*, which is all about resisting temptation, having faith and turning negative choices into steppingstones toward a positive life. I was still struggling financially and didn't have a big budget to spend, but I got the right support from the right peeps and that's all that mattered. We hit the streets of Dandenong which set an authentic tone to the narrative, then shot some scenes around my mates gym in Noble Park. The video was straight up fire!

My training was going better than ever with the new adjustments I'd made to my routine. Ray and I grew to have a tight bond and I continued working with our team in the corners of fighters including Kane who was the main event at Hisense arena in Melbourne, packing out the stadium with well over the 10k person capacity. The feedback I was getting on my new music from my inner sanctum of hip hop advisors was better than ever, they were genuinely feelin' it and agreed going solo was a step in the right direction. I dreamed of rapping in front of the same crowd as the fight at Hisense arena. What a fucken mad rush that would be!

I'd drive Ray to the fights when my team members were fighting so we could be extra organised and discuss game plans. One day he mentioned he was gonna try and lock me in for another fight in early 2017, but I'd have to get my weight down close to around 165 lbs and fight as a super middle weight. He asked me a little more about my personal life and I told him about some of the hard stuff I'd been through. He responded with some powerful words which I'll never forget: "Always remember, son, tuff times don't last, but tuff people do, you're a winner, never stop believing in yourself!". Those words were great to hear. It was time to embrace some positivity!

DO IT FOR THE LOVE, FROM THE HEART, GLOVE UP

Final Fight, *Don't Take It Personal* **(2018)**

Final Fight

My next fight was officially locked in and I wasn't going to let anything sabotage me getting the 'W' this time. I was really looking forward to jumping back in the ring, I was determined to leave no stone unturned and offer no excuses. Life was getting better. The months were flying by. Technically speaking I was already an inactive fighter, given it would be 18 months since my pro debut until I stepped back into the ring for fight number two. Again, I would need to shake off the cobwebs, meaning the nerves, but I was a professional now and that's what pros do ... Get focused, keep cool and get the fucken job done!

I felt a lot more comfortable and in control of my life. I just needed to be more disciplined with my diet coz my weight would sometimes fluctuating back up into the cruiserweight division. I needed to rely on skill more than muscle. I wasn't entering a wrestling ring; it was the boxing ring. The squared circle. Not only did I need to get the job done this time, I didn't want to let my team, or my sponsors down.

My training went well over the next few months. I was loving every minute of it. I was looking sharp during sparring and in the best shape of my life. I'd work footwork and repetition drills with Ray and Stuart, who was an ex lightweight fighter who'd fought and trained in the UK. He had a few tricks we'd work on, to improve my inside-fighting. All was on track. I hadn't touched drugs or alcohol in a long time, and I felt a lot better mentally. I continued to focus on four things: family, friends, music and boxing.

I came to the realisation that anger is a dangerous emotion and that being assertive is better than being aggressive. If your mind is clouded with emotion, it's difficult to think straight and a fighter doesn't need that kinda distraction, they need to focus on fighting at their best. I cut out sugar and complex carbohydrates from my diet completely. Even from vegetables like carrots or sweet potato. I didn't eat anything at all after 5 pm. I was living on water and small portions of lean protein and fresh, mostly green vegetables throughout the day. But, still because of my muscular physic, I was roughly about 10 lbs overweight leading up to the fight. Ray advised fasting. I wasn't allowed to eat or drink anything at all for 24 hours before the weigh in. I'd never been that disciplined with my diet in my life. I'd best describe it as a euphoric feeling. It was like I was on a natural high, thriving on the sacrifices. Stuart asked how I was going. I said "Great, I'm gonna win this inside the fourth round." The number four gave me balance, it made sense coz I was also born in April, the fourth month of the year ...

I made weight coming in right on 165 lbs, just under the weight limit for super middleweight. When I stepped off the scales, I felt like I'd already won. But as I shaped up to my opponent for the cameras, I quickly reminded myself I hadn't won anything yet. When I got home, I tried to relax the best I could, this fight was about getting in there, enjoying it and putting on a great show for my supporters. With that in mind, I laid down and had a great night's sleep.

I was much better prepared going into this fight and arrived in the change rooms early. Ray was happy about that and taped my hands up right away, so we could focus on the fight. Big Tony, for the first time in my life came over and shook my hand, and wished me all the best! I was dressed in my shorts and robe at that point, and the gesture meant a lot. I felt more accepted than I'd ever been in my life. Everything was going smooth. Maybe a little too glossy ... "Now don't you be trippin', this is your night!" I told myself.

But the nerves creeped in again like the Mumu curse was still with me, and I started to feel that surreal feeling I'd felt during my last fight. As if I was on a bad acid trip. So, my warmup was average. Ray was shouting, "Switch on son and wake the hell *up*." I started sweating like mad. Those fucken cobwebs! Although I'd trained my ass off over the inactive period, nothing quite prepares your mind for the tension, nerves, pressure, and expectation of the night, unless you're fighting frequently. Still, I was not going to let that bullshit become an excuse. I was fighting a boxer from Thailand who was on his professional boxing debut. In my mind, I was fighting someone of the calibre of Sugar Ray Leonard. I suddenly snapped out of the bad trip, self-sabotage type mentality and gave myself a reality check. I told myself, you're a great fighter, now get the fucken job done!

It was time to get out there. My track *How We Do* got the

joint bangin', along with the roar from my supporters. They'd packed out the ringside tables, general admission and a private VIP mezzanine level. It was showtime.

The referee laid down the instructions, the bell rang, and we were underway. I started the fight cautiously, throwing long jabs with hands up high and in close. I took a few of the guy's shots on the back of my gloves and couple came through on the top of my head. He didn't really have much power coming through. I just felt a bit stiff and not completely comfortable. He was a southpaw and a little unpredictable. No doubt he came from an experienced Muay Thai fighting background coz he threw an illegal spinning back fist which scraped the top of my head. I had to relax, switch on and get busy. Ray gave me another massive spray in the corner, "Mate you're fighting like you're scared! What the hell is wrong with you! You're a much better fighter than what we're seeing out there, you eat guys like this for breakfast normally!"

Ray was right, I was fighting like I was scared of failure, I needed the wakeup call. I thought about my mandrill vision. I had to control my mind and summon the strength to win this fight. It wasn't just gonna happen coz I wanted it to, I had to *make* it happen. I started to relax and fight the way I should have been fighting, and I felt I'd worked out his rhythm. Still, when I went to the corner after round two, Ray wasn't impressed, "Mate, what the fuck is going on out there? Smash this bloke, would ya?!" I thought about my prediction to finish the fight in round four!

Round three, I reverted to my strengths, went out and enjoyed myself. I wasn't having any trouble with the guy this round, I just wanted to enjoy doing what I loved! When the bell rang, I went back to the corner and this time Ray was impressed. "That's a helluva lot better, now stop playing around and get the job done!" he said.

Round four, I came out of the corner jabbing, bobbing, and slipping my way inside, then boom, I landed a big right hook to my opponent's body followed by a short left hook, which sent him crashing to the canvas. The dude was a tuff competitor though, and to my surprise he got up. I didn't want to rush in too eagerly this time, so I cautiously covered up while he threw some survival type punches, which I caught with my gloves. As he tired, I got my way inside again, this time dropping him with a right uppercut to the chin.

It was ruled a TKO 0.59 seconds into the fourth round, making the stoppage by one second still in the 10th minute of the fight. Just like my birthdate: fourth month, 10th day … The mandrill had climbed the tree top, and as the referee raised my glove and I looked through the ropes of the boxing ring to the cheering crowd, I knew I had found my paradise. There would be no turning back.

Just as they were for my days in court, my mum and dad were again in the same room. Sitting on tables with friends and family ringside on the opposite sides of the boxing ring, in the neutral corner. I wondered, am I more like my mum or am I more like my dad? The answer was neither. I was me. Benny El Toro.

It had been an entertaining fight, which the crowd seemed to enjoy. I finally started feeling comfortable inside that ring. I felt like I wanted to go on and fight again. I was just starting to shake off the cobwebs. I'd be a lot more relaxed next time round, get more prize money, more sponsors, more fans. But my trainer Ray didn't see it this way. Right after the fight we had a quick debrief. He said, "retire with a win son!" I understood. It was time to move on. Well at least that's what I told Ray. Deep down it was like my heart had sunken to the bottom of the ocean. I turned my head a different direction so that Ray could not tell I was fighting back tears. My childhood dreams of becoming a World Champion would never eventuate. The voice of reason scolded my spirit like an old school teacher, the naughty kid inside desperately wanted to say something smart, to prove the teacher wrong, but my faith insisted that I took this one on the chin, no matter how much it hurt. It's all part of a bigger plan and boxing will always be with me.

My entire boxing career, I never got dropped or knocked out and nothing will ever change that. I was tuff and I never felt pain. Any fight I ever lost was on points and it was because I wasn't focused, and my head wasn't right. But I never got hurt. The game is more a battle of the mind than it is physical. Words have hurt me far more in my life than getting hit ever will. Words stay in your head. What I've learnt is if your mind is strong the words can't hurt you. I realised, as a rapper that my words could change the world and change people lives for the better, just like my idols words had changed mine. My voice and my words had always been my calling.

Diamond in Da' Ruff

ife after Boxing is never easy for any fighter. I asked myself what would fill that void?

Would I get on the rack and fall off the rails? Hit the booze and get into blues? Become a bikie and live like a pikey? Sounds fucken crazy right? But to be frank in many ways that's how it is. There isn't a lot of support out there for retired boxers, and those demons, they come a calling. I walked away undamaged, but let's face the facts, I made those decisions coz it was right for me and chose to listen to the advice I was given, coz it made sense. Whose there for all the ex-Olympians and title contenders, who fought and fought until they couldn't fight anymore? In the best-case scenarios, its family, but the reality is if family's not solid, it's very easy to fall through the cracks.

Boxing is one of the most brutal things us humans do, so why do we do it? All the years of sacrifice, pain, commitment, trauma, inevitable damage and not a helluva lot of cash for most. People say, we all make choices, but fighting isn't just a choice for some of us, it's life. So, you take away that, you take away the oxygen that we breathe. People sometimes ask me why did you stop; don't you miss it? Of course I do, being a fighter has determined who I am my whole life. But for me, the fight didn't start or stop in the ring, I was fighting for a better life and I had found a sport that accepted me for who I was and that's what I loved. But I always knew there was a little more to my story and it wasn't to rely on my fists. The biggest weapon I have and always did have was my *words*, to be specific, the ability to tell a story with a loud voice to back it up. It was time for me to get back into the studio, I had some music to make.

With my first LP finished and waiting to be released, I started on my second LP, *Don't Take It Personal*. Before a rehearsal one night I was having a yarn wit' Beanz at his pad 'bout tryna pull a crowd for the upcoming launch gig. I said, "I got a great idea man, I'm gonna put up some training photos on Instagram and promote our events that way. Might help get some more ladies down to this show, my brother." He said, "Really man?" And I said, "Yeh bro, you must have some like thirst trap photos in ya phone somewhere man? Haha!" "Nah, fuck that Bro, I'm not really into that shit," Beanz said. I said, "Fair enough man, I was just messen' with ya anyway."

Regardless, I logged back into IG and before I could upload a photo I noticed in my notifications a pretty looking girl I'd never seen before had liked our flyer. Boom, just what I was talking about! I was intrigued by this mysterious IG Girl. I reached out right away, slid into her DM and asked if she would like to come to the show, she responded with "I'd Luv 2 xx." Then I kinda got distracted after that and forgot about the whole IG thing for a while. We had a rehearsal to get through, Beanz and another mate were my support act and the hype men for my set. We planned on nailing it!

I dropped *The Impeccable Word* a week before the launch gig, along with the video, and managed to lock down some community airplay right across Australia. I got some dope reviews and also an artist spotlight with the community radio association showcasing upcoming multi-cultural artists. Times had changed since I dropped *King Hits* in '09. Everything was now so much more dependent on social media. Success was gauged by hits, views and likes. The entertainment world had become a bunch of number crunches and the hustle had gone up a notch or two.

The fight was far from over. As much as I felt I'd reached paradise when my glove was raised by the referee after my last fight, I still also had a massive climb ahead of me, but I knew it would all be worth it, I realised that paradise is what you make it!

I was back at the recovery club for *The Impeccable Word* launch gig. It was my first gig in years, I'd moved on from the acid trip type sensation I'd felt before entering the boxing ring and was on top of my nerves. A coupla tequila shots definitely took the edge off though, shame I couldn't have hit the bar before my last fight, I thought to myself. The venue was packed out, it was a little different to the bouncer gigs, coz there was heaps more chicks. I definitely wasn't complaining. Apart from Beanz and his mate, another pro boxer: Lucas performed with his band, setting the tone for a soulful and memorable night. Again the boxing connection was closely tied to my music. I started my set with *Coconut Crusher*. The lyrics, "shit's about to get real in here", almost blew up the speakers and our energy got the whole crowd up and moving.

Beanz pointed out the mysterious IG girl and he pulled her up on stage. She was a little shy, but I was happy to see she'd made it like she said she would. We hit the afterparty at Beanz's pad, until the mysterious IG girl and me headed back to mine to do little after partying of our own ... Wink, wink, nudge, nudge! But first I made it clear that I wasn't looking for anything serious, I was just focused on what I had to do, and she said she understood, she was on the same page having come out of a serious relationship not long before that night. But there was something different about that night, a strong spiritual sensation in the air. A priceless gift would come my way ...

THREE AMIGOS

I was still in contact with my Mexican American FB friends and over the past few years a boxing manager: Charlie fell into my friendship circle. I noticed one of his fighters had fought GGG for a WBA world middle title in Panama. He'd posted that he was starting up a record label, so I started to send him through some of my tracks. He responded with a coupla thumbs up to acknowledge he liked the tracks, but I didn't hear much more from him after that.

I continued on my everyday grind; praying, keeping myself fit, training my clients down at my gym. I was really feelin' the direction of the new LP. I was mixing up the beats and rapping with a variety of different flows. I also started singing on some of the tracks, which I'd never really done before, but I felt I needed to do something a little different, try and make some noise. Hip hop was continually evolving, it had well and truly crossed into every genre of music, so I decided to evolve with it. I was loving the process and was flyin' through getting my second album done, all was on schedule for the 2018 release date. I had the time up my sleeve to get some more videos cut, and got asked to play at some gigs around Melbourne, one of them as the headline act at a popular hip hop club in the city. This led to some interviews on local Melbourne radio and stuff like that: it was great, my name was getting out there and my profile was growing as a solo artist.

I was still a single dude and now I was loving life. I'd finally found the balance between work, play, passion, and spirituality. The mysterious IG girl and me kept in contact, but it was her friendship I cherished more than anything. We had made a pact, that night we hooked up, meant nothing too serious, however there was some news she needed to break to me. "I'm pregnant," she said.

Not for one moment did I regret hearing those words. We agreed to be co-parents and friends regardless of what the future held. I inevitably found comfort in embracing what society deemed an unconventional family arrangement. Coz, you know why? Fuck society! I ran my own ship; I did things my way and that's the way it is! After all, mandrills live in a democracy without a boss dictating what they can and can't do!

The day of my son's birth was something I'll never forget. When I first laid eyes on my boy I could tell he was fucken *huge*, at least double the size of any other baby in the ward. My kid was the infant heavy weight champ of the hospital, so we named him accordingly. I touched his hand he gripped my finger with such power – I was amazed – and he wasn't gonna let go any time soon either. I knew this kid could be anything!

ROUND 2 MUSIC

In March 2019 we ran our next event which was all about showcasing Melbourne's upcoming raw rap talent. We closed out the show with a dope set. The momentum was building and there was mad love from all the fans; it was a great turn out that day, with more of a festival vibe compared to our other events. I was relentless with my push to get a hit and as soon as *Don't take it Personal* dropped I was right back in that studio again working on my third solo LP, *Assumptions*.

I started working with a new producer who was getting a lot of his tracks placed on Netflix through an agency. And his beats were fresh, so I was feelin' it. We got an idea to create an epic boxing track, something like I'd never recorded before. So, we did. The beat was fucken bangin'. I reflected on my boxing career and my experience as a trainer, and wrote the track *Nothing Comes Easy*.

The boxing community embraced the track and we shot the video at a gym in the Northwest suburbs of Melbourne; The owner Sam, was also a muso, a big North Melbourne fan and had developed one of the strongest fighters stables in Australia, so we had a lot in common. The video turned out to be 'the real deal'.

Everything was going so well, but there were simply no benji's coming back in from my music and I needed that to change. I found myself hustling again, but this time I wasn't pushing anything illegal. I was just pushing my music and dealing with all the trials and tribulations associated with the game. Then, just like fishing down the Yarra River as a kid, something finally hit the line.

I'd sent Charlie *Nothing Comes Easy* via email and he was impressed. As soon as he heard the track, he contacted me to fill me in with some amazing news. His plan was to premiere the track on a radio station he was involved with in California and see what the feedback was like. I couldn't fucken believe it! After all those years of hard work and dedication, I was finally getting an opportunity to break through in the USA! I thanked Charlie and ended the call, then as I walked outside, I closed my eyes and prayed. I looked up to the sky and at the top of my voice screamed out, "THANK YOU!" It was the happiest I'd felt in a long, long time.

Nothing Comes Easy premiered on KCAA radio on a Friday night, California time. The experience was fucken unreal, and I could watch the livestream over FB too. After the track finished the host, Angel Baby, asked Kid Frost what he thought about the track and he answered, "It's cool." It was the first time I'd ever heard my song played on US radio. It was a dream come true! Having a Californian legend of the rap game review my track was surreal.

My next move was to finish off the album coz Charlie and the team were keen to hear more tracks. I was advised to pitch it to US college radio and run a campaign. I liked the idea and I bought myself some studio equipment, so I could work from home and put the finishing touches on the LP. Some of my mates, like Gypsy Brown, would help out with the production, simply for the love. It was much more efficient working that way. Once *Assumptions* was complete, I released the LP across

US college radio. It was well received and peaked at #21 across the NACC hip hop charts.

Angel Baby played more of my tracks on his show, and the response was great. Charlie called me up on a Saturday afternoon, Melbourne time, and said, "Benny, we gotta get you over here man to record some songs, they are loving your style out here man. I've just signed up a DJ by the name of DJ Bobby B, you guys would be great working together." I nearly dropped the phone, I was trembling ... "Hello ... Hello Benny, are you there?" I said, "Sorry Charlie, I'm lost for words, this is one of the greatest moments of my life, please send me the details!" Charlie said, "Man, don't worry about the details, just grab ya' self a flight, I got you, we need you out here right away. If we wait any longer people are gonna forget your name man!" I said, "Okay bro, thank you, I'll be there!"

Straight after Charlie called, I was literally standing beside a travel agency inside a shopping centre! Without any hesitation I went into the shop, right then and there and I bought a return flight to LAX, scheduled to fly out in January 2020. As I walked out the travel agent's door, something dawned on me. Ahhh shit! My US Visa application denial from years ago... surely that couldn't come back to bite me now, right?

It was just before Christmas, there was no way I'd have time to go through the whole visa process again. I decided I was gonna have to take a risk, keep things on the down low and not declare that I had been denied a visa in the past. Yesterday is history, tomorrow is a mystery, and the present is a gift from God. So, I just said, "Fuck It!" and kept on walking.

I was determined to fulfil my destiny.

The next few weeks I was busy preparing for the trip, but I was trying not to think about the whole visa situation, keeping the anxiety at bay and staying cool. I was too embarrassed to talk to Charlie about the risk. I had well and truly moved on from all that juvenile shit I'd gotten up to in my past. Benny Blanco from the Bronx was a distant memory …

I thought back to my rapping as a kid and the first time I heard rap on the radio in Melbourne; it all seemed like a fucken fairy tale. It was a significant breakthrough, my dreams of making it as a rapper in the USA were coming to fruition. I asked myself, would my flight to LAX signify the mandrill's climbing of the massive tree, or had I already climbed the tree when the referee raised my glove after my last fight? Truth be told, it didn't matter, and maybe that was the point. It had all been about finding acceptance in myself, never giving up and using my voice to tell my story to the world. I knew my words could change people's lives and that's what I loved about hip hop the most!

I was beyond stoked that I had found a team that could get my music out to the world. But still the system don't like my kind, I prayed every night that all would be okay. This was the best shot I had at making it to the big time, and I was hungry to show the world what I was made of. But I knew I was gonna have to own my hasty and impatient visa mistake if things fucked up and I got refused entry into USA.

It was departure day. Getting onto the plane was the easy bit – it would be getting through customs in the US that could put a hold on my dreams. On the plane I slept like a baby, and in between meals I worked on a new track in the notes of my iPhone, based on my experience. It was a 15 hour flight; when I arrived at LAX I was jet lagged AF!

I nervously waited in a big line to checkout of the airport through customs. I felt like everything was going in slow motion. Finally, I was at the passport scanners. I took a deep breath and placed my passport on the screen. Something wasn't right. The worst of the worst-case scenario of my life at that moment was about to go down ... Shiittt! ... There was a fucken issue with my passport.

Customs officials escorted me to the interview room, I was told I would not be allowed to make any phone calls or communicate with anyone until further notice. My dream had turned into a nightmare, my paradise felt like hell. Was this the end of the road for Benny Sinclair? As I sat in the interview room and awaited the decision, I prayed and reflected on my childhood and all that had brought me to that point in my life. Boxing reflected my desire to fight, search for a better life and discover myself. Music had always been there with me; it stems from my soul. But I felt like I was just getting started and I still had so much to rap about ...

So, I told the US customs officers my story ... And ya wanna know a little something? ... They were fucken cool wit it!

WHEN THE HUSTLE GETS U DOWN IN CALI LIKE MY VIBE

In Cali, *Released by Round 2 Music* (2020)

Photograph by Marty Camilleri

CPSIA information can be obtained
at www.ICGtesting.com
Printed in the USA
BVHW081928140223
658501BV00013B/277